RADIO & TV PREMIUMS

Jim Harmon

A Guide to the History and Value of Radio and TV Premiums

Published by

**krause
publications**

700 E. State Street • Iola, WI 54990-0001
Telephone: 715/445-2214

Please call or write for our free catalog.
Our toll-free number to place an order or obtain a free catalog is 800-258-0929
or please use our regular business telephone 715-445-2214
for editorial comment and further information.

Library of Congress Catalog Number: 97-073027
ISBN: 0-87341-518-3

Printed in the United States of America

Table of Contents

ACKNOWLEDGMENTS

I would like to thank my former publisher Jeremy Tarcher for the opportunity to write the first book primarily on radio premiums, my 1973 release, *Nostalgia Catalogue* (long out of print, and only a very general guide to value); writer/editor Richard O'Brien for having me contribute a section on "Premiums" to his authoritative *Collecting Toys* omnibus volumes first for Books Americana and now Krause, and for his help in advancing a book of my own on premiums to those publishers; Amy Tincher-Durik, enthusiastic editor at Krause, and her predecessor Elizabeth Noll; writer Tom Tumbusch for advice and information; fan expert Jack Melcher who lead the way with an early "fanzine" premium price guide; collector Joe Young for many favors; Dave Amaral, Lloyd Nesbitt, Rev. Bob Neilly, Judge Douglas Due, the late Redd Boggs, and the late Ron Haydock; and to the late Charles Claggett, who created the Tom Mix radio series and developed the use of the premium to the utmost, for sharing an all-too-brief portion of his time with me.

Personal thanks to cartoonist Shel Dorf and his employer, the late Milton Caniff, for the gift of some one hundred Sunday comics radio premium advertisements of Tom Mix, Jack Armstrong, etc. that had been attached to forty years of file copies of *Terry and the Pirates*; the late journalist Manny Weltman who gave me some of his personal childhood premiums; to collectors and dealers who have always given me a fair deal on buying and selling premiums: Ted Hake, Jerry Cook, Bob Hritz, Ed Praeger, and others whose names I can't remember under the pressure of time restraints.

Thanks to my stepdaughter, Dawn Kovner, for taking probably the majority of photographs in this volume, to Felicia Cano for the photo of the Tom Mix Mystery Picture Ring, to April Kinchloe and Canoga Camera for developing the film, and to anyone who may have taken a picture for me over the years.

Finally, thanks to my wife and partner, Barbara Gratz Harmon, who took some of the photos, helped design, and completely typed the listings of premiums. Without her, this book would be impossible. Moreover, without her (and sometimes, even with her), I would be impossible.

J.H.

Special acknowledgment is made to Mr. John K. Snyder, Jr., of Diamond Galleries, for his advice on the "high end" collectibles. The final judgment, however, is that of the author, Jim Harmon, and should be considered only as an informed opinion.

Prices go up and down based on transitory events like the TV interview of some old star who played a famous character, on personal choices, on whims. No one should pay prices over one thousand dollars without the advice of several experts in the field. Counterfeits are not unknown, and some real items can be misrepresented to be something else. Reading this book will tell you *something* about the value of premiums, but certainly not *everything*.

INTRODUCTION

The collecting urge is in almost everyone. Most people save the books they read, instead of merely throwing them away after they have finished. Some people save theatre or movie ticket stubs. One of the most frequent things collected are those of childhood. Toys have become some of the top collectibles. This book concerns a very special type of toy that was given away free or for a very nominal charge that only covered the cost of the item, without any profit to the supplier.

These were the premiums offered by radio and TV programs, mostly aimed at children, for a boxtop from the cereal sponsor's product and sometimes, but not always, "ten cents to cover the cost of handling and mailing." Sometimes another part of the sponsor's product, like the inner seal from a jar of Ovaltine, was requested, and coinage went up over the years to twenty cents, thirty five cents, fifty cents, and for some of the last offers even one or two dollars. A recent

A collection of nostalgia including Buck Rogers Atomic Ray-gun, Tom Mix gun and telegraph sets, Captain Midnight statuette, and clock from movie star Ken Maynard's home.

breakfast cereal box offered a wonderful "gift" for only $7.95.

This book concerns itself with the past when radio and early TV shows offered items on the programs themselves. I don't try to cover every small plastic item enclosed in cereal boxes up to the present day. There might be some interest in such a book someday, but it has been my experience that these small items are generally not kept, are so cheaply made they will not survive, and no one has any great interest in them. Only items connected with some famous character or program have any established value.

As to that value: The standard method is to say an item, like a badge, has a certain value in just "good" condition (I'll use $8.50 as an example) and is worth twice as much in "fine" ($17.00) and again double for "mint" ($34.00). Dealers do not generally use figures like that in pricing for their lists or catalogues and collectors follow their example. Premiums are usually priced in "round" numbers. If you see a price like $67.50 that probably means it is a

hundred dollar item but this particular example is damaged in such a way to take away a third of its value.

I have not always followed this mathematical method of pricing. I have on routine items, but where a premium is particularly sought after, and that usually means particularly expensive, tried to put a price such as a dealer or selling collector might put on it. Condition is not so critical on premiums as, for example, old time comic books which are made of paper and subject to water, insect, and sun damage. A metal ring can lie in a drawer for forty years and look brand new after a little buffing. I have seldom seen a Tom Mix brass compass and magnifying glass in less than "fine" condition. Maybe somewhere there is one beat into a lump by the hammer of some long ago kid, but I've not seen it. Only paper or light cardboard items like the model buildings from the Lone Ranger Frontier Town show wear and tear.

Some premiums are worth a minimum value, but only gain a few points for "fine" or "mint" condition. A coupon for a Flight Com-

Toy guns—left side, Tom Mix wooden gun, cylinder spins (1935); values in Good, Fine, and Mint: 85, 160, 300 (top) and Orphan Annie water pistol (bottom); right side, Buck Rogers Atomic Pistol (store display item) and Gene Autry toy gun (store display item)

mander's Badge from a 1942 Captain Midnight manual could be worth $10, but if you doubled it for "fine" and re-doubled it for "mint" you would have a value of $40. I believe this would be an exaggerated price for a small piece of paper.

I will let you in on one of the Big Inside Secrets of collecting premiums or anything else. The varying prices for "good," "fine," and "mint" are mainly there for arguing points. The item you want is priced at the "mint" grade—a premium, a comic book, a coin—but you might argue that in your opinion it is really only "fine." The seller might not budge, or if he or she wants to make the sale he or she might give in to you and sell it at the "fine" price, or he or she might compromise at a price between "fine" and "mint."

It hasn't become a standard method of haggling over a price, but I have used it to argue between buyer and seller what plateau the premium is to be sold at. If all of your friends are wealthy—and possibly celebrities—and are interested in collectibles mostly for investment purposes, hoping to buy now and resell later for a profit, you can expect to buy and sell at the highest level. If you are attending a flea market sale in the parking lot of a junior college, where people (mostly men) of middle age or more are seeking items that they fondly remember from their childhood, you can expect to deal for less money.

A few years ago, at a civic auditorium show, I bought a store item of associated interest to my premium collection. It was a Marx wind-up Lone Ranger, on a rearing Silver, spinning a wire lariat. I paid $100 for it. At the next table, another dealer was selling the same item for $950. The best practice is never to comment favorably on a price until the deal is done, but I was sure this dealer must have seen his competitor's price. "Some people here want a lot more for this Lone Ranger," I said. This man took my money, and shook his head. "I'm never going to live long enough to get that price." Sure enough, at other shows, I've seen that other Lone Ranger stay in that dealer's collection and go up to $1,600, but bring in no

real money. The moral is: Be realistic. What is the most money you have ever sold an item for? What is the most money you have ever paid? Do you personally deal with millionaires or average people?

In recent years, the same people who have raised the selling price of 1940s Golden Age comic books into the range of tens of thousands of dollars have attempted to do the same with certain premiums, especially rings. Some of these sales are arranged publicity ventures. Sales are arranged where an equal amount of money changes hands. I buy your Brick Bradford belt buckle for $100,000 but you buy three of my Nyoka bracelets for $33,000 each. (A hypothetical example.) The ring that has brought in fabulous sums in recent years—first $18,000, then $43,000 on resale—is a 1938 Superman ring offered to a few contest winners. Significantly, it is a comic book premium and part of that world of fabulous prices, not a real radio premium.

There is a change from previous listings of toys and premiums in other publications where they were placed under the year they were first offered. If the reader were so knowledgeable that he or she could identify the item to the exact year it was offered, he or she probably would not need a book such as this. The character who is the source of each premium can often be identified by the name itself ("Captain Midnight") or a recognizable symbol like Tom Mix's TM-Bar brand. Sometimes it gets a little harder, but if the premium is decorated with six-guns, spurs, and lariats, you can assume it comes from a Western show, not *Space Patrol*. A ring is listed in an alphabetical grouping of rings for the run of the show under each program title. And so on for badges, boxes, knives, telescopes, etc.

One of the few terms used in this book you might not recognize immediately is "bounceback." This refers to a premium that is offered in the same package as the premium one ordered from radio spots. Usually this was the only place this second item was advertised. Orders for it were bouncebacks from the first order. The Tom Mix Captain's Spur Badge was such a bounceback item. Usually, these bouncebacks were not very successful because they lacked the constant pressure on the listener of the daily commercials and even involvement in the storyline of the original premium. One can assume that sponsors wanted to see if listeners required the pressure of the broadcasts or if they would simply order anything offered to them. The necessity of the broadcasts were proved. Some Jack Armstrong bouncebacks showed a pathetic number of responses—in the mere dozens!

You will find detailed information on the more important premium-issuing programs, but concerning other shows about which little need be said, I have said little.

It was radio, more than TV, that gave us these wonderful toys that were "free as the air" that brought us news of their availability. The intervening years have brought rarity and value to them, but generally speaking, they are still obtainable for a price within reason and a patience for the hunt.

Jim Harmon
Burbank, CA, 1997

ARMSTRONG OF THE S.B.I.—
See "Jack Armstrong,the All-American Boy"

AMOS 'N' ANDY

Primarily known as a comedy serial, the earliest stories in serial form also contained elements of crime, suspense, and romance beginning August 19, 1929 (after appearing in the same format as "Sam and Henry" since 1926 for a rival broadcaster). It can't be denied that most of the shows, either as a serial or in the complete half-hour comedy show it became, would seem objectionable by today's standards. The two lead characters spoke a broad dialect, often invented and not reflective of the way Afro-Americans spoke at that time, and the characters were ignorant in the extreme. But the level of prejudice was so high in that era, Freeman Gosden ("Amos") told the present writer "It was the most sympathetic presentation Charles Corell ("Andy") and I could get on the air. If it were any more favorable to Black people, we would just have been forced off the air."

Always, Amos was presented as the "nicer" fellow of the two. In later years, he spoke almost flawless English, was a good husband and father, and a hard-working businessman. Andy was always trying to take advantage of his buddy—trying to get work or money out of Amos—so that he could spend his time loafing and chasing women, like his secretary, Miss Blue, whom he talked to on a cross-wired intercom: "Buzz me, Miss Blue."

Shortly, the two men met a con artist who completely eclipsed Andy. He, George Stevens, known as the Kingfish (after the Southern political boss Huey Long), was the head of their lodge, the Mystic Knights of the Sea. He was crafty enough to pull the schemes on Andy that Andy had tried to pull on Amos. Occasionally, Andy and the Kingfish would join forces and try to con Amos, but since, as W.C. Fields pointed out, "You can't cheat an honest

Freeman Gosden (left), radio's "Amos." Courtesy Eddie Brandt's Saturday Matinee.

man," Amos' lack of larceny in his soul always saved him. Both Kingfish and Amos were played by Gosden. Sometimes they appeared in the same scene and talked to each other.

In the early years, Amos and Andy moved from the Deep South, "reluctantly" because of the wonderful life they had there (so ran the script), to Webber City, a fictional suburb of a Mid-Western city, possibly Chicago (where the broadcasts from station WGN originated). In the beginning, the two ran the Fresh Air Taxicab company—so called because their one cab was missing a roof and several other parts. Amos continued to run the cab company into the '40s and '50s, and presumably expanded it into a fleet of taxis. Andy dropped out to concentrate on his own harmlessly shady endeavors.

A map of Webber City was one of the earliest premiums when the series became sponsored by Pepsodent tooth paste. A letter from Amos and Andy came with the colorful map, urging listeners to buy Pepsodent and related products because that would "help us a lot"— an appeal flatly illegal by today's advertising standards. Another premium was the script of the fifteen minute serial episode in which Amos married his long time sweetheart, Ruby, although the ceremony was interrupted by certain dramatic events.

The later half-hour series concentrated mostly on the Kingfish and his long-suffering wife, Sapphire, and her mother, "Mama," whose joint efforts were to get Kingfish a job, while his sole effort was to keep from working.

The series provided the inspiration for other dialect humor in early radio, including the "rube," *Lum and Abner*, and the Jewish *Goldbergs*, not to mention helping inspire romantic daytime serials—soap operas—such as *Ma Perkins* and *Just Plain Bill*, and even children's adventure serials such as *Jack Armstrong, the All-American Boy*. The series influences daytime and nighttime soap operas and mini-series today on TV, even if the callow scripters are unaware of the ultimate source of inspiration.

Amos 'n' Andy was the most listened to, most imitated, most important series in the history of broadcasting. The premiums are only a faint reflection of this landmark program.

AUNT JENNY'S REAL LIFE STORIES

From January 1937 to late 1956 the cheerful kitchen of everybody's Aunt Jenny was visited by announcer Dan Seymour—"Danny"— not the immensely fat actor of the movies with same name, although his picture is mistakenly used at times to represent the trim announcer. It is a wonder Danny kept his figure with all the cakes and pies made with Spry, the sponsoring shortening that Jenny plied him with before and after every show. He had to sample everything, and at times lent a hand adding some apples to a pie shell.

The baking started, and Danny and the home audience could settle down and listen to Aunt Jenny tell one of her stories about something that happened to someone in her home town of Littleton. Like Mary Worth in the comic strips, Aunt Jenny usually did not play too prominent a part in the story—it was about one of her younger friends and a problem in their love life. Unlike most soap operas—daytime serials—of the time, whose storyline might last for years, the events here were wrapped up usually in a week of daily episodes. The program had a magazine format, and was constantly turning a new page.

From time to time, Aunt Jenny (Edith Spencer and later Agnes Young) would offer some piece of costume jewelry like a locket, a broach, or a pin. Many other soap operas did this as well. Almost none of these pieces were identified as coming from Aunt Jenny, or anyone else, though. They were not fixed in memory as those items offered on the various juvenile shows. Nobody can remember them.

Only those items showing pictures of Aunt Jenny advertising Spry can definitely be identified with the show.

BABE RUTH

Babe Ruth was considered THE great American baseball player, just as Louis Armstrong was THE great jazz performer, and Ray Bradbury is THE science fiction writer. He had various radio shows from the '30s into the '40s; often they involved a sports quiz with kids. He spoke well for an athlete of his era and was able to deliver dialogue well in the short radio dramas he often performed (as he did in the motion picture *Pride of the Yankees*).

Often described as a "big kid" into middle age, he listened to *The Lone Ranger* and *Tom Mix* almost every day. One of his last appearances on radio came on the *Mix* program when he was promoting the biographical film about his life in the late '40s, even as he fought the throat cancer claiming his life. The episode is one of the some thirty known to have survived from the *Mix* series. In it, the train carrying Babe Ruth stops in Tom Mix's home town, Dobie, and Tom (Curley Bradley) and Sheriff Mike Shaw (Leo Curley) come aboard. They talk about the new movie coming out, and Babe is given an honorary Dobie Sheriff's badge (recently a premium offer). Tom and Mike ask Babe to stop by again, but there is a false hardiness in Mike's voice that tells the story.

BABY SNOOKS

Fanny Brice was a comedienne when being "ethnic" was no sin. Fanny was definitely Jewish and her act was built around that fact. The big budget movies about her life told mostly of her romance with gambler Nickie Arnstein, but she had many other boyfriends, not all Jewish, among them (from what he told me) cowboy actor Tim McCoy.

While she could sing comedy songs in dialect ("Second Hand Rose") or plaintive torch songs ("My Man"), Brice became most popular in later years for a character she played in a sketch for the Ziegfield Follies stage show. Baby Snooks was the most precocious brat of all time, originally specifically Jewish, but that element became generalized. She first did it on radio as a series on *Good News of 1938*. The half hour originally was shared with comedian Frank Morgan who told windy, tall tales for fifteen minutes in a routine patterned after Jack Pearl's *Baron Munchausen*. Eventually, Snooks was given a whole half hour until Brice died in 1951, in mid-series. Morgan had it paired with another sketch, "The Bickersons," featuring Don Ameche and Francis Langford for *The Old Gold Show*.

Only a few premiums were offered over the years. Kids were supposed to want a Jack Armstrong flashlight so they could be like Jack, but few kids wanted something of Snooks' so they could be like her bawling, whining, trouble-making self.

BATMAN

Batman, the Caped Crusader, and his sidekick, Robin, the Boy Wonder, appeared regularly on radio beginning in 1945 as supporting characters (we would call them "guest stars" today) on *The Adventures of Superman*. (See "Superman" entry.) The two were obviously planned to "spin off" (another modern term) to their own show, and a pilot or audition program was produced, but their own series never actually made it to radio. In less than five years, television was beginning to force many established shows off sound broadcasting, and there was little incentive to try anything new. Perhaps something innovative might have helped, and a few things like the *X Minus One* science fiction dramas were tried, but not a series with Batman.

Robin was encountered by Superman first. The Man of Steel found him unconscious, floating in a rowboat—his x-ray vision revealed the colorful scarlet vest of the Boy Wonderunder the sports clothes of young Dick Grayson. When revived, the youth told Superman that Batman was missing. "Missing... the most glamorous figure in all the world, save Superman himself..." announcer Jackson Beck intoned. As a child I was an avid reader and I knew "glamour" was not confined to movie stars like Lana Turner alone, but I don't know if all the kids listening understood.

The mighty Man of Tomorrow could find anyone, and he soon discovered the Dark Knight, Batman, as a figure in Zolton's Wax Museum. Superman quickly discovered a heart beat slowed almost to a stop in a state of suspended animation. He soon freed Batman and together the two heroes quickly captured the mad scientific wizard, Zolton, who was turning great American scientists into wax figures to be revived in Nazi Germany to help their cause.

Thereafter, Batman appeared in about every second serial story on the *Superman* radio show, sometimes with Robin and sometimes without him. Batman and Robin were often called upon for help when the Man of Steel was threatened with Kryptonite, the element from his destroyed home planet that could weaken him, and even theoretically kill him, if he was exposed to it long enough. It was the Dynamic Duo who aided Superman in his fight against his greatest foe, the Atom Man, in whose very veins flowed deadly liquid Kryptonite. Batman was played by a variety of actors, including Stacy Harris (earlier radio's Jack Armstrong), Matt Crowley (who played Buck Rogers, Dick Tracy, and Mark Trail at various times), and even future movie star, husband to Bette Davis on screen and off, Gary Merrill. Robin seemed to have always been radio juvenile Ronn Liss.

In the comic books, Batman appeared on the cover of *Detective Comics* No. 27 in 1939, and in the lead story inside, only about a year after the first appearance of Superman in *Action Comics* No. 1 in 1938. Almost immediately, the Man of Steel had his own club, the Supermen of America, with a membership card and certificate, and a badge. It was probably thought one club per publishing company was sufficient, but by 1942, DC publications had changed its mind and offered another membership kit for the Junior Justice Society of America, an offshoot of the regular Justice Society of America featuring a group of heroes including Hawkman, Hourman, and the Spectre who appeared not only in their own comic books, but also joined together in *All Star Comics*. Both Batman and Superman were honorary members of the Society. They didn't appear in every issue, but did once in awhile for special events, such as raising money for a Red Cross drive in *All Star* No. 7. The membership certificate of the Junior Justice Society was bordered with head shots of the regular members about the size of 25-cent piece and with smaller dime-size pictures of honorary members Batman, Superman, Flash, and Green Lantern. So, contrary to some published reports, Batman was connected to this group, and the Junior Justice Society Membership Kit would be the first comic book Batman premium available.

In 1943, a *Batman* movie serial of "Continued Next Week" episodes appeared in theatres. It seemed incredibly cheaply made and shoddy, even for a medium not known for sufficient budgeting. Yet the *Flash Gordon* serial from 1936 has been added to the Library of Congress' National Registry of Films, recognized as a "National Treasure." It may be the only chapterplay ever so recognized, although a few others—*Flash Gordon's Trip to Mars*, *The Lone Ranger*, and *The Adventures of Captain Marvel*—probably deserve recognition. Certainly *Batman*, and its sequel of six years later, *Batman and Robin* in 1949, do not deserve honors, due to many problems not the fault of the second serial's director, Dean of Chapterplay Directors, the present writer's dear old friend, Spencer Bennet. These movies did provide a few pin-back buttons and membership cards as collectibles.

It was not until 1966 and the appearance of the *Batman* TV show that many new toys and premiums began appearing. With Adam West and Burt Ward as Batman and Robin, the series made literal transfers of material from artist Bob Kane's comic book pages. It provided a low type of humor known as "Camp" in certain select circles. The general public seemed to enjoy the laughs; often young children and some adults did not realize it was supposed to be humor and accepted it all as colorful adventure. Most of these items were store toys, but cereal box backs and write-in ads did provide a few genuine premiums, mobile cut-outs, and giveaway comic books. Similar offers connected to the big-budget feature films continue to this day.

"Supermen of America" comic badge

BLACK FLAME OF THE AMAZON

This series was an early 1930s radio adventure serial about the exploits of real life explorer Harold Noice along the Rio Vaupes in Columbia, South America, and his encounters with the wild natives and greedy whites turned modern pirates. Despite the blood-curdling storylines, the premiums held educational content, notably the map of the region.

BOBBY BENSON

Bobby Benson was always the lead character in this Western drama series, but it went by a variety of titles. In the early days—from 1932—the show was sometimes called *The H-Bar-O Ranch* or *The H-Bar-O Rangers*, after the sponsor, H-O Oats. After more than a decade, producer Herbert Rice and original writer Peter Dixon revived the series in 1949 and it became *Bobby Benson and his B-Bar-B Riders* or sometimes just *The B-Bar-B Ranch*.

Bobby was a very young cowboy, a child of perhaps ten to twelve. (Bobby Jordan, later leader of the Dead End Kids on screen, was probably the first young actor in the role; Ivan Curry and others were in the '40s). He had inherited the ranch in the Big Bend area of Texas from his old uncle. While the ranch hands called him "Little Boss," things were really run by the foreman and apparently Bobby's legal guardian, Tex Mason (originally future movie star Tex Ritter). There was also the Indian, Harka (who called Tex "El Tejuano"), and the sturdy cowboy Irish, the boasting, skinny Windy Wales (played in the '40s series by comic Don Knotts).

Although the fictional series gave Bobby more authority and autonomy than a real-life child would have, it told many nice little moral lessons where both Tex and Harka employed mutual respect and understanding to solve any problem.

The '40s series was not a serial but a complete half-hour story every broadcast. One program concerned Bobby accidentally releasing a prize bull while playing a joke on Windy. Troubled with guilt, Bobby vowed to recapture the dangerous bull by himself. Harka would not tell on Bobby—he instead followed him into mountain lion country, only to get bitten by a rattlesnake. With the dedication of father and son, Bobby and Harka applied Indian lore to stave off death until Tex and the B-Bar-B Riders arrived to rescue them, and incidentally, recapture the bull. Bobby vowed no more practical jokes for him.

Despite being very popular, in those days of diminishing radio drama, the series never got a regular sponsor. It was sponsored from time to time for a few days or few weeks by such things as Christmas balloon-made animals one could send in for. Most of the premiums were made by the show's producers to prove its appeal to potential sponsors. One of the best premiums was a 45 rpm record with a seven-minute dramatization of the show, similar to those produced of *The Lone Ranger*.

The thirty minute series was moved around, filling many open time slots on the Monday through Friday adventure hour, 5:00 to 6:00 P.M. As many old favorites like *Tom Mix* and *Captain Midnight* were discontinued in the face of television in the early 1950s, the B-Bar-B program was brought in to replace them. For a short time the half-hour show was on an incredible eight times a week—Saturday and Sunday afternoons, Tuesdays and Thursdays at 5:30 P.M., Mondays, Wednesdays, and Fridays at 5:00 P.M., and an added different show Monday nights. For the sake of variety, not every episode featured Bobby Benson. Some stories dealt with Tex Mason in his mysterious rider role, the Lemonade Kid. (Later, Tex would assume a more threatening secret identity, the King of the Outlaws, but he always really worked for law and order.) A few episodes were carried by Harka and Windy Wales working alone.

In the midst of all these shows, there was also a five-minute Bobby Benson series featuring another Tex, Tex Fletcher, singing and Windy telling tall stories. This capsule show appeared on Sundays, Tuesdays, and Thursdays, and perhaps other times. A local WOR New York TV show also appeared—a half-hour expansion of the songs and jokes format.

The very last Bobby Benson radio series was a quarter-hour in 1955 where Bobby appeared alone and introduced kiddie records, such as seven minute dramatizations of Walt Disney's TV hero, Davy Crockett. It filled out the hour (with a quarter-hour newscast) of daily half-hour reruns of *Sergeant Preston of the Yukon*. When Quaker dropped sponsorship of those, Bobby Benson was told to ride into the sunset, still the Kid Cowboy after surviving three decades of broadcasting.

BUCK JONES IN HOOFBEATS

Hoofbeats was a syndicated transcription series in 1937 starring Western movie star Buck Jones. Although he had started in the silent movie era working in Tom Mix vehicles before getting his own series, Buck had a strong, masculine voice and was able to project emotion as well as humor. His acting ability may have been limited, but he had some as opposed to none in many of his contemporaries. He was okay as a radio performer. Although the Buck Jones series was very brief, he did have the distinction of actually portraying himself on radio. The *Tom Mix* series ran for decades, but the actual movie star never supplied his own voice for the broadcast series. Mix was impersonated by a string of actors. Mix might have portrayed himself as Buck Jones did, but in point of fact, he never did.

The Jones series, *Hoofbeats*, seemed to be aimed at a more adult audience. The title suggested an epic film of riders of destiny pushing the frontier ever onward. Orchestrated music supplied the bridges and the dialogue was more mature. The single known surviving example of *Hoofbeats* is a quarter-hour serial episode involving Buck and his horse, Silver, coming to the aid of a family in a covered wagon in the days of the Old West. The pioneers are an old gentleman and his grown daughter, who shows a most decorous interest in our stalwart hero. There was no kid sidekick or overly humanized horse to set the then standard of children's adventure shows. Yet the sponsor was a breakfast cereal, Grape Nuts, and the program offered badges, rings, and toy premiums, also advertised in Sunday comics section ads very similar to the Tom Mix campaign.

Another similarity to the Tom Mix series was that the narrator and commercial spokesperson called himself "The Old Wrangler" on both the Jones and Mix series. It was a colossal blunder. The producers of the Buck Jones series evidently never even listened to a single episode of the show they hoped to compete with. While it is not known for a fact, one might conjecture that the Jones series was of so short a duration because Ralston-Purina,

Movie star ice cream lid featuring Buck Jones

owners of the Mix radio series and the character "The Old Wrangler" may have threatened legal action. It was even a worse "sin" because it had Ralston's "Old Wrangler" selling a rival breakfast food. The two actors even sounded alike, each with a rich baritone voice.

The popularity of Buck Jones nearly equaled that of Tom Mix and it would have been a reasonable expectation for the Jones series to run a good many years, but such was not to be.

BUCK ROGERS

In many ways, Buck Rogers was the first adventure hero for kids to be on national radio.

Orphan Annie had been around since 1930, but to be gender specific and perhaps not "po-

"Buck Jones in Silver Spurs" movie poster

litically correct" for these days, she was a heroine. She was also a little girl, and originally her "adventures" around Simmons Corners were pretty tame—planning a surprise birthday party, searching for a missing pet, etc. Buck Rogers was a grown man, capable of taking part in a rousing fist fight, or even firing shots at an enemy. One could say the level of violence was rising, or that radio's young audience was demanding stronger meat for its entertainment.

The *Buck Rogers* program was unique in that it was science fiction, set five hundred years in the future. In 1932, the year the series began, fantasy had not been widely accepted by a pragmatic America. The Western or detective story magazine was what filled newsstands with hundreds of titles. Only three or four fantasy or SF magazines were around at any one time for years. Perhaps one or two movies of a "fantastic" content were made a year. And on the radio airwaves, there were only less than half a dozen series, and those were more supernatural than science fiction in nature.

As a newspaper comic strip, *Buck Rogers in the Twenty-Fifth Century* had made a big hit with young readers with its rocket ships that looked like a plumber had put them together in his backyard, and stories of a future at once optimistic and dire in its predictions. Kellogg's cereals first brought the comic strip to radio. The company probably thought it didn't matter whether it was set in the past like a Western, or set in the future as it was—what counted was that the kids liked it.

Science fiction subjects have always created a fan following (witness the more recent phenomenons of *Star Trek* and *Star Wars*) with a desire to band together in clubs. The Buck Rogers Club for Boys and the Wilma Deering Club for Girls were actually started by the listeners, not the sponsor.

The comic strip was written by Phil Nowland (who used material from an earlier novel he wrote for the pulp magazine *Amazing Stories*) and illustrated by Dick Caulkins. Both men tried to keep up with the radio version; Nowland submitted story ideas for scripter Jack Johnstone to flesh out, and Caulkins did special illustrated booklets—premiums—for the show. But over the years, their input to the radio series diminished and it became a thing unto itself.

Probably reflecting the problems science fiction had in being accepted in the mundane era of the '30s and '40s, Buck Rogers did not stay in one time period on one network the way such slightly later adventure series such as *The Lone Ranger*, *Tom Mix*, and *Jack Armstrong* did for nearly twenty years or more (with perhaps a few alterations). Buck and his friends moved around, changing time slots and sponsors. It went into syndication for Popsicle bars, repeating the original quarter-hour scripts, now in recorded thirty-minute chunks, once every Saturday. There was a final live daily fifteen-minute series on the Mutual network in 1947. The program went "beyond rocket power...beyond the atomic bomb...beyond the future..." A premium offer was for an "atomic-charged" Ring of Saturn which glowed in the dark.

Curtis Arnall, the first actor to portray Buck on the air, explained how a strange gas in the lowest part of a mine had caused Buck to sleep five hundred years, from the twentieth century into the twenty-fifth. Arnall got a lot more publicity than the leads in most afternoon adventure serials. He appeared in costume as Buck and was photographed for the newspapers, at the openings of various scientific exhibits, at the New York World's Fair, and elsewhere. He certainly looked the part, and could have played Buck in a movie, given the chance. For some reason, he dropped out of the part—and apparently out of broadcasting.

Matt Crowley was next to assume the role, and he continued getting great publicity. He appeared in costume as the only non-cowboy on a premium series of full-color photos (color photography was rare in those days) for an ice cream product, appearing alongside such great stars as Buck Jones, Tom Mix, and John Wayne. Radio performers rarely appeared in such famed company. Later, Carl Frank and John Larkin as-

This advertisement for the Buck Rogers radio show appeared on a Post Toasties box in 1946

sumed the flying belt of Buck, but apparently did not leave behind such great photographs.

The female lead in the series was Adele Ronson as Wilma Deering, one of the earliest female astronauts in fiction. I met Miss Ronson more than fifty years later at the Newark Friends of Old Time Radio Convention, and fantastic indeed, she looked as if no more than half a dozen years had passed since she first traveled in space.

With their mentor, wise old Dr. Huer (Edgar Stehli), Buck and Wilma fought the dastardly plans of Killer Kane. His name may have made him sound like a small time crook, but he operated as a futuristic Hitler. One of his aides was the muscular, but none-too-bright, Black Barney. Eventually, Buck won him over to the right side, an accomplishment of dubious value, considering Barney made things worse as often as he helped.

In the final post-World War II series, Buck met a giant robot, the first among a planet full of robots, known as One. After One was opened up and reprogrammed by Buck, he became a staunch ally. After a final encounter with Killer Kane, in which Buck gave him the whipping of his rotten life, Buck, Wilma, and Doc, along with One, were sailing through space, en route to their home on Earth. Everybody was saying how great they felt, and even One offered that he was especially well lubricated that day. It was hard to see what they were so happy about after the announcer told the listeners that *Buck Rogers* would be going off the air. "Check your newspaper for the announcement of our return." I once said I was still looking, but actually, I gave it up after eight or ten years.

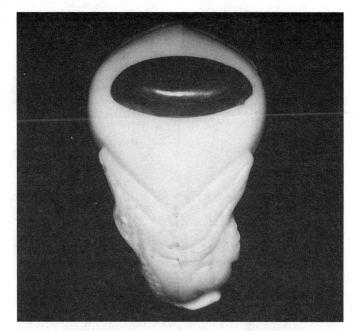

Buck Rogers glow-in-the-dark Saturn ring with a red stone (1945). Values in Good, Fine, and Mint: 150, 300, 550.

My patience was rewarded in part. That was not quite the end of *Buck Rogers* on radio. The small Liberty radio network in the '50s got permission to remake the old scripts but not to use the original character name. The old stories reappeared as *Brad Steele, Ace of Space*. The dramatic series originated on a Dallas radio station, so that everyone in outer space spoke with a Texas accent. This series was on for some months in harness with another quarter-hour show with old time Western movie star Ken Maynard narrating stories of the West. But Buck in disguise and Ken past retirement age couldn't hold out against TV for long, and hoofbeats and rocket trails faded into the sunset.

BUSTER BROWN GANG (STARRING SMILIN' ED MC CONNELL)

Smilin' Ed was another, perhaps the foremost, example of presenting a "favorite uncle" type as a teller of tales. Ed could do more than tell tales—he sang and played the piano, mostly songs for children with a moral about using plenty of soap and water. In the opening half of his thirty minute show, he had music and childish humor involving his animal sidekicks, Froggy the Gremlin (who was a trouble-maker) and Midnight the Cat (who was very nice). Then he would tell a story, often with recurring heroes such as Robin Hood or the Elephant Boy of India. Once a year lion trainer Clyde Beatty would make a personal appearance and act in a story about one of his adventures (anticipating a 1950 series of his own that offered no premiums).

The Buster Brown Shoe Company brought the show to TV about 1950 with McConnell and a filmed story. The early sequence offered the animals from radio held in place with wire, which is unacceptable by humane standards of today.

After the overweight McConnell's death, Andy Devine took over the hosting. It became *Andy's Gang*. The animals were still wired down.

CAPTAIN GALLANT OF THE FOREIGN LEGION

One of the screen's great action stars, Buster Crabbe (who had played Tarzan, Flash Gordon, Buck Rogers, and Billy the Kid in movies) chose Captain Gallant to come to TV. Unfortunately, it was not very popular and did not last. It seemed to have it all: Crabbe's real life sub-teen son, "Cuffy," as a kid mascot, a comic sidekick from Westerns, Fuzzy Knight, and Crabbe himself looking sharp in a Legion uniform. Despite the trappings of a kid show, many of the stories took

a serious, adult turn, and involved a court marshal trial, a philandering husband, and the like. Perhaps camels were just not a likable as rangeland horses. One wished Crabbe could just have continued as Flash Gordon on TV. Of course, as he once told me, he wanted the parts Clark Gable got. "I could have been a big star then," he said. But to anyone who was a kid in the '30s or '40s, there will seldom be a bigger star than Buster Crabbe.

CAPTAIN MARVEL

The chief rival of Superman in the comic books—and one who surpassed him in sales for a time—did appear briefly on radio. In the early '40s, *Captain Marvel* was heard on the air; newspaper radio listings and the fading memories of a few people can attest to the fact. The lawsuit by the Superman publishers against Captain Marvel's publisher for plagiarism probably put an end to the radio show. No recordings or scripts are known to have survived.

Captain Marvel, like Superman, was a super-powered man. He was strong enough to bend iron bars. He could fly like a bird, and bullets could not harm him. The difference was that while Superman was a grown man who removed his civilian outer clothes to reveal his fighting uniform when danger threatened, Captain Marvel, when not his red and gold garbed super-self, turned into his natural

form, a young boy named Billy Batson. He had been granted a mystical power to change into the mighty Marvel by saying the magic word "Shazam" and could return to his normal boy body by repeating the word. The changes came with a blinding flash of lightning and a crash of thunder. The change was so startling most people never realized where Billy went or where Captain Marvel came from.

The appeal of the radio series must have been the same as the comic magazines. If the program had been allowed to continue, it probably would have been as popular as *Superman* or *The Green Hornet*. As it was, Captain Marvel fans had to follow him exclusively in the comic books— save for one twelve chapter movie serial made in 1941 before the legal action of the Superman outfit made any inroads.

The serial is considered among the finest chapterplays ever produced and ordinarily would have generated a string of sequels. Former Western star Tom Tyler played the World's Mightiest Mortal and young Frank Couglan, Jr. played Billy Batson in the William Witney and John English directed Republic production. The story had Billy being granted his powers in the Far East—instead of the comic's strange tunnel of an old subway in the big city. A golden idol of the Scorpion could be used as a death ray by focusing the sun's rays through a set of lenses. A living symbol of the idol, also known as the Scorpion, appeared and mislead the native people into thinking he was their ancient god. The true protector of the idol and its followers, the spirit of Shazam, re-emerged from the fog of time and granted Billy the powers of Captain Marvel. The red-suited fighter fought the false Scorpion in the primitive land and crowded civilization until the false prophet was brought to justice.

The comic book series seemed to make up for the lack of premiums from the short-lived broadcast series. Premiums, the giveaway-type offered over the air, were presented in the pages of the comic book and in a series of letters from Captain Marvel mailed to those who joined his fan club. The letters themselves, and some special item like a post card that could be dipped in water to reveal a secret message, were free. There was a low charge for other items, but the intent was obviously to publicize the fabulous Captain Marvel when other manufacturers were turned off by the Superman law suit. The most valuable of these offerings were the small statues of Captain Marvel, his sister, Mary Marvel, and his adopted son, Captain Marvel, Jr. They have sold for more than two thousand dollars each.

There was a set of comic buttons, similar to the ones from Pep Wheat Flakes offered by Superman, but Captain Marvel offered buttons of his fellow Fawcett characters, Golden Arrow, Ibis the Invincible (a magician), Radar the International Policeman, and others. There was even a beanie cap to wear them on.

The early episodes of the World's Mightiest Mortal in *Whiz Comics* and *Captain Marvel Adventures* magazines were mainly concerned

Captain Marvel tie clip (store item)

with his battle against "the world's wickedest scientist," Dr. Sivana. Of course, Sivana had his own viewpoint. He considered himself "Rightful Ruler of the Universe." He must have seen it as a battle of "Right" versus "Might," but no loyal fan of Captain Marvel could agree with him. Sivana was definitely not a nice person and was ready to kill every man, woman, and child on Earth to achieve his ambition of ruling the universe. He came up with a variety of inventions to accomplish this, many of which were weapons against Captain Marvel.

There was at least one villain even worse than Sivana, a villain so powerful that even the self-styled Rightful Ruler of the Universe was reduced to working for him. This was the mysterious "Mister Mind" who headed the Monster Society of Evil. This dictator appeared in a twenty-five chapter series that appeared for a two-year period until 1945 in the publication *Captain Marvel Adventures*.

During the long story, Captain Marvel battled many of the same villains he had fought by themselves, but now they were in the employ of Mr. Mind: Captain Nazi, a superhuman created by German science to challenge America's heroes, Ibac, a creature with powers nearly as mighty as Marvel's who drew his source from pure evil, and the dastardly Sivana—all were our hero's worst enemies. What kind of villain could command a crew like this? Was Mr. Mind a giant robot? A powerful goat-headed monster? As he searched the chief villain's home planet, Marvel brushed a small worm off his shoulder. Big mistake. The worm was Mr. Mind. His power was in his great mind, not his body.

Two very valuable Captain Marvel special edition comics

Mary Marvel, Captain Marvel Club (Values in Good, Fine, and Mint: 50, 100, 150), and Capt. Marvel Jr. shoulder patches

Even after his tiny form had been revealed, Mr. Mind gave the mighty Captain Marvel the fight of his life, with the help of his Monster Society members, many of whom seemed to have crocodile heads and sort of human bodies. But finally Mr. Mind was captured, tried by a legal court, and Scotch-taped into the electric chair. The end.

Much of the appeal of Captain Marvel lies in the humor infused into the comic book stories by the chief artist, C.C. Beck. He also edited the stories and changed them around to suit himself. When a torrent of wind knocked young Billy Batson off his feet and upside down, his dialogue balloon of speech was also upside down: „¡dɪǝH„ And a moment later Billy spoke his magic word to turn himself into Captain Marvel and that was also inverted. Touches like that added a unique charm.

After years of being out of business from the '50s to the '70s, Captain Marvel was brought back to life by the company that had killed him—Superman's DC comics. If DC wanted to imitate itself with another Superman-like character, it could. The revival produced some pin-back premiums, and both a live-action and animated cartoon series for Saturday mornings on TV. Even C.C. Beck was brought back to the comics to do the art. But DC did not have Eando Bindo and the rest of the writers Fawcett had. Beck did not like the scripts so he quit. The revived series, now titled *Shazam!*—because another character was calling himself "Captain Marvel" by this time—limped on for a time and saw several revivals. Finally, in the '90s, artist/writer Jerry Ordway did the best revival yet, capturing much of the spirit of the original, but with the more sophisticated plots and characterizations expected by modern fans.

Unusual Captain Marvel and Mary Marvel shoulder patches

CAPTAIN MIDNIGHT

The *Captain Midnight* afternoon adventure series was on Monday through Friday for most of its duration (only three times a week in the beginning), syndicated fall 1938 to spring 1940; Skelly Gasoline was the sponsor. The network series was then broadcast on Mutual, September 1940 to late December 1949; Ovaltine was the sponsor.

Captain Midnight was the most mysterious and glamorous of a long line of aviator heroes on radio. He first flew through the airwaves in the fall of 1938, on only a small web of Midwest stations, sponsored by a local gasoline brand, Skelly. At first, Captain Midnight was not as colorful as his name. People in the story referred to him by his real name, Jim Albright, usually nick-named "Red." But as time went by, everybody began referring to him by his secret code name, "Captain Midnight."

The name began years before. An American Flying corps captain was given a high priority assignment. The outcome of the First World War depended upon it. The thing had to be done before twelve that night. The hours passed with glacial slowness for the staff officers waiting behind. Hope and despair shared the air. Then...very faint...now stronger, all heard the engine of a single plane. "And it is just midnight," one officer said, as the church clock began to strike. "Yes," Major Steele said, "And to me, he will always be...Captain Midnight!"

Publicity photos for the new radio series now showed Captain Midnight, dressed in black leather flying togs, eerily lit in shadow. A costumed, double-identity superhero was born, concurrent with Superman and Batman in the comic books.

Created by Robert M. Burtt and Willfred G. Moore, *Captain Midnight* was one of several aviation-themed programs the two had on radio. The announcer on their earlier show about a teen-aged flyboy, *Jimmie Allen*, became the lead actor on their new *Captain Midnight*. He was the commanding-voiced Ed Prentiss.

Prentiss told the present writer he did the first year of the Midnight series and considered the part his. The show went on summer hiatus. He read that auditions were being held for the next season. He assumed that meant for supporting characters, not for Captain Midnight himself. He was wrong. The sponsor's representative gave the title role to another Chicago actor, Bill Bouchey ("Boo-shay"). After another year, auditions were held in the fall of 1940. Prentiss showed up for these, and regained the part for almost another ten years.

The Wander company, makers of Ovaltine, bought the show from Skelly gasoline for national sponsorship over the Mutual Broadcasting System in 1940. Paul Barnes replaced Prentiss for the final six months in late 1949 when it was tried unsuccessfully as a half-hour complete adventure.

More than any other program on radio, Midnight fought a single villain, a man well-named Shark. He was Ivan Shark, a man originally suggested to be of mixed European and Asian bloodlines, and certainly exhibited the alleged least favorable aspects of both races. He owed allegiance only to himself. He might work for the Nazis or the Japanese high command, but his long-range goal was to promote his own plans for world conquest. The actor chosen for this important role was Boris Aplon, who had a long relationship with the Ovaltine company. He had played the beloved Daddy Warbucks on its earlier series, *Orphan Annie*. After the era of radio drama, he often worked in various stage companies of *Fiddler on the Roof* in supporting roles and sometimes the lead. Aplon was a talented man and was well aware of it.

With the help of his sinister daughter, Fury, and his henchmen including Fang and Gardo, Shark was a near constant menace to Captain Midnight, his young lieutenants, Chuck Ramsey and Joyce Ryan, and his mechanic and general assistant, Ichabod "Ikky" Mudd.

Skelly gasoline began offering the premiums that could be picked up at its various service stations. There were stamp albums, photos of Midnight and pals, and a winged badge for the Flight Patrol which preceded the Secret Squadron (which came when Ovaltine picked up sponsorship).

With Ovaltine, the big premium offer each year was a new Code-o-graph badge (for decoding and encoding messages) featuring a distinctive element—an early one came with a photograph of Captain Midnight which you could replace with one of yourself, and then there was one with a magnifying glass, another with a police-type whistle, and so on. With each badge came a handsome full-color manual with paintings of the heroes and villains of the show, and information on secret signals and the like.

Other items were offered from time to time. The most sought after came during an adventure in South America when the show offered the Mystic Sun God Ring. This ring has become one of the rarest and most valuable of all radio premiums.

In the beginning of the Midnight series, Shark was the constant opponent week after week, but then as years went by, Shark went offstage from time to time—captured and imprisoned, or thought killed in some explosion. Other villains would call for Captain Midnight's attention, be they the Axis military forces dur-

Captain Midnight 1946 code-o-graph mirro-matic badge. Values in Good, Fine, and Mint: 70, 140, 275.

A Captain Midnight Secret Squadron manual

Captain Midnight 1948 code-o-graph pocket piece mirro-flash badge. Values in Good, Fine, and Mint: 60, 125, 200.

and his closest associates saw Shark flee into the ice and snow, only to encounter a polar bear—a hungry one.

Finally, kindly announcer Pierre Andre asked all of the listeners to never forget Captain Midnight and his healthful food drink sponsor, Ovaltine. The heroic captain would fly again, in just a few years, in a new TV series starring Richard Webb—new Code-o-graph premiums were offered—but it was over and out for the memorable radio program.

"Happy Land-i-ings..." echoed a final closing.

Back view of the 1947 Captain Midnight code-o-graph badge with the dial on the side of the police whistle. Values in Good, Fine, and Mint: 5, 100, 200.

ing World War II, or criminals who attempted to modernize cattle rustling out West.

But Shark would come back, time after time, until that final instance, the last episode, now in the half-hour format adapted by all the radio adventure serials before succumbing to TV. Secret Squadron planes had spotted his arctic headquarters from the air, and Midnight

CAPTAIN VIDEO

One of the earliest space heroes on TV was the aptly named Captain Video. In the earliest days of nation-wide television, the character appeared as host Monday through Friday afternoons on the Dumont television network to introduce old films. Oddly the films he was chosen to introduce were not old space films like *Flash Gordon* serials (shown elsewhere), but old cowboy movies of Johnny Mack Brown, Jimmy Wakely, and the like. Captain Video would come on screen, tell the audience that

there was a big solar storm threatening some of his Video Rangers out near Pluto, and he would have to keep track of what was happening to them. In the meantime, he would check in on one of his Video Rangers on Earth—in the state of Texas, in fact. The captain would turn in his super-powered TV to Texas in time to reveal Jimmy Wakely being falsely arrested on a charge of rustling!

In time, Captain Video would get a sidekick, the youthful Video Ranger, and other cast members. We would see him acting out a space story between peeks at the Wild West. The Western clips became shorter, and disappeared during a Saturday morning series of more adult science fiction stories.

During the afternoon serial, Powerhouse candy bars and other sponsors offered premiums after the type radio had been giving away for decades. The Rite-O-Lite ray gun was a popular item.

The very earliest serials on the series that ran from 1949 to 1956 were written by such mainstays of radio drama as George Lowther (who had written for both *Superman* and *Tom Mix* on radio). Because of a lack of budget, much of the TV show was like radio. Captain Video would describe a battle between two fleets of space battle cruisers as he and the Ranger looked out the portal of his own space craft and flashes of light from laser cannons

and exploding space craft lit the faces of the two uniformed watchers. Eventually, both the daily serials and the Saturday show were written by some of the leading SF writers of the day, including Damon Knight and Jack Vance. They were eager to get their feet in the door and many did go on in the new medium, such as Knight who would later write for Rod Serling's *Twilight Zone*.

The best known Video was Al Hodge who had played the Green Hornet on the radio nearly a generation before. His Ranger was Don Hastings. They were involved in a really innovative TV program, going from a bare-bones gimmick to a nicely produced TV drama. *Captain Video* may have been the best show the fledgling DuMont television network had—which may have been the reason why the TV set manufacturer had to take its network off the air, leaving no space lane for Captain Video.

CHANDU THE MAGICIAN

Chandu, which began in 1932, was a very early serial on radio. It involved not only adventure and fantasy, but also elements of atmospheric Near East music as well. Frank Chandler had learned real occult magic from an Old Yogi in a distant land. Throughout half the world he was known as Chandu, a master magician. He could use hypnotism (not unlike Mandrake of the comic strips) to make his enemies think they were being attacked by a cobra or wild men of the desert. But with Chandu, it was more than hypnotism. He could actually transport his body through space and go from Cairo to London in a few breaths.

He took his whole family with him on his adventures. To provide listener identification, there was his somewhat matronly sister, Dorothy, and niece and nephew, Betty and Bob Regent. Mr. Regent, the children's father and Dorothy's husband, was among the missing at first—long a captive of Chandu's evil counterpart, Roxor.

Gayne Whitman was the suave Chandu in the early years of a syndicated series. The pro-

gram was revived in 1949 on a regional West Coast Don Lee network with a young actor, Tom Collins, in the title role. In at least one episode, Gayne Whitman returned to play a minor government official. He chose not to take name credit, unlike every other actor in the cast. He probably did not wish to admit to "slipping" to a supporting role.

The daily episodes were slightly rewritten for a more modern interpretation of the Harry A. Earnshaw originals. After less than a year, the old and most current sponsor, White King soap, adapted the show into a complete half-hour story once a week. At first, the series retained all the old magic, but the show began to become routine, a simple detective story where Chandu performed one magic trick an episode. By then it was deemed worthy of being heard nationwide on the whole ABC network.

Not unexpectedly, virtually all the premiums were for one or more feats of parlor magic the listener could perform "just like Chandu."

CHARLIE MC CARTHY

Charlie McCarthy was the feisty Irish street kid dummy of ventriloquist Edgar Bergen. For one sketch, Charlie put on a tuxedo with a top hat and monocle, a complete contrast to his personality, but the clothing stuck. Edgar was a very reserved man who told me during an interview at the Brown Derby "I sometimes wish I could be accepted by people as readily as Charlie is." Of course, it was through Charlie he could lose his reserve and say whatever outrageous things he could think of.

His radio sponsor, Chase and Sanborn coffee, offered a number of premiums for Charlie's fans, the best of which was a cardboard figure of Charlie with a moving mouth. I recall as a child I desperately wanted that paper "dummy." For some reason, I did not get it. Either I couldn't get the Chase and Sanborn label I needed, or if I sent for it, it just was lost in the mail. For a long time, I tried to make my own paper "Charlie" from pictures of him in magazines and the mail-order catalogue. Years later, I was able to buy one of the Chase and Sanborn originals, and even to buy a full-size semi-professional dummy of him. But it wasn't as good as getting one of those cardboard "Charleys" in the mail would have been.

THE CINNAMON BEAR

The story of Paddy, the Cinnamon Bear, and how he helped a small boy and girl find the Silver Star that had topped their Christmas tree for as long as they could remember took twenty-six episodes. It took them all on a long fairy tale quest that involved a trip to the workshop of Santa Claus at the North Pole. Some people remember it with a fondness beyond all other radio programs. Fortunately for them, all episodes have been found and transferred from transcription disc to cassettes for all to enjoy.

As for me, I thought it was kind of cute, but I really resented the fact that it took a month of Hop Harrigan off the air just at the point where Hop was about to dive his plane down and rain .45 automatic slugs into cockpit of Japanese ace, Baron Matsubusi.

This exclusive, authorized set of six audio tapes contains all 26 original episodes of The Cinnamon Bear *with the original music (1979).*

THE CISCO KID

O. Henry's "Robin Hood of the Old Southwest" was just about as cleaned up for radio as a choir boy on Sunday. In the original literary piece, a short story, Cisco is a bandit who escapes being captured by wearing his girlfriend's dress and scarf. Certainly, the radio Cisco would never behave in so unmanly and unheroic a manner. The movies were a bit ambiguous on the point, but the radio made it clear that Cisco and his chubby sidekick, Pancho,

Charlie McCarthy and Edgar Bergen. Courtesy Eddie Brandt's Saturday Matinee.

were falsely suspected of being bandits. What they really wanted to do was help capture the bad guys. Sometimes the motives of the Lone Ranger and Tonto were suspected too.

New York announcer and actor Jackson Beck was the first Cisco of record out of New York in the early 1940s. In less than ten years, TV would come on the scene, and screen actors Duncan Renaldo and Leo Carillio began playing Cisco and Pancho on half-hour complete stories on both radio and television. Location work on the films soon made it impossible for them to make all the then-live radio shows, so they gave over their radio roles to Jack Mather and Harry Lang.

The filmed TV show and the transcribed radio series have played off and on, on their various media, right up to the present time. If bigots ever had any prejudice against Latinos, they could never sell it to us fans of the wonderful Cisco Kid.

Cisco Kid "Pancho" tab badge

COUNTERSPY (DAVID HARDING)

The *Counterspy* series was another creation of Phillips H. Lord, who also came up with *Gangbusters*. A wartime creation, the show was based on real life director of the Federal Bureau of Investigation, J. Edgar Hoover, and his fight against spies and saboteurs—an obvious conclusion, but never admitted. Harding (actor Don McLaughlan) had the help of his loyal agent, Peters (Mandel Kramer). Peters did most of the leg work, posing as a member of a subversive band or whatever, but Harding showed up at the end to help make the arrest. (The real Hoover did that only once, when a crook repeatedly questioned Hoover's courage.)

During the period when the *Counterspy* series was on in a time slot Tuesdays and Thursdays, alternating with *The Lone Ranger* for a young audience, a few premiums were tried.

DEATH VALLEY DAYS

Among my earliest memories of radio comes *Death Valley Days* and its "early morning bugle call" summoning the twenty-mule team wagons that would deliver the cargo of borax from Death Valley to the cities of the West, and then on to the rest of America.

The Old Ranger was the leading citizen of that tortuously hot section of desert. He had always lived there and always would. He knew everything that had happened and he would see everything that would happen. He had stories.

When I was a very small child I thought the announcer said the narrator was "the Old Wrangler," the character from my favorite afternoon serial, Tom Mix. So he had two shows. The Wrangler idea caught my attention, but I soon caught on that the Old Ranger was a different guy, but a pretty interesting fellow himself. He told stories about outlaws like Sam Bass, the building of Scotty's Castle in the desert, and some really oddball stories like the one where some telegraph lines picked up voices and transmitted them through an old army bugle as a sounding box—before the invention of the telephone.

Only a couple of years ago, my wife Barbara and I visited Scotty's Castle for the first time, and our guide—in my own mind—was the Old Ranger. He was reasonably old and his name was Jack and he was a Park Ranger. He declined to wear the regulation uniform and dressed in some Western-style duds he had thrown together. We told him it was our first visit to the Castle but that we had been to other parts of Death Valley several times. He said, "I guess you've seen about all there is to see then." I could sense he was baiting us. "I think it would take far more trips than we've had to see all that the Valley holds." Jack nodded, more friendly now. "I've lived here forty years, slept on the sand dunes, watched them load the borax, and I've only begun to see Death Valley."

Some of the tales from this pioneering radio and television series were preserved in various premium booklets by the Old Ranger, and these radio scripts have been adapted into booklets that even now are being offered for sale in the newly designated National Park.

DICK TRACY

Chester Gould's comic strip creation *Dick Tracy* made a fine afternoon thriller for kids and a lot of grown-ups who listened along. It began in 1935 and was on NBC in 1937. This was a great period for the show. Ned Weaver gave Tracy a rich, quietly authoritative voice, and the scripts were by George Lowther, one of the top writers in radio. He went on to write the broadcasts of *Superman* for a time, and then *Tom Mix* from 1944 to 1950. He tried a number of unusual things in a run of surviving episodes. He introduced versions of other popular radio heroes as villains combating Tracy. There was a mysterious cloaked figure called The Unknown who was clearly an alternate version of The Shadow. And only a few episodes later Dick Tracy and his sidekick, Pat Patton, went out West and encountered a Phantom Rider who was clearly a menacing version of The Lone Ranger.

It was not only the content of Lowther's scripts that was fine, but he developed an interesting format. As a writer myself, I have analyzed such things, and I have found that what Lowther did was put two usual quarter-hour serial episodes into one. Many episodes of other serials stalled around until the climax but Lowther, in six or seven minutes, offered as much content and characterization as most serials would take for the whole chapter, and built to a strong subclimax. Then he finished that day's episode by building to a stronger climax. As a result, the *Tracy* show moved twice as fast and had twice the content of most other serials.

The *Tracy* show became so popular that it was decided to try the program as a "prime time" venture in the evening. It was tried in 1939, and as memory serves, they were good shows. But maybe the adult audience was scared off by the comic strip name, thinking it would be too juvenile. At any rate, the show went off the air and stayed off for about five years.

Dick Tracy returned during the war years and one of his first jobs was tracking down those who counterfeited ration books. The show was never the same to me. What was missing I now know were the scripts by Lowther who was then writing *Mix*.

In a few more years, Tracy would be on at night again for a half-hour. This time the daily serial was not discontinued—there was also a Saturday night show with an entirely different plot and a more light-hearted, even comic, attitude.

Some of the more outlandish characters from the comic strip, like Gravel Gertie, appeared.

But soon both versions of *Dick Tracy* were gone from radio again, pushed aside in the afternoons of 1948 by more popular new shows like Sergeant Preston in *Challenge of the Yukon*, ironically in the half-hour format for action shows pioneered by the Tracy show.

GENE AUTRY

Gene Autry was at one time the most famous cowboy in the world; he was an actor and singer and star of screen, radio, records, stage, and rodeo. He would add TV to the list and even do an original cable show in the 1990s when most of the stars of his era, the '30s and '40s, were dead. (One notable exception is another hardy cowboy, Roy Rogers, who with his wife, Dale Evans, guest starred on Autry's cable show, as Autry returned the favor on theirs.) At this writing, as Gene approaches age ninety, he is still making personal appearances and is active as part owner of the Anaheim Angels baseball team.

I have always loved Gene Autry, as far back as my memory goes. Needless to say, I would go to see every Saturday matinee that offered a Gene Autry. I was a sickly kid, and my mother and father would hide the movie ads from me if an Autry film was scheduled during a period I was too sick with whatever was going around to attend. If I found out about it, sick or not, I would scream and cry in hopes of going.

I really did not care for a lot of singing to the leading lady. Some of the story lines confused me, like *South of the Border* where Gene's girlfriend becomes a nun either because Gene did not return from his secret assignment when he promised (song) or because her brother had been a bandit (film). Yet there was enough riding and fighting to satisfy me each time.

Gene was my favorite. I liked Hopalong Cassidy and Johnny Mack Brown, but Gene was No. 1. Critic William K. Everson said that Gene celebrated the common man. I was a fat kid with a round face. I couldn't believe I could grow up to be as slim and handsome as Roy Rogers, but I did think I might look something like Gene. So in the way of small boys, I fused with my hero, and it was "we" who sat in Champion's saddle and rode hard after the bad guys.

From an early age, I also was fixed on Tom Mix as a hero—reading articles about his supposed real life adventures, listening to the radio show about him, and seeing some short Mix films on my 8mm toy projector. But Gene and Tom rode similar horses (in fact I would learn that Tom's last "Tony Jr." was the same horse—real name "Lindy"—as the first one Gene called "Champion"), they wore similar costumes, and the two of them sort of blurred together as my cowboy hero.

It was Gene, though, who was real and alive for me in the movies and every Sunday night on radio. Tom Mix was a private myth I did not talk about much. (One schoolteacher told my mother it was "abnormal" that Jimmie had a "dead hero.") The two cowboys had came jarringly together one night in 1940. Gene had gone through his radio show—singing a few songs and doing a little ten or fifteen minute adventure story. While he prepared to announce his final song, Gene said, "I want to dedicate this song to one of the great Western pioneers, who has gone to join Buffalo Bill and Kit Carson in that land beyond the sunset... a man who will never be forgotten—Tom Mix." He then sang "Empty Saddles in the Old Corral."

I was six. I understood Tom Mix was dead. But maybe I didn't understand what death was. I didn't cry. But somehow I felt I had to go next door and tell my mother, who was visiting my aunt. I told her. "I always liked him," she said. "He was so handsome before he broke his nose." I think I was looking for something more comforting.

The Tom Mix Ralston Straight Shooters show was then in its seventh successful year on radio. I didn't then know his name, but Russell Thorson was playing Tom. I had this fantasy that with Tom gone, maybe the story would go and everything would be the same except instead of Tom Mix it would be Gene Autry sitting on the horse, waiting to fire the shot to start the current sequence about a modern land rush. But Monday came, and it was still Tom up there on Tony. I had gotten in a little late and missed most of an announcement. My father told me it said that the name and voice of Tom Mix would live forever. The radio series, with one long break, did continue another ten years.

Gene Autry went on as well. Except that when World War II came, Gene quit the movies to become a transport pilot in the then Army Air Corps. He risked death from being shot down by enemy planes or groundfire, as some so-called movie heroes contented themselves with selling war bonds. Somehow, Gene managed to continue his radio show, with the show now being listed as *Sgt. Gene Autry*. The Western story "half" (actually the drama usually only took about a third of the program) disappeared. Sometimes there was no story; at other times it was about some wartime event. I drifted away from the *Gene Autry* show for a few years, but after the war when Gene returned to the screen and to Western adventures on the radio, I came back too.

Premiums did not come back, because they had hardly been there at all. His radio sponsor contented itself with Gene saying: "Try delicious, healthful Wriggly's Doublemint gum. I like it." That was the entire commercial content of the program—not time enough to pitch a giveaway. Yet other companies (none a competing gum company) like Quaker and Pillsbury did give out various comics and the like.

The radio series could never be as gripping a dramatic experience as the hard-riding action of *The Lone Ranger* or the mysterious rangeland cases of *Tom Mix*, but the show itself was always enjoyable. The "story" segment near the end was the highlight of the show for me. The cast included such performers from other Western radio shows as Howard McNear, Forrest Lewis, Leo Curley, and Janet Waldo. The story might concern Gene driving his trail herd into a strange town. A gambling hall girl, who seemed to want to be a friend, warned Gene of a plan to rustle the herd, and offered to show him a safe route. She turned out to the leader of the rustlers, but Gene was too smart for her and had the sheriff waiting. But sometimes the younger audience did not even get its small dose of adventure. Sometimes the story was a comedy sequence where Gene had to pose as the father of a girl's baby for some innocent reason. At other times, the story was just a character study of some Western type, such as the old newspaper editor. Often the story set the stage for a fitting closing song.

Earlier at Melody Ranch there was music—Gene singing with Carl Cottner's band and the Cass County Boys trio. Usually the only women around were the Blue Bonnets, the back up singers. After a couple of songs, Gene was interrupted by the comedy side-kick. Johnny Bond and Pat Buttram usually alternated doing the bit. One segment had Pat asking Gene for advice on filing his income tax. For advice on

Gene Autry movie giveaway

A Gene Autry advertisement from 1942 for a Univex Camera

money matters he certainly came to the right man, the fabulously wealthy Gene. On a very few occasions, screen funny man Smiley Burnette put in a guest appearance. (Smiley had his own successful radio show in syndication.)

After the story and the final song, announcer Charlie Lyons would ask us to listen again next week and to see Gene's latest movie at our local theatre, telling us the title which would change every few months. When the title of the film remained *Riders of the Whistling Pines* for a year, I realized that was going to be the last Autry theatrical film.

But Gene kept appearing on TV in his own half-hour show and producing other TV Westerns like *The Range Rider* and *Annie Oakley*. There were personal appearances at state fairs and rodeos. And the radio show kept on, years after many favorites had left the air. But in 1956, there came a special broadcast without a live appearance of Gene. Lyons read a telegram from Gene saying the press of other work was making him give up the radio series. Lyons spoke for the sponsor, Wriggley's gum: "You've been the Doublemint man for a long time, Gene, and you are always welcome back if you change your mind..." He didn't, but Pat Buttram and most of the rest of the Melody Ranch gang continued for a time with a show called *Just Entertainment*.

After radio, I continued to follow Gene on TV. He had his own TV station in Los Angeles, KTLA, Channel 5 and he continued to show reruns of the TV series, as well as his movie features cut to one hour.

Gene Autry "Gene Autry Adventure Comics and Play-Fun Book" in-store giveaway

Over the years I made several attempts to arrange a meeting with Gene Autry to talk to him for my various books on movie serials (he made one of the historically more important, the science fiction/Western *Phantom Empire*) and of course radio. He always seemed unavailable.

Finally, in the '90s, I attended a Golden Boot Awards dinner where many of the old Western stars appeared, including Gene. After the awards had been given to many people, Eddie Dean was playing the guitar and singing, asking Monte Hale and others to join in. Finally, he hit the familiar strains of "Back in the Saddle Again" and Gene Autry began to sing along. It had been many years since Gene had sung in public. A stroke had made it difficult for him to speak, but he sang effortless and beautifully. The crowd was leaving after a long and tiring program, but all stopped to listen. "... Back in the saddle again, out where a friend is a friend..." Tears began streaming down the faces of men and women alike. We waited until Gene had finished, and then a thunderous ovation came forth, worthy of a

presidential nomination. Eddie gave a quizzical angle of the head. Gene said, "Naw... I've been lucky enough for one night."

I wrote Gene a letter. "Listening to you sing the other night was like seeing Babe Ruth hit one over the fence... Joe Louis deliver a knockout punch...It was seeing a great American do what he did best..." Gene wrote me back a nice note about that said he would have time to grant me an interview after baseball season. But with Gene, baseball season never ends.

A year or so later, I finally met Gene face to face when he appeared at the placement of a star on the Hollywood Boulevard Walk of Fame for his long time comedy partner, the late Smiley Burnette. The once magic name of Smiley no longer produced a great crowd. I got through the line to Gene, asked him to sign a photo, and shook hands with him. As he turned to go back to the group for the installation, he turned back and wished me "Good luck." A small gesture it was, but too large an effort for many celebrities to make to fans who have supported them (in more ways than one) all their careers.

Superman and Gene Autry play money

Over the years, I've kidded Gene in various writings about all his money and his once ample waistline, but I've always been a fan and at an age that makes me a Senior Citizen I'm still in the front row for any endeavor he makes from his Autry Museum of Western Heritage to his continuing interest in the always striving Angels baseball team. He has lived long and prospered and hopefully he will continue to do so until he joins Tom Mix in that land beyond the sunset.

GREEN HORNET

The Green Hornet was, in effect, the Lone Ranger brought into modern times. There was appeal to the character, but somehow the magic was not as great. A fiery horse with the speed of light seemed more exciting to most than a super-powered automobile called Black Beauty. Knockout gas fired from a pistol lacked the power of silver bullets aimed with unerring accuracy.

Yet the figure of the man with the gas gun, the lower half of his face masked, dressed in a dark hat and overcoat, persists. There were other modern urban masked avengers, in pulp paper fiction magazines, comic books, and a few movies, but probably none of them reached the millions that this popular radio show character did.

It was early 1936. George W. Trendle wanted another success to follow that of the *Lone Ranger* which began just three years earlier. It was his idea to put a character like the Lone Ranger into modern times. He gave the concept to writer Fran Striker to flesh out.

There were precedents. The Shadow was a masked character who prowled the popular fiction magazines known as "the pulps" (for the cheap pulp paper they were printed on).There was also a radio series of The Shadow, but he was different in the medium at that time—only a mysterious narrator of crime stories.

It was unexplored territory Striker entered to bring a double identity character to radio. There was no Batman in the comics yet, nor any other cloaked phantom hero regularly appearing in films. The radio writer devised no elaborate costume for his hero. He would merely wear a mask along with clothes like people of his time wore, just like the Lone Ranger. It was not unusual that his hero wore a hat—most men wore felt hats in the '30s. A long coat was standard dress for the cold winters of eastern cities. He carried a gun, but like the Lone Ranger whose silver bullets were never aimed to kill, this avenger would avoid the possibility of inflecting death by using a gun that could not kill—one that fired only a knockout gas, a variation on the tear gas guns some people carried in real life for protection.

What would he be called? There was an old movie about a mysterious character called The Bat. That had been used. Another menacing flying creature? The Hawk, perhaps. Maybe an insect, not a bird. There had been villains called the Scorpion. Maybe...the Hornet. Hornets buzzed around everything, angry and threatening. The most angry were green. The Green Hornet. Two words. Like the Lone Ranger. That was it. The Green Hornet.

The crime-fighter would work at a newspaper, so he would be able to hear of crimes quickly and learn where his help was needed. It was the same basic idea that the creators of Superman would have a few years later. But instead of being a reporter, like Siegel and Shuster's Clark Kent, Trendle and Striker's Brit Reid was the boss—the publisher of the paper, the *Daily Sentinel*.

He had taken the paper over from his elderly father, Daniel Reid. As the years passed in real time, it became established that this man was the same Dan Reid who had ridden with the Lone Ranger in the days of the Wild West, when he was only a teenager. In the radio show's beginning in 1936, the time sequence was right. If Brit was in his thirties, his father could be in his sixties and could have been in the West of the 1890s, some forty years before.

Brit worked at the *Sentinel* with others. There was his pretty, loyal, smart secretary Lenore Case. Brit called her "Miss Case." The reporters jauntily called her "Casey." As years passed, she began to suspect the double life her employer was leading, and at long last, she was permitted to be given the secret of the Green Hornet. The reporter who seemed to get all the best stories was Ed Lowry. The city editor was Dunnigen. And there was another character named Michael Axford. Originally, he was hired by the elder Reid to see that the young publisher, Brit, stayed out of trouble and to be his bodyguard. When Brit got tired of him hanging around and interfering with his activities as the Green Hornet, he was made a reporter. It was not an ideal job for Axford because he seemed too dumb to read or write, but then he could call in the stories to rewrite, and as an ex-cop he had contacts down at police headquarters. It became Axford's reason for living to capture the illusive menace, believed to be a criminal by most, the Green Hornet.

At his exclusive apartment, Reid ran a compact household. He only had his valet, Kato. The youthful Oriental was a man of many talents. Not only was he an excellent valet but he was also a master mechanic and inventor. It was Kato who invented the gas pistol and who designed the Black Beauty, the "sleek, super-powered car of the Green Hornet." Although Reid lived in a good neighborhood, just behind his apartment building there was a supposedly abandoned building. In the earliest stories, the place was described as an abandoned "livery stable." After all, only twenty years before, there had been as many horse-drawn vehicles on the streets as automobiles.

Eventually, the place was used as a warehouse, or rather not used, because it was a "supposedly abandoned warehouse." But in reality a secret passage in the back of Reid's clothes closet led to this secret hiding place of the Black Beauty. When the Hornet and Kato took the car out on a mission "a section of the wall raised in front of the car, and closed behind it," and the Hornet was gliding down a dark side street toward his rendezvous with danger.

Most of the crooks the Green Hornet encountered were not master criminals, but political crooks trying to swindle money out of the city treasury, or kidnappers, or bank robbers. It often seemed he did not have foes worth his mettle.

During World War II he concentrated his efforts on spies and saboteurs. He saved ships and factories from hidden bombs; he captured the spies who threatened a kindly old professor with harming his family in Germany in order to get the plans to the old man's secret weapon he was building for America.

The war affected the real world of radio production at WXYZ Detroit. Lee Allman, sister of production chief Jim Jewell, told me she suspected the Japanese actor who played Kato in the early years to actually be a spy for Nippon. While the vast majority of Japanese-Americans were entirely innocent of any harmful intent against America, there may have been a mere handful who served their former country. This "Kato" also ran a restaurant near the navel base in Detroit. Lee Allman noticed him eavesdropping on the conversations of naval officers before Pearl Harbor. After the attack on Dec. 7, 1941 the man simply disappeared off the face of the earth. Miss Allman suspected a visit by the Federal Bureau of Investigation.

In the storyline of the radio series, it was the Japanese ancestry of Kato which disappeared. After years of being described as a "faithful Japanese valet," Kato became Filipino. Perhaps he was a Filipino of Japanese ancestry, which is not uncommon. Some say Kato became Filipino the day after the Pearl Harbor attack, but evidence indicates he was described as Filipino a year before.

The first Green Hornet, Al Hodge, had an excellent voice, one that stood him in good stead along with his impressive looks some fifteen years later as the hero of another medium, Captain Video. Hodge complained in later years that the Green Hornet director, Charles Livingstone, had him read every line with increasing excitement, which was not always appropriate. So sometimes a line would go. "I'm going out, Miss Case. I'll be gone for half an hour! I'M GOING TO GET A SHOE SHINE!"

Not as many premiums were offered on this series as some of the other cornerstones of radio. One reason was that it did not always have a sponsor. *The Green Hornet* moved around quite a bit over the dial, trying to find an ideal spot, and it was often sustaining (no product advertising). It was not really a program for children, and like the Lone Ranger, the Hornet tried to attract an older audience too. Frequent pitches for premium toys would not fit the more adult attitude.

Of the premiums that were offered, the most popular among collectors is the Green Hornet Seal Ring. Just as the Lone Ranger left behind a silver bullet for identification, the Green Hornet left his seal—apparently a paper sticker. During the ring promotion, he left his seal by imprinting it on paper with his ring. It was a classy method, harking back to tales of knights and kings who sealed documents with their rings, and probably should have been kept as a permanent part of the mythos, but was not.

When listeners got their rings, they could see an embossed image of a hornet on the gold-colored top of the ring. The whole image was not left behind when the ring was pressed to a soft surface but certain bumps outlined a sketchy picture of a hornet in what appeared to be pin pricks.

Below the metal top, there was a base of whitish glow-in-the-dark plastic which contained an obvious "secret " compartment, big enough to hide a folded paper message or one nickel to keep away from the school bully, perhaps. A handsome band with intertwined G.H. initials completes this highly sought after ring. The ring, the premium most closely identified with the character, was the best-looking in the run of the series.

Though not as imaginative as The Shadow, or as thrilling as the Lone Ranger, the Green Hornet still prowls the imaginations of many a grown-up radio listener as he imprints his seal, gives an evil-doer a final blast of gas, and goes off into the night, the Black Beauty trailing away with the fading sound of a Hornet buzz.

I LOVE A MYSTERY

I Love a Mystery began in 1939, as a quarter-hour Monday through Friday serial, first on the West Coast only. It became a half-hour weekly serial on NBC coast-to-coast, 1939–1942, and a quarter-hour Monday through Friday, 1943–1944. It was retitled *I Love Adventure*, with half-hour complete stories in 1948 on ABC. It came back as *I Love a Mystery* and moved from Hollywood to New York studios, new cast, Mutual, 1949–1952, Monday through Friday, quarter-hour, new dramatizations of previous scripts.

CAST

Jack Packard	Michael Raffetto (1939–1943, also 1948)
	Jay Novello (1943)
	John McIntire (1943–1944)
	Russell Thorson (1949–1952, also 1954)
	Robert Dryden (1952)
Doc Long	Barton Yarborough (1939–1944, also 1948)
	Jim Boles (1949–1952)
	Jack Edwards (audition episode, 1945)
	Parley Baer (audition episode, 1954)
Reggie York	Walter Patterson (1939–1941)
	Tom Collins (1948)
	Tony Randall (1949–1951)
	Ben Wright (audition episodes, circa 1954)
Jerri Booker	Gloria Blondell (1940–1942)
	Athena Lord (1951–1952)

Others: Les Tremayne, Mercedes McCambridge, Forrest Lewis, Luis Van Rooten, Sarah Fussel, Elliot Lewis, Cathy Lewis, Barbara Jean Wong, Page Gillman, John Gibson, Don Douglas, Frank Bresee

Announcers: Dresser Dahlsted (1939–1944), Jim Bannon (commercials, 1944), Frank McCarthy (1949–1952), others

Creator/Writer/Producer/Director: Carlton E. Morse

Assistant Writers: Michael Raffetto, Barton Yarborough

Director: Mel Bailey (New York, 1951–1952)

Organists: Paul Carson, Rex Corey, others

Three comrades in adventure...three beautiful girls in a decaying old mansion menaced by a murderer who announces each killing with the sobbing cry of a baby...a lovely debutante whose touch brings death to every man in her life...vampire bats, big as men, winging through the ancient ruins of a sinister temple...these were all part of the best remembered and most loved of all the adventure serials of Golden Age radio, *I Love a Mystery*.

Carlton E. Morse (1901–1993) created the series in the late 1930s. Morse attributed the quality to a kind of universal greatness that he did not possess but which worked through him and all creative people. The appeal of the epic adventure lies in the power of children's imagination. Yet the series also reaches the minds of adults encountering recordings of the program for the first time. *I Love a Mystery* is a timeless work of popular art on the same plateau as works of literature, including Conan Doyle's stories of Sherlock Holmes.

Morse attributed much of the success of his programs to the actors who voiced his scripts. He not only gave the actors words to speak; the actors themselves gave back to him their own personalities, which fueled the development of the fictional situation they were in.

Michael Raffetto was an attorney admitted to the bar, as well as a radio actor, notably as thoughtful eldest son Paul Barbour on Morse's other great serial *One Man's Family*, but he was also the gruff, no-nonsense man of action who was Jack Packard, the leader of the Three Comrades, Jack, Doc, and Reggie on *I Love a Mystery*.

Barton Yarborough was born a Texan, but he could drop his Southwestern drawl when needed, for instance to play an Englishman on some radio shows and as Dr. Frankenstein's assistant in the film *Son of Frankenstein*. He sounded like a generalized American as brother Cliff Barbour on *One Man's Family*. But the dialect poured back when he was Jack's sidekick, Doc Long. It is reported that Yarborough did not have to do much acting to portray Doc's unrelenting appreciation for the fairer sex.

Walter Patterson was a former subject of South Africa, but he had the cultured tones of a well-schooled Briton. He became the idealistic young Englishman, Reggie York, the third member of the trio.

Many other West Coast actors took other parts in the series. One of the best, who also worked in the New York series ten years later, was Mercedes McCambridge. She played everything from an aging spinster in a wheelchair in Morse's story "Island of Skulls" in Hollywood to a whimpering beauty who thought she was always being threatened by the invisible "They" in the New York broadcasts of "The Thing that Cries in the Night." She was the only major performer to work the show from both coasts and to win an Academy Award for her film work.

Carlton Morse was in New York in 1949 to write and produce a TV series of *One Man's Family* in what was then the home city of television broadcasting. While there, he also sold a radio series of *I Love a Mystery*. He could not use his usual West Coast players but recruited a new cast of professionals then in New York.

Russell Thorson had worked for Morse before. He had played Paul Barbour's brother-in-law on *One Man's Family* and a ship's captain on *I Love Adventure*. A decade before acting for Morse, he had impersonated cowboy hero Tom Mix. Curley Bradley was Tom's sidekick, Pecos, and would go on to take over the title role of Tom Mix in the radio series. Bradley reported Thorson was shy, sensitive about an acne-marked face, despite his commanding voice. Thorson did go on to appear before the camera as many an honest sheriff or rancher in TV and film Westerns. He was among the vigilantes who took a rope to Clint Eastwood in *Hang 'Em High*.

Jim Boles played many different roles on the New York stage, including Abraham Lincoln. On radio, he portrayed Western characters on *Tennessee Jed* and *Bobby Benson's B Bar B Riders*. "I knew I had Doc when I first heard Jim Boles read," Morse said. I met Boles once at an AFTRA meeting and I found he also *looked* the part of the bony faced, skinny man I imagined Doc to be—although he could have been taller.

Tony Randall came from Oklahoma, and he tried out for Doc, thinking he had an authentic

I Love a Mystery *photo (same as giveaway photo) (c. 1940). Values in Good, Fine, and Mint: 50, 70, 95.*

Western accent. But years of stage work gave him a more cultured tone, one more appropriate for Reggie York, the part he actually got.

A prominent regular in New York was Les Tremayne, one of the great actors of radio, formerly the leading man on *First Nighter* and star of *The Thin Man*. Tremayne was heard as the crippled boyfriend, another victim of beautiful Sunny Richard's curse, in "The Million Dollar Mystery" and as the mad man, Cooper, who experimented with exposing human beings as the prey of mountain lions in "The Fear that Creeps Like a Cat."

The program's first adventure began in China, before World War II. The three men had joined the Chinese forces to fight the invading Japanese. These three were together behind a barricade, resisting an overwhelming attack. They vowed if they survived and got separated, they would join up again a certain establishment in San Francisco's Chinatown they all knew the next New Year's Eve. Then fire and shell and smoke covered all. Come New Year's, the three all showed up—but the cops were chasing Doc.

The program's first premium, a photograph of the actors playing the three heroes may have put a jinx on future giveaways. Those who received the photo complained the actors did not look as they imagined Jack, Doc, and Reggie—a common complaint about radio actors and their characters.

A number of fans of the series believe the greatest adventure told involved an ancient climb of stone steps leading up a mountain peak in Central America, known as "The Stairway to the Sun." This stairway led to a lost plateau inhabited by life from every era of the world's history, from prehistoric dinosaurs and cavemen through mystic priests of fabled lost continents to beings of tomorrow evolved into super-men who secretly guided the destiny of our planet.

This was a story considered when the present writer, Jim Harmon, revived *I Love a Mystery* commercial cassettes, mainly distributed by Metacom in 1996. "'Stairway' is one of my best, Jim," Carlton Morse said. "Get into the spirit of the *Mystery* show with something else before you try that." So we did "The Fear that Creeps Like a Cat," about an island where deranged scientists experiment on people, using mountain lions, from the original Morse scripts, produced, edited, and directed by Harmon, featuring original cast member Les Tremayne as Jack, young Tony Clay as Doc, and Frank Bresee as Reggie York, with the talents of the great announcer Fred Foy, and radio's Sky King, Jack Lester, plus Art Hern, Barbara Gratz, and others.

The story of greatest appeal Morse wrote is another entry, the greatest single adventure serial in all of Golden Age radio, "Temple of Vampires" on *I Love a Mystery*. Jack, Doc, and Reggie were flying their plane down to Central America in search of new adventure. With them was Sunny Richard, a "client" from a previous story, who was coming along to try and forget a web of menace that had surrounded her. It wasn't after too many hours in the air when they discovered, in Reggie's words, "a blooming stowaway," a little boy named Hermie who had been ditched in the plane by a vagabond of a father.

The group had little time to get to know the stowaway before the plane developed engine trouble and Jack had to put it down with what Doc called "about the prettiest piece of landing an airship as anybody's going to see."

But they had come down in the middle of the rain forest, and Sunny did not like it.

At the window, Doc yelled "Holy jumpin' catfish!"

"What is it, Doc?" Sunny wanted to know.

"A doggone cathedral…"

"Cathedral…" Sunny murmured.

"Good Lord," Reggie said. "A New York skyscraper rising right up out of the jungle!"

It was their first sight of the Temple of Vampires.

The plane was too hot to stay inside, and the ancient structure offered some shelter. The small band made their way to it through the jungle full of menaces just out of sight.

In that old place, they quickly discovered two beings, Manuel and Angelina, who claimed to be priest and priestess of this "Temple of Vampires," as they named it. These two robed ones could come and go from ledges a hundred feet up the sides of the temple, as if they could fly—fly like bats.

It didn't take some of the smartest operatives of the A-1 Detective Agency in Hollywood long to find out the secret of the seeming ability to fly from ledge to ledge. There was a spider-web of ropes throughout the stone rafters of the ancient structure. With these robes, the priests could swing, Tarzan-style, from one side of the temple to the other. In the pitch black, they had seemed to fly.

Leaving Reggie to guard Hermie, Jack and Doc used the swinging ropes to cross over to Manuel's private quarters next to the chamber where the priests kept the sacred giant vampire bats. They rescued Sunny, whose own fists had taught the supposed holy man some respect for American women. But the valiant girl gave out at the prospect of swinging across the void between ledges in the dark. She fainted. While Jack got the unconscious girl on his back, Doc went to check the ropes. His footsteps diminished in the darkness, and then Jack heard the crack of two revolver shots and a high-pitched shriek.

"Doc...Doc...what's the matter?"

"I got him, Jack," Doc said from the distant dark.

He came closer. "Did you hear the flapping of wings as he went over?"

"What was it—what happened?"

"Just one of them big He-Bats a-sittin' there on the ledge making sucking noises at me."

Jack listened and looked hard. "They're out on the ledge?"

"That one was. I let him have it and he high-dived off the ledge."

"It's time we were getting out of here. Is your rope all right?"

"Right as rain!"

"All right then," Jack said. "Let's go."

The two used the ropes in the great dark chamber. Jack got Sunny to Reggie's keeping, but returning he ran into Doc and their ropes got twisted, leaving the two adventurers clinging to the ceiling "like a couple of flies," in Doc's words.

It was then that the earthquake struck, beginning to shake the old building into a pile of dust and rocks. The Temple of Vampires had stood for centuries, but it was not going to stand forever.

The complete story is available on commercial cassettes, and is *I Love a Mystery* at its best.

JACK ARMSTRONG, THE ALL-AMERICAN BOY

The *Jack Armstrong* show was one of the earliest afternoon adventure serials for boys and girls on radio in 1933. It stayed around until 1950 under its original title and for one more year with an altered title and format as *Armstrong of the S.B.I.*

He was originally a high school boy who went to Hudson High and was on the basketball team, the football team, and just about any sports team you could name. Sometimes he had to deal with gamblers who were trying to fix the game to ensure their profits. (I hadn't heard that there was a lot of betting on point

spreads for high school games, but maybe things were different in 1933.)

Then into Jack's life came Uncle Jim Fairfield, uncle to Jack's schoolmates Billy and Betty Fairfield. Uncle Jim was a fabulous individual, a designer and builder of planes, a retired captain in military intelligence, a world traveler. He asked Jack and his niece and nephew to join him on some of his trips to exotic locales. After obtaining parental consent, Jack went along. The elder Fairfield always treated Jack just as well as his own relatives. Out of respect, Jack always referred to his mentor as "Uncle Jim" even though he was no

Charles Flynn as Jack Armstrong the All-American Boy, 1939

blood kin. Sometimes you got the impression Fairfield would have preferred Jack to be his nephew rather than the bungling Billy.

The show was a creation of the prolific writer Robert Hardy Andrews. The first Jack was played by Jim Ameche, brother of Don who became a movie star. Don Ameche also appeared on the series for a while as a coach, but the similarity in voice to the two brothers was confusing, so Don had to pull out. Jim Ameche himself would depart for other work eventually, and over the years Jack would be played by Stacy Harris, St. John Terrill, Rye Billsbury (Michael Rye), and for the longest period, most of the last ten years, by Charles Flynn.

With Uncle Jim leading the way, Jack and the Fairfields visited Africa and sought the Elephants Graveyard, where old pachyderms went to die, and conveniently piled up a fortune in ivory tusks. Around 1940, a visit to the Philippines involved Jack Armstrong and his friends in a search for Uranium U-235 and the secret of atomic energy. (Atomic energy was a theoretical possibility for a long time and the subject of any number of speculative adventures in science fiction magazines and thrillers in other medium such as this Armstrong story.)

In the late 1940s a new character appeared on the program, Vic Hardy, head of the Scientific Bureau of Investigation, another thinly disguised version of the real life J. Edgar Hoover, head of the FBI. Soon Hardy would drive away great old Uncle Jim and become the new father figure for Jack, Billy, and Betty. The series was never the same.

Not only did the story content change to capturing criminals instead of exploring exotic lands, but so did the format of Jack Armstrong. It was the first of the afternoon serials to change from fifteen minutes Monday through Friday to a complete half-hour story several times a week. It alternated with the adventures of flying cowboy Sky King. At first times were divided equally with Jack on Monday, Wednesday, and Friday, and King on Tuesday and Thursday the first week, but then the following week, King would be on three times starting Monday, and Jack would be twice starting Tuesday. It was a little confusing, and so it was worked out to have Jack Armstrong on in the three day spot, and Sky King on Tuesday and Thursday.

Now a full-fledged government agent, it was admitted that Jack Armstrong was no longer a boy. Now the introduction went: "Jack Armstrong, the All-American"—period.

There were some good stories during this period—I particularly remember one about Jack and his friends flying through a hurricane to try to tame the monstrous wind by seeding it with dry ice as a government experiment. But a lot of the innocent fun of childhood was gone from these stories about federal police. It was not much of a surprise when the Armstrong show dropped the mantle of a children's program and became a full-fledged adult evening series as *Armstrong of the S.B.I.*

Of course, the original conversion to the half-hour and the second conversion to an adult series was just to help compete with TV. In the end, even Jack Armstrong could not defeat that foe of all the great radio heroes.

I would prefer to remember Jack Armstrong not as a government agent, but when he was younger and more idealistic, when he wanted to discover atomic energy so he could "do big fine things for all the world."

LITTLE ORPHAN ANNIE (RADIO ORPHAN ANNIE)

Little Orphan Annie was, in 1930, the first nationally successful afternoon radio serial for kids. It probably became the first because *Annie* was the most successful newspaper comic strip about a kid—a girl in this case. Harold Grey never really aimed his cartoon strip at children. It

Radio Orphan Annie water pistol—this was a give-away, but was also sold in stores

was full of his extremely conservative political views, and obviously he hoped to persuade adults—voters—to his side. Whether you agreed or not with his philosophy, he created many memorable characters and situations. Only some of these made the radio series, which simplified everything for the young listeners.

In the beginning the little orphan girl was stuck living in the farming community of Simmons Corners with Pa and Ma Silo. Her best friend was a farm boy, Joe Corntassel. Annie helped arrange a surprise party for a pair of twins in one of the earliest surviving recorded episodes. She helped Joe raise a pig to try to win prize money at the local fair. This was pretty tame stuff when other serials had begun to take listeners to Africa with Tarzan and to Egypt with Chandu the Magician. Annie's foster father, "Daddy" Warbucks, came on the scene and carried Annie and Joe off in his airplane to exciting places all over the globe.

The Shake-Up Mug was not the first Annie premium, but it was the most significant. Kids eagerly sent in for something that would use the sponsor's product, Ovaltine drink mix, to make something resembling a soda fountain treat. Many differing models were offered over the years. Actually the mugs began before radio with the children's storybook favorite, Uncle Wiggily, who gave them away in Ovaltine print ads. The Shake-Up Mug went beyond Annie, and was offered by Captain Midnight on radio and TV and by Howdy Doody on TV. Both Captain Midnight and Annie offered Shake-Ups in revivals into the 1980s.

With her Shake-Up Mug in her suitcase, Annie helped Warbucks fight modern pirates in the South Seas. She worked against a gang of tough kids in the big city who all wore black leather jackets (in a curiously modern touch). But for all that Annie (actress Shirley Bell) did, for all the Mugs and Code-o-graphs she offered, she and her dog Sandy were just not exciting enough to compete with Dick Tracy and Tom Mix.

In 1940, Ovaltine gave up on Annie and hired a two-fisted war hero, Captain Midnight, to sell its product. Quaker Puffed Wheat and Rice became Annie's sponsors. Maybe there was life there yet. But taking no chances, it added to the cast a two-fisted pilot, Captain Sparks, who could have been mistaken for Captain Midnight in a failing light. Soon, he dominated the show, but even Captain Sparks couldn't pull out of this nosedive, and Annie left the air forever in 1942—but not before offering some great new premiums from Quaker.

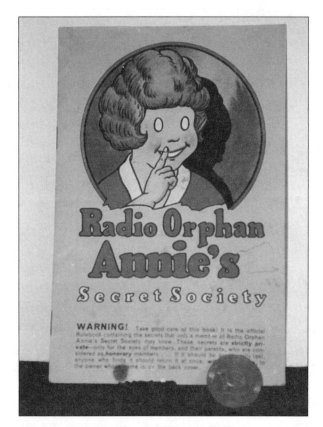

Radio Orphan Annie Secret Society manual (year unknown)

LITTLE ORPHAN ANNIE OVALTINE SHAKE-UP MUG

The Little Orphan Annie Ovaltine Shake-Up Mug is essentially a cup with a picture of Orphan Annie on it with a rounded top one could take off and put on again. While the top was on, and the cup was filled with milk, ice, and a measure of chocolately Ovaltine powder, you could shake up a tasty drink similar to the one the soda jerk shook up with ice cream down at the corner drug store.

This was Annie's gift to all of her listeners. It was one of the earliest radio premiums and definitely one of the most significant. It had been preceded by sheet music of Annie's theme song and a Beetleware drinking cup, but it is the shake-up mug which is remembered best.

While the mug was mentioned on the show, in the story, as well as in the commercials, it never played as important a part in the storyline as Jack Armstrong's Pedometer or Tom Mix's compass-magnifier. It was hard to figure out a way Annie's shake-up mug could save her life—unless she was real, real thirsty.

But, generations of kids liked it. It was a drinking mug of their own. Even when the whole routine of mixing up Ovaltine wasn't followed, it was a special glass for drinking milk or sometimes an unauthorized Coke or Pepsi.

Kids saved them, even into their adult years. That's why there are still a good many shake-up mugs around today. Lift a mug in a toast to the child you once were, or the children of now nearly seventy years ago who have gone even past being grown-ups, on into the great unknown, to the last adventure.

A 1935 advertisement for "the very latest Little Orphan Annie Shake-Up Mug"

PREMIUM SPOTLIGHT

Yukon Land Deed

The most famous in-box premium from the Golden Age is the Sergeant Preston Big Inch Land Deed, which gave the possessor one square inch of Yukon gold territory—or so the carefully worded advertisements on radio and on the cereal boxes led kids (and adults) to believe.

In the early '50s, young listeners of *Sergeant Preston of the Yukon* with the adventures of the Mountie and his wonder dog, Yukon King, munched a lot of Quaker Puffed Wheat and Rice to get these handsome certificates. You could open up the Quaker box and pull the deed out, without having to send in a box top and a coin or waiting, seemingly forever, to have the mailman deliver it. I had one deed, taken out of a cereal box when I was a kid, and elaborately inscribed "James Harmon" on it.

Like all in-box giveaways, it was pretty inexpensive—just a piece of paper with some nice lettering and pictures on it. But Quaker was selling an *idea*, a *dream*. You had a piece of the gold country, the land you heard men fighting and struggling for on the *Sergeant Preston* radio stories. If one inch of gold property was good, twelve deeds equaling a square foot would be even better. If you ate enough cereal, you could get rich!

Years passed. Most deeds got thrown out with old comic books and prize rings. But there were always the few kids who kept their premiums (or there would be none today).

In the '60s and early '70s there spread a rumor that these old Big Inch Land Deeds had increased in value by an exponential ratio, that these deeds might be worth hundreds, maybe thousands of dollars. Advertisements for them began appearing in leading newspapers and magazines. Rumors circulated that certain people had paid a hundred dollars or more for a single deed. I was offered deeds as a premium collector, with the asking price averaging fifty dollars. Without any firm information, I had my strong doubts that these pieces of paper

This offer for the "Prospector's Pouch with 1 oz. of Klondike Land" came with the Klondike Land Deed.

had any high dollar value. My feeling at the time was that as a collectible, they might be worth ten or fifteen dollars.

The way radio sponsors worked was known to me. They sent out many letters signed "Tom Mix," but they were not authentic signatures or autographs. These letters continued years after the real, original Tom had died. I did not believe that a cereal company was giving away genuine pieces of gold property.

Yet, the legend persisted. People were acquiring vast holdings of gold property, inch by inch. There were even newspaper and TV stories about it.

Finally the *Wall Street Journal* contacted me about the Yukon one inch land deeds. I told them that as a writer about premiums and a collector I believed these deeds only had a modest collectible value of perhaps twenty-five dollars now due to the notoriety. The reporter shared some information with me. The *Journal* had done research and found the Quaker company had bought some land of little value through a subsidiary company. The "deeds" actually represented shares in this company. The shares were good for many years and were not guaranteed in perpetuity. After decades, the company became disbanded and the land reverted to the government through non-payment of taxes. By about 1970, the deeds had no intrinsic value, other than as collectors' items. The *Journal* ran a front page story about the Yukon one inch land deeds and credited me prominently, although I had learned more from them than they from me.

I have not heard in recent years of anyone seeking these deeds for any amount above their collectible value, but somewhere there may be someone eagerly hoarding such deeds, believing that somehow, sometime, they are going to make him or her fabulously rich.

Sergeant Preston Deed of Land (back view)

Sergeant Preston Deed of Land (front view)

THE LONE RANGER

A man lie in a shadowed cave, near an almost smokeless fire. He was wounded, as the bandages revealed—he had an injured shoulder, and other bandages masked his face. He wore a Texas Ranger star on his shirt. A shadow fell across him, and though wounded, his form stirred alertly.

"Where am I? Where are my friends?" the injured man asked.

"You in cave near Bryant's Gap. Wounded in big fight. Other Texas Rangers all dead," a stalwart Indian told him. "You lone ranger now."

"The Lone Ranger... The others were my friends. One was my brother. I'll avenge those deaths."

"Me help you," the Indian said eagerly. "We meet before. When we just young fellers. You save Indian boy's life. Now me save you. We took vow—always to be Kemo Sabe."

The injured man raised himself on his elbows. "Kemo Sabe—faithful friend—trusted scout. I know you. You're Tonto!"

This retelling of the origin of *The Lone Ranger* is based on both the 1938 movie serial and the 1941 radio episode called "A Girl to Aid." When the movie serial came out there was no established radio origin for the famous Masked Man even though the radio series began in 1933.

The radio series' chief writer, Fran Striker, did confer with the movie studio, Republic, and contributed ideas to the screenplay, according to Fran Striker, Jr.'s fine book about his father, *His Typewriter Wore Spurs*. It is probable that it was Striker who suggested the Lone Ranger was the only survivor of an ambush of Texas Rangers, or else he would not have accepted it so fully for his 1941 radio script. Striker did not use other elements from the serial, such as there were five suspects who may have really been the Lone Ranger.

Striker had another piece to the origin in this first telling, something that was later dropped from the official version. In that first origin script, "A Girl to Aid," a mysterious young woman was at the ambush site even before Tonto, and it was she who directed the Indian to where the last of the rangers lie wounded. This girl would figure prominently in the Masked Man's longest serialized radio adventure, one about a mysterious band of traitors to America called the Black Arrow. But she was not a vital part of his origin, and she was left out of later retellings.

The story of the Lone Ranger went on, as he pursued the instigator of the radio show's ambush, Butch Cavendish, leader of the most powerful outlaw band in the West. The Lone Ranger vowed to bury his identity with his fallen comrades. He would be a man unknown. He would wear a black mask fashioned from his brother's vest.

When the Masked Man's faithful cow pony, Dusty, was lost to an outlaw bullet intended for his rider, he had to seek another mount. There were stories of a great white stallion who lead a band of wild horses in a hidden valley. The Ranger and Tonto went there, and eventually the Lone Ranger won his great mount, his partner in a thousand adventures, the owner of the thundering hooves like no others ever to beat the plains—Silver.

At first, Tonto rode double on Silver, but then he tried a series of horses. First there was White Feller who resembled Silver. Then a traditional Indian pony, Paint. And at last, a mount who could keep stride with Silver, the intelligent Scout.

The Lone Ranger and Tonto tracked down one man after another from the Cavendish gang, the men who ambushed the Texas Rangers in Bryant's Gap. Finally, only Butch Cavendish was left and at last he was cornered and captured. The killer somehow escaped the gallows with a life sentence at hard labor.

The Masked Man's avowed mission was achieved. But he knew he could not stop, not while there was banditry and injustice anywhere in the West. Tonto would be at his side. "Long as you live... long as me live ... we ride together," the Indian promised.

There were many other criminals who would feel the impact of a silver bullet against their gun hands. The Lone Ranger fashioned these bullets from ore, which came from a secret silver mine he owned with his brother. Their precious metal would be a constant reminder to shoot sparingly and to always remember the high cost of human life.

No criminal in the West was safe from the Masked Man's justice, be his scheme the stealing of a single ranch or the annexation of a state. He would expose a confidence man trying to fleece a young girl of her inheritance, or help a young man falsely accused of bank robbery. Some of these crimes seemed too minor for this heroic figure. The story seemed to fit him better when it was of a grander scale, like the time the Lone Ranger was on a special mission for the President on which "the future of the West depends," as often happened.

According to author Fran Striker, it was the Lone Ranger who fought to establish the Western Union telegraph lines to join the nation together, at the special assignment of President Lincoln. He also gave hard riding aid to the building of the Union Pacific railroad.

He fought shoulder to shoulder with Buffalo Bill against renegade whites and Indians to protect the wagon trains of pioneers, opening up the West to the hungry and the needy.

General Custer lead foolhardy attacks on Indian forces, both larger and commanded by wiser leaders than he. The Masked Man tried to save Custer from his folly, but even the Lone Ranger could not always prevail.

When Custer's gallant old foe, Sitting Bull, had to surrender, it was the Masked Man saw to it that he was given fair and honorable treatment, for a time at least.

He helped Wild Bill Hickok tame the town of Deadwood, by disguising himself as another Hickok, letting the lawman be in two places at once, leading his enemies to confusion and defeat.

Knowing that no man is all bad, the Lone Ranger tried to get young Billy the Kid to give up his criminal rebellion, but it was Sheriff Pat Garrett's guns that delivered the final message.

The Lone Ranger was everywhere, helping and protecting good men, and fighting evil men. "More than any other man, it was the Lone Ranger who finally succeeded in bringing law and order to the West."

Premiums were a part of the Lone Ranger program from the start. Photographs of the Masked Man were offered when the series was only on a few regional stations. With Silvercup bread as a sponsor, new offers were made. Variations of the silver bullet were offered a number of times, as was the black mask.

A ring was one of the most popular premiums—in fact, by actual number it is the most successful premium offer in the history of radio, with about three and a half million offerings distributed. This was the Lone Ranger

A Lone Ranger card

Atom Bomb ring. The front part of the ring looked like a silver bullet, connecting it to the Lone Ranger, and the back part had red fins like a bomb. When the rear was removed in a darkened room, the wearer of the ring could see flashes of light from a low grade radioactive element—a true scientific demonstration. With the Atomic Bomb constantly in the news, hailed as one of the most important events in human history, combined with the timeless appeal of the Lone Ranger himself, it is no wonder the ring was so popular. While the ring cannot be considered a rare collector's item today due to its large circulation, it is still a highly desired item, more so than many a less common premium.

The radio story of how the Lone Ranger became involved with atomic energy demonstrates the appeal of the ring. One of the Masked Man's greatest exploits happened in 1945 (listener's time). The Masked Man's mission was to save the secret of "the power of the Sun" for America from enemy agents.

The Lone Ranger received a letter from a high government official, which gave him a secret mission. The paper had been damaged in an attempted theft. He was told to meet a certain stagecoach and to meet a man "wearing a silver bullet..." The rest of the letter was missing.

Heroic Police Officer Frank E. Swain was appointed the first (and only) Honorary Lone Ranger. He had his own Lone Ranger uniform, insignia, seals, etc. for non-profit appearances.

The Masked Man and Tonto talked over what was meant by "wearing" a silver bullet. Was it pushed into his gunbelt, concealed among dull gray lead bullets? Perhaps it was on a rawhide thong around his neck. No matter. Their first task was to meet that stagecoach and then look for the silver bullet on the person of their contact.

When they finally found their government man, they saw he was wearing a silver bullet on a finger ring. The Masked Man and Tonto learned that their mission was to get a radioactive meteorite through to a group of government scientists, who would begin research on a great project that might not be completed even within the century in which they lived, but which would be vital in the coming century for the survival of the United States. This endeavor was code named "Project Andromedia."

There were four episodes in this adventure, continuing the story on the thrice-weekly program into a second week. Remembering the story before recordings were uncovered, my imperfect memory had it lasting many weeks. The atomic energy story made a strong impression on listeners. In the end, the Masked Man captured the enemy agents after a fight in an eerie cave that reflected the unusualness of this Lone Ranger adventure. The last scene ended not with the Lone Ranger riding away with a "Hi-Yo Silver," but with the two, the Lone Ranger and Tonto, watching from their campsite as a shooting star crossed the night sky, wondering where the meteor would land and what it would bring.

Children at home, looking at their premium rings, combining elements of the Old West and the most challenging of futures also wondered what lay ahead.

There were other serials in the history of *The Lone Ranger* program, which was best known as a story complete in half an hour. Besides the long-running series about the Black Arrow, there was a three-parter about the Son of Silver. Another series took the Masked Man to the Barbary Coast, and had him fighting those who shanghaied men as sailors against their will.

The Lone Ranger Atom Bomb Ring (1947). Values in Good, Fine, and Mint: 40, 80, 125.

The most significant serial was in 1942 when the Lone Ranger found his nephew, Dan Reid, who was long lost after an Indian attack on a wagon train. The Masked Man and Tonto found him living with kindly Grandma Frizby. The two men helped Grandma Frizby and Dan battle a gang of crooks who were trying to take over the entire territory. But the fight was too much for the old lady. As she prepared for her final sleep, she told of saving Dan during the wagon train attack where his mother had perished. The photo she had saved of Dan's parents pictured his father, Dan, Sr., and mother, Linda. They were the brother and sister-in-law of the Lone Ranger. The Masked Man promised the old lady to take Dan as his own son, and he revealed his character and identity to the dying pioneer by answering her last request to see his unmasked face.

"It's a good face," she said.

Dan was given a good education at a boarding school so he was not in every story following, but he joined his "friends" on frequent holidays, appearing perhaps in one episode out of six, once every two weeks of the three-times-a-week programs. While the Masked Man wanted him to be educated for the challenges of the coming twentieth century, Dan just wanted to ride with the Lone Ranger and Tonto.

This was the history we heard from the loudspeaker, but behind the speaker, behind the microphone, there was another history.

At WXYZ Detroit, station owner George W. Trendle had the head of his production staff, Jim Jewell, phone a writer named Fran Striker who was having some success writing a Western series called *Covered Wagon Days* for a Buffalo, New York station. Jewell wanted Striker to write a new series Trendle envisioned, another Western. Jewell had written a number of episodes of a series called *Curley Edwards*, about a cowboy who sometimes disguised himself with a bandana, mask to be a secret avenger. Trendle wanted something better.

A production staff meeting was called at WXYZ in late 1932. Trendle told me in 1968 there was no give and take in these meetings: "I was the boss. What I said went." Yet these talented professionals were there to do more than listen to Trendle talk. They contributed ideas, but Trendle had the final word.

Researcher Dave Holland revealed that one of the earliest recorded recollections of that meeting came from Jewell to free-lance writer Tom Eldredge.

As a boy, Trendle, had liked the silent movies of Douglas Fairbanks, Sr. as the masked Robin Hood, Zorro, and those of daredevil horseman Tom Mix. There wasn't any prominent evening Western radio series, and there was room for a new character combining Zorro and Tom Mix and other elements, but he needed a name more distinctive than Curley Edwards.

"Zane Grey had a book about 'The Lone Star Ranger'," program director Jim Jewell recalled.

Station manager Harold True nodded thoughtfully. "Not bad. There was a movie too. But that was Zane Grey's title. How about changing it to... The Lone Ranger!"

Trendle spoke: "That's it. Jim, I want you to get up some scripts about this Lone Ranger."

After the conference, Jewell sent Striker a letter (a copy still exists): "Will you write up three or four Wild West thrillers using the central figure the Lone Ranger...(include) all the hokum of the masked rider, rustler, Killer Pete, heroine on the train tracks, fighting on the top of box cars,

Indian badman, two gun bank robber, etc." Jewell's cynical attitude was one Striker never had—Striker's characters were real to him, even one as noble as The Lone Ranger.

Striker selected the tenth episode of his existing series, *Covered Wagon Days*, and rewrote it to be the first episode of the new *Lone Ranger* series, according to the research of Dave Holland. The first introduction ran: "Throughout the entire West, in those turbulent days, were circulated stories of a masked rider, a picturesque figure that performed deeds of the greatest daring. A modern Robin Hood... seen by few, known by none. Whence he came and where he went, no one ever knew... The daring adventures of the Lone Ranger, the mystery rider, will be presented in this new series of programs." In the story, in a few brief appearances the Masked Man dealt out justice to claim jumpers.

Actually, WXYZ owner Trendle liked the second script written by Striker better, and it was the first performed. In this one, the Masked Man was riding his to-be-famous horse Silver.

In this first broadcast the Lone Ranger was out to clear Jeb Longworth of a false murder charge by the real killer, Cal Steward, whom the Masked Man confronted.

A Lone Ranger restaurant giveaway

CAL: Folks around here aren't going to be troubled by you any longer. I'M GOING
TO KILL YOU RIGHT NOW, LONE RANGER!
SHERIFF (Distant) : Oh no you ain't, Cal Steward. PUT UP YOUR HANDS... I HEARD ALL THAT WAS SAID, AND I GUESS IT'S YOU THAT'LL BE TRIED FOR THE MURDER OF HIGGINS, NOT JEB!
RANGER: You see, Cal, it takes BRAINS sometimes to out guess GUNS! I was so sure that you'd take advantage of me when I was unarmed, and so sure of your boasting nature, that I left a little note for the Sheriff to be by that window tonight, if he wanted to hear the confession of the REAL MURDERER! ...I think I'll be leaving... COME ALONG, SILVER... THAT'S THE BOY... HI YI .. (HEARTY LAUGH) NOW CUT LOOSE... AND AWAY...

The Lone Ranger's call to horse was not quite right. Striker experimented with "Yi... Yi... Yippee" and others, but it wasn't until the twelfth script that Striker typed out "Hi Yo Silver... Away..."

Director Jim Jewell wrote another piece of the Lone Ranger vocabulary into the scripts, getting it from the name of an Indian-styled boys camp back in 1915—Kamp Kee-Mo Sah-Bee. According to the director it meant "trusty scout," becoming "Kemo Sabe," the friendly name the Masked Man and Tonto had for each other.

It was Jewell who suggested on February 15, 1933, in a letter to Striker: "It might be a good idea also to (give the Lone Ranger a partner), an Indian half-breed who always stands ready...to help him..." The writer made him a full-blooded Indian and named him after the Tonto National Park on a map. In Spanish "tonto" means wild and uninhibited, similar in connotation to the name "Wild Bill."

The true relationship of the men who called each other Kemo Sabe was established in a late episode when the Lone Ranger and the local sheriff are waiting for Tonto.

SHERIFF: I'm looking forward to meeting Tonto...
RANGER: He's one of the finest men I've ever met, Sheriff. I owe my life to him many times...
SHERIFF: Any man would be proud to have a friend like Tonto...

Tonto spoke imperfect English. This was radio. The dialect helped listeners imagine

PREMIUM SPOTLIGHT
Lone Ranger Frontier Town

The first, and for many years the *only*, radio premium to sell among collectors for one thousand dollars or more was the complete Lone Ranger Frontier Town. "Complete" is the tricky word. It is hard to get everything together for the whole set. It was complicated even in 1948.

The first any kid back then saw of Frontier Town was a few of the buildings flattened to be cut out and assembled from the back of a Cheerios cereal box from the store. (Actually, the front was pretty good too—a painting of the six foot four radio actor, Brace Beemer, who played the Lone Ranger, probably from a photo. Ironically, the largely unseen Beemer was probably the most physically impressive man who ever played the Masked Man on stage, screen, or radio. Curley Bradley, radio's Tom Mix, who had a friendly rivalry with Beemer, once said of him "Brace Beemer could have picked up one of these movie Lone Rangers and shook him like a rag doll.")

You may have seen your first Frontier Town Cheerios box, but you had not seen your last if you wanted the whole set. You needed not one or two boxes, but a total of nine to get the parts you needed. That meant eating a lot of cereal fast. Counting on your mother getting the right number box was a long shot. Kids had to go the grocery themselves—or probably to more than one store to find all the numbers in stock needed. The offer did not last forever, and probably you would have to swear on a Bible to eat all that stuff if you could stock pile some boxes ahead.

My wife, Barbara Gratz Harmon, tells a sad story. The little building interested her. Her mother usually bought Cheerios, so the boxes came in, but Barbara's mother would not let her cut out the models until the box was empty. But when the box was empty, her mother would throw it out. It was a catch-22. She did manage to grab a few boxes and put together a few houses, but her mother did not believe in useless toys lying around, and occupants of the town had to be gone by the sunset. She has some boxes herself today, thanks to collector Joe Young and me, and of course a partnership in my complete set. But it probably isn't as much fun now as it would have been back then.

If you were lucky enough to have indulgent mothers like mine, you could get all of the nine boxes. But that was not the end of it. You had to send in a box top and a dime for four different envelopes. Each one consisted of a map or placement diagram for a quarter of the town, and additional buildings not on the boxes to punch out and put together. There was the Northwest section, the Northeast, the Southwest, and the Southeast. Forty cents! We are talking money here—enough to buy four comic books, or enough to go to the movies four times. Despite patient parents and some cast money, you needed the staying power of continuing interest. Many kids must have become bored with the little cardboard models before they built their complete Frontier Towns. Some persisted, as proved by the number of total sets that continue to come on the market.

The whole town assembled is pretty impressive. It is approximately eight feet square and has four large "maps" with colored terrain with dozens of small model buildings placed on them. Children might have set up the town on the floor of their rooms, or in a corner of the living room. As a boy, I had my town on a dinner table out on a screened-in porch of our house. Using a method I do not now endorse, I glued all of the parts together. Chilly spring gave way to hot summer in Illinois and my mother wanted the table back to serve meals on our airy screened porch. With me, childhood was giving away to my teen years. I had no place to put the one-piece Frontier Town and besides, I was getting past the things of childhood. With some regret, I gathered up the paper and cardboard Frontier Town and stuffed it into the trash can.

When I decided I wanted my Frontier Town back twenty years later, it took me a good many years and hundreds of dollars to reassemble it piece by piece (but it was cheaper than buying it as a complete set).

Where are collectors supposed to put the Frontier Town today if they can get the whole set together? Some people have a house big enough to devote a whole coffee table to the town, but most wives prefer not to have their whole house, or even the living room, devoted to their husbands' collections. I have heard of one man who did what I did as a boy and glued the maps together, glued all the building in place, and hung the whole works on the wall. I don't recommend this, because the gluing devalues the original condition of the collectibles. I don't have a solution. In my own case, I have some of the cereal boxes and some of the buildings put out on the shelves of a display case. Once in awhile, the whole thing is assembled so I can take a photo or display it to a visiting collector like you.

Lone Ranger "Authentic Ground Plan Map for the NORTHWEST Section" from Frontier Town

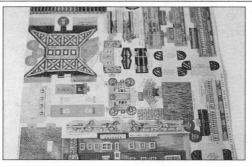

Lone Ranger Frontier Town—Southeast Section (1948). Values in Good, Fine, and Mint: 125, 250, 500.

what the character was supposed to look like. Dialects were everywhere in early radio: Irish, Swedish, Italian, French, Jewish, Hillbilly, etc. They added color to a medium without sight.

The part of Tonto was played from first to last by John Todd, an Irish actor, on the stage, on radio, wherever there was a job. He took the part in his sixties and did it to the end of the series, when he was in his eighties. Some say he dozed off sometimes during the last few seasons of shows. Sometimes when nudged, whether the scene was on the second floor of a hotel, or the deck of a Mississippi riverboat, Todd would give a cry: "Gettum up, Scout!"

Director Jewell selected the theme music, the "Ride" section of the *William Tell Over-ture*—a 1927 RCA Black Seal record by Rosario Bourdon and the Victor Symphony. The trumpet call that is the first sound you hear opening *The Lone Ranger* radio show begins cleanly (not coming out of the final pastoral notes of "The Storm" sequence) because it is at the start of one of the 78 rpm recording sets. (These old records only run some three or four minutes each, as those over forty know.) This trumpeting became a call to adventure for decades. Rossini's immortal music suggests a man riding, riding on through every danger, on a mission of destiny.

The other music was memorable. Over the years, a number of people contacted me, their hobby being trying to identity every classical selection on the series. The big problem was that it was not all classical. Some selections were background themes from the 1938 *Lone Ranger* movie serial. Alberto Columbo, William Lava, and other Republic staff composers and arrangers supplied them, in a contractual agreement that allowed Trendle to use the movie music on radio. The most complete source of musical identifications is Reg Jones' book, *The Masked Man and His Music*.

It has often been said that *The Lone Ranger* premiered on January 30, 1933. That dates the regional Michigan Radio Network's first broadcast, but a detailed description of every minute of the presentation reveal no drama of the Masked Man. The *Detroit Evening Times* for

February 2, 1933, offers a more definitive date. "'The Lone Ranger'... makes his bow (to-night) in a new dramatization series to be heard three times weekly on WXYZ starting at 9:00 p.m. today..."

Who played the very first Lone Ranger? Fran Striker's original script for Episode 1 survives and his handwriting states "Lone Ranger...Stenius"—George Stenius. He later became well-known in Hollywood as a writer-director under the name George Seaton. George W. Trendle has mentioned "a man named Deeds" as the first Lone Ranger, but "Deeds" (if that is his right name) only substituted in the role later, perhaps only once. He had trouble with both alcohol and putting up with Jewell's bullying direction. Trendle's memory was fuzzy on several matters.

Jim Jewell remembered hiring Stenius for the Lone Ranger role after seeing him in a stage play in Detroit. Jewell was not only responsible for hiring Stenius/Seaton, he was the reason Stenius left after only two and a half months. The radio director so praised his writing ability after seeing some plays he wrote, the man took it to heart and took his talent to Hollywood.

Front view of Cheerios box with Lone Ranger Frontier Town

When Jack Deeds did not work out, and after Jewell found out he couldn't do the job himself (with the Scandinavian accent he inherited), he auditioned all the men in the drama club at Wayne State University. Earle W. Graser (pronounced "grah-zer") won the audition on Sunday, April 16, 1933, and played the Lone Ranger the first time Tuesday, April 18. Graser had a naturalness that gave warmth to his powerful baritone voice. Many think he was the best man to ever to play the Masked Man. For the better part of a decade he was the Lone Ranger to a nation of children and grown-ups. On April 8, 1941, Graser was killed in a traffic accident.

From the beginning, an important man at WXYZ, one time station manager and sometimes announcer Brace Beemer had posed for the photos of the Lone Ranger, and had made personal appearances on horseback (he was an expert horseman). He was a towering, barrel-voiced figure, well over six feet tall. He commanded grown men in the First World War when he was thirteen years old—he misrepresented his age and quickly earned sergeant stripes. He wanted to play the part on the radio that he was asked to visually represent. He had the voice for it. As a matter of fact, he sounded a great deal like Earle Graser. Perhaps Graser was selected by Trendle and Jewell because his voice was like the one they heard from Beemer when he was in costume (without their realizing it). Beemer was the narrator and commercial announcer on the show, alternating at times with others. A fine actor was dead, but the Lone Ranger lived forever. "The show goes on," Trendle said. (Someone has pointed out the reason the show goes on is that otherwise one would have to refund the audience its money.) Could Al Hodge quit his role of the Green Hornet to replace Graser? How about another deep-voiced announcer, Jay Michael? (His voice was too familiar in villain roles, although there came a few times he played the Ranger in emergency situations.) Charles Livingstone, the director following Jewell who left for greener fields in Chicago, made what seems the obvious suggestion: Brace Beemer.

Beemer and Graser sounded so much alike that experts today listening to old shows sometimes argue which is playing the role on a particular recording. Beemer's voice got more authoritative and commanding as he continued in the role.

Beemer used that voice sparingly at first. Trendle told Striker to introduce Beemer into the role carefully; the audience would have to learn to accept him.

In the first episode in a series of five introducing Beemer, Tonto was told by their old friend, Mustang Mag, that the Lone Ranger had been badly wounded. She told Tonto and all that listened: "I want you to know that I'm sure of one thing... The Lone Ranger is goin' to ride again!"

There were a few words from the Masked Man, some scrawled notes, and Tonto carried out the Lone Ranger's plans to prevent a range war. "Ride for us both" was about the first complete sentence from Beemer as the Lone Ranger.

Finally, there came a matter that Tonto could not handle alone. Though not completely at all of his power, the Lone Ranger struggled from his bed. Did he seem taller, sterner, a grimmer angel of vengeance for evil men? His voice now suggested that. He had to save a wagon train loaded with gold from destruction by an outlaw band. "We'll be riding again, Silver," Brace Beemer as the Lone Ranger said.

It was a long ride. In 1943 the WXYZ dramas were moved to the Mendelssohn mansion at Iroqois and Jefferson in Detroit. This old millionaire's home became the "Jefferson Studios." The living room became Studio D. The fireplace and flowered rug were retained, and RCA model 44 microphones were added. The sound effects department, which could make you hear a white horse coming, was moved to the converted sun porch. The acoustics were fine. For a dozen years the Lone Ranger (unmasked, in an open shirt and sports jacket) acted out the Old West in a rich man's mansion along with all the other actors, actresses, and the greatest of all announcer-narrators, Fred Foy. In a second floor room, Fran Striker worked far into the night on scripts. It lasted for even five years into the age of television and Clayton Moore and

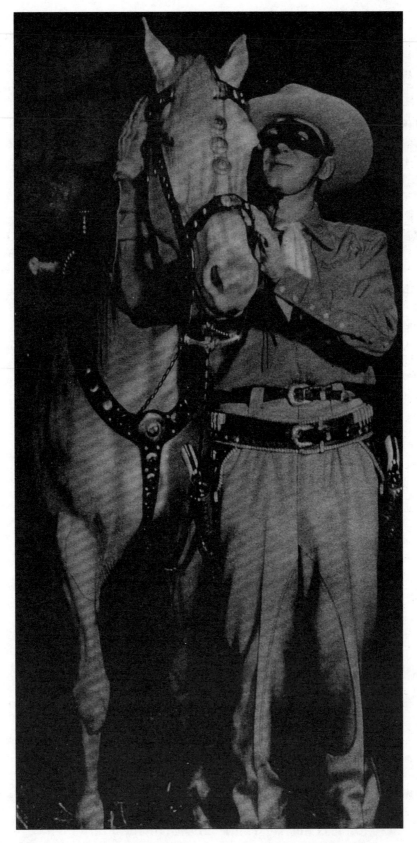

Radio's Brace Beemer as the Lone Ranger with his Silver, c. 1950

then John Hart for one season on screen as the Lone Ranger. But finally there was a sale by Trendle of the Lone Ranger, Inc. to the Wrather corporation, and the radio show that many connected with it, the one they thought would simply go on forever, was gone.

The final live show was on Friday, Sept. 3, 1954. Then there were years of network reruns until 1959 and syndicated reruns to local stations to the present date.

The ride of the Lone Ranger and Silver is not over. They ride on in the dreams of several generations who encountered them in any incarnation. I can hear them and see them in my imagination now.

The Lone Ranger is riding on through the night, wind cutting his cheeks beneath the mask, astride a great white stallion which seems to have the speed of light, whose silver-shod hooves thunder across the plains like no others.

A full moon lights the mountain trail and the prairie land in the valley below. Most things are starkly visible with a cold, bluish whiteness. But the shadows cast by tall rocks are black as an inkwell.

The Masked Man urges his great horse on, feeling the muscles of the magnificent steed rippling between his calves, pulling ahead, over and over again, eating up the miles. The Ranger urges the horse ever onward, with a whispered word, a solid pat, and occasionally, a full-throated "Come on, Silver!"

He can see their shadows on the roadbed, seemingly cut from cloth, black as his mask. Now they cross flinty rubble and Silver's hooves strike flashing yellow and red stars from the mineral deposits. Both horse and rider are blowing clouds of white steam into the night, as the flashes are struck below. To a crouching, watching coyote, they appear as some locomotive device from another world, coming onward, ever on.

"We've got to make it, Big Fellow," the Lone Ranger shouts. "They're counting on us ... Tonto...Dan...The President...The whole future of the West! We're going to make it! Hi-Yo Silver!"

THE SHADOW

The Shadow began as a nameless voice of mystery on *Street and Smith's Detective Story Hour*, CBS, July 31, 1930, and was named "The Shadow" in the first season. He appeared on *Street & Smith's Love Story Hour*, Blue Coal Radio Revue. The Shadow series began January 1932, then went to twice weekly, CBS, October 1933–Spring 1935. Originally the narrator of drama only, the double identity format of Lamont Cranston, socialite, and The Shadow, crime-fighter, began September 26, 1937, Mutual, and ran to December 21, 1954. It was revived in syndicated reruns, from 1963 on.

CAST

The Shadow (Host)	James LaCurto (1930)
	Frank Readick (1931–1935)
The Shadow/Lamont Cranston	Orson Welles (1937–1938)
	Bill Johnstone (1938–1944)
	Bret Morrison (1943–1944, 1945–54)
	John Archer (Fall 1944–Spring 1945)
	Steve Courtley (Fall 1945, six episodes)
Margot Lane	Agnes Moorehead (1937–1938)
	Margo Stevenson (1937 Summer Series)

Marjorie Anderson (began 1938)
Judith Allen (1944–1945)
Laura Mae Carpenter (1945)
Lesley Woods (1945)
Grace Mathews (1946–1949)
Gertrude Warner (1949–1954)

Police Commissioner Weston   Ray Collins
Dwight Weist
Santos Ortega

Moe "Shrevie" Shrevnitz   Alan Reed
James LaCurto (the original Shadow)

Other Cast Members: Ralph Bell, Everett Sloan, Richard Widmark

Directors: Clark Andrews, Jerry Devine, others

Writers: Harry Engman Charlot (1930), Edward Hale Bierstadt (1937), Alonzo Dean Cole, Alfred Bester, Max Erhlich, others

Consultant: Walter Gibson

Music: Rosa Rio, organist, others

The Shadow is one of the immortal characters of popular entertainment. For long periods he seems to survive only in memory, but then he reappears in some form or other, most recently in the major motion picture starring Alec Baldwin in 1994. Another radio creation, the Lone Ranger, has been more consistently promoted over the decades, but even without new appearances in any media, the Master of Men's Minds comes back like a bad dream—sometimes garbed in a slouch hat and somber cloak, at other times cloaked only in darkness, as unseen as a remembered threat.

The Shadow first appeared on the air as only the narrator/host of anthology stories about other characters. His position was similar to that of Raymond, the host of *Inner Sanctum* or of Alfred Hitchcock on his dramatic TV series.

On *Street & Smith's Detective Story Hour*, Thursday, July 30, 1930, The Shadow first sent his mocking laugh out over the air. He was so mysterious he did not even have a name. The author of the scripts, Harry Engman Charlot, eventually gave him the name of The Shadow. (Only a few years later, September 28, 1935, Charlot, thirty-five, was found dead by poison in a cheap hotel on the Bowery. Not even The Shadow knew how or why.)

Radio fans began showing up asking for "The Shadow Detective Magazine" or "that Shadow monthly." This was not fulfilling the aims of *Street & Smith's Detective Story* to sell more copies through the radio show. But to fulfill a demand, the company developed and published *The Shadow* magazine. Since it was not enough to have him merely introduce the stories as on the air, The Shadow (who was always referred to with a capitol on "The" as if he were a deity) was given his own adventures as a mysterious avenger, written by pulp wordsmith Walter Gibson under the house name Maxwell Grant.

From the earliest years, the commercials for Blue Coal and other products on *The Shadow* occasionally offered premiums, including photos of the radio Shadow, free copies of the magazine, and two different rings. These items were not featured in the dramatic entertainment portion, unlike juvenile shows such as *Dick Tracy* and *Tom Mix*. It may have been felt by a sponsor or producer that the show was "too adult" to actually have Lamont Cranston use some Shadow toy in the story, but during the first decade or so the stories were so wild, this would not have seemed totally out of place.

Early on, Walter Gibson was consultant to the radio show and gave advice to the first radio scripter, Edward Hale Beirstadt. The two most significant changes in the radio series from the novels of The Shadow were the introduction of the feminine interest, Margot Lane, and the character's ability to employ literal invisibility (and not merely glide about the camouflaging shadows in his funeral cape).

In the early years of the radio series, the Master of Darkness was given stories suited to his fantastic persona, for example tales of dark fantasy and eerie science fiction.

The first script, "The Death House Rescue" (Bierstadt, author, September 26, 1937), was a more or less mundane tale of last minute reprieve of wrongly convicted man from the death house, but by "The Temple Bells of Neban" (October 24, 1937), The Shadow was delving into his Far Eastern origin, explaining how he achieved his near-supernatural hypnotic powers. For a summer series in 1938, the Master of Men's Minds displayed how he could read the thoughts of others in "Power of the Mind" and in a tale of a Caucasian man setting himself up as lord of an island of the South Seas, "The White God," The Shadow revealed he could control the actions of others with his mental powers.

Welles went on to greater fame as host, producer, and frequent star of radio's *Mercury The-*

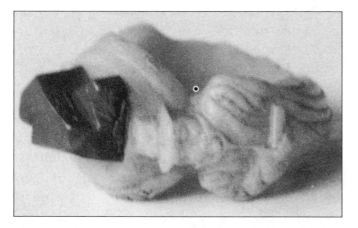

The Shadow glow-in-the-dark blue coal ring (1941). Values in Good, Fine, and Mint: 375, 562, 750.

atre on the Air and beginning in 1940 to 1941 in a brilliant, if stilted, career in Hollywood motion pictures beginning with *Citizen Kane*.

When a less famous actor, Bill Johnstone, took over the starring roll in the fall of 1938, the style and quality of the scripts did not change. "Night without End" (October 16, 1938) concerned the efforts of a scientist to block out the sun and produce perpetual night, until the city paid a huge ransom. Another mad scheme involved causing the death of anyone who made an E flat sound in the busy city, an early anti-Noise Pollution campaign. Newsboys eagerly whispered the headlines about "Murder in E Flat" (November 4, 1938).

Margot Lane was at the side of Lamont Cranston through all of these adventures, a friend and companion to the wealthy young man about town who had a secret side to him. For all her fidelity, she was usually awarded only some peril from which The Shadow would rescue her.

I have met a number of the actors who played The Shadow. The original in the role (as a full-fledged central character) was Orson Welles. Several years before his death, he was trying to get a TV talk show on the air which he would host. I think it safe to say he "over-produced" the pilot, taking what should have essentially been a live show, only delayed on tape, and tried to edit and rearrange it like a movie to make it better. Long after the original guests, including Burt Reynolds and Dolly Parton, had taped their segments, Welles recruited a studio audience to produce audience reaction shots to nonexistent guests. A number of people in the business or connected to it were invited, including myself. For a limited time, it was somewhat interesting to see the Great Man direct and in fact be directed by him. Welles singled in on me and asked me to come down in front, and for some reason, asked me to sit on an apple crate, my knees touching his. It was a silly position. For several hours, I sat toe to toe with the great Orson, his glare daring me to interrupt his concentration with some remark. Later, from actor Tony Clay who saw the completed tape, I found that I had actually been doubling the back of Burt Reynolds' head. Apparently our hair and jackets were similar.

As time went on, Welles berated the crew and constantly dwindling audience to produce some vision he had of the perfect talk show. Finally, an end was called and after hours of non-paid crate-sitting, I asked a question of

---

PREMIUM SPOTLIGHT
THE SHADOW BLUE COAL RING

One of the rarest and most valuable premium rings is The Shadow Blue Coal "glow-in-the-dark" ring. This ivory-like plastic ring has "carved" figures of the cloaked Shadow on both sides of the band, which holds up a jagged blue setting—a lump of *The Shadow* sponsor, Blue Coal. (Most people never stop to think what this rough "stone" is supposed to be, but clearly, Blue Coal is the intention.) In the dark, the band (only) glows in the dark—if charged by sunlight or a bright lamp.

It is rare because it was a premium on a series with a large percentage of adult listeners, many of whom probably felt they were too "grown-up" to send for a radio ring. (Not everyone felt this way—I know many listeners, mostly male, who continued to send in for premiums into their twenties, including myself.)

A ring was often associated with The Shadow. In descriptions of the Master of Darkness in novels in *The Shadow* magazine, and on covers and illustrations and in illustrated advertisements for the radio show, he is depicted as wearing a fiery red Gerisol ring. His gestures are emphasized by the ring. While the radio premium did not resemble this red stoned ring, it reminded one of The Shadow usually wearing a ring of some sort.

Because the premium ring is plastic, it does not seem as worthwhile as the heavy metal rings of other characters like Tom Mix. The plastic is also vulnerable to too much heat from sunshine or a steam radiator. Many have been made lumpy or completely destroyed by such heat sources. But the original owners who have preserved their own rings (as I have) or the collector who is able to find one is lucky to have the best and best-known premium from perhaps radio's most famous program.

---

the Great Man for my radio research. He turned and marched from the room without a word. I learned something of Welles' genius, and a lot more about his graciousness.

I met Bret Morrison a number of times over a twenty year period, but never really got to be friends with him the way I have some radio era actors. His voice was beautiful, but Bret was the opposite of The Shadow in appearance. Not tall and lean and black haired, Morrison was of only average height and rather plump, and bald. He signed a number of autographs for me over the years. The first one said "May I be the only Shadow in your life."

I asked Morrison about the actors who had temporarily broken his long run as The Shadow. They came in when the producers had refused to meet his salary demands ("Not that they were all that high," he said) and he left to follow other work—he even sang in nightclubs for a time.

One of the actors who replaced Morrison for part of a season of *The Shadow* was John Archer, who appeared in Anthony Tollin's Shadow re-creation for the convention of the Society for the Preservation and Encouragement of Radio Drama, Variety, and Comedy—SPERDVAC—in the Los Angeles area in 1987. Also a well-known movie actor (*Destination Moon*, for example), Archer is more visually like Lamont Cranston than Morrison, and his vocal performance is excellent too. He projects a sincerity and very masculine kindness.

The original *Shadow* radio series had also been performed before a live audience. "When I became The Shadow," Morrison told me, "I would slip behind a screen (some sources say an enclosed announcer's booth) so I would be invisible to the studio audience too. That part went over, but even though I was slender in those days and had my hair, I often got the impression the audience was disappointed in my appearance." Of course, no one could live up to certain mental images in the minds of listeners, but vocally, Morrison may have been the best performer. (I was fortunate enough to see Morrison perform as The Shadow, but only in parody sketches for various Frank Bresee productions.)

Bret Morrison as the Shadow, c. 1946

"The Shadow Knows" 1963 radio re-run giveaway

It is Bret Morrison's voice I hear in my imagination when I read a printed script such as "The Final Hour" (Jerry McGill, October 31, 1954). As the hours ticked off to the midnight hour of execution, The Shadow went to Walker, the witness whose perjury was sending young Jim Martin to the chair, rather than the real killer, Marty Barton...

SHADOW: ... An unseen presence speaks to you.

WALKER: (Dazed and frightened) Speaks! Yes. I am hearing it or I'm going crazy!!

SHADOW: The voice is as real as the fear and remorse that are slowly destroying your mind, Sam Walker.

WALKER: What...where are you?

SHADOW: Not behind you. Not in dark corners of this bar. I am right here, in front of you, close enough to touch you.

WALKER: (Verge of panic.) No! It can't be. It's my mind!

SHADOW: Of course! For I have the power to remain unseen, invisible to the eyes of men with tormented minds such as yours. But I am real...

WALKER: Who...Who are you?

SHADOW: Many men and women, such as you,

have known me as the Shadow.

WALKER: The...Shadow!

After even more pressure, Walker broke and agreed to tell the truth. This was the show only nine weeks from the last of all. In a Yin and Yang kind of Fate, this story so near the end had the same theme as the very first broadcast adventure of *The Shadow*—saving an innocent man from execution.

These later episodes were recorded on magnetic tape which could be, and were, erased and reused. The older shows were on transcription discs. It was the survival of these old discs that allowed long time radio syndicator Charles Michaelson to revive *The Shadow* on radio beginning in 1962, with WGN Chicago being the first station to air the nostalgic old favorite. Michaelson found great success with *The Shadow* and eventually added many other favorites including *The Lone Ranger*, *Gangbusters*, and others.

The Shadow is a mythic figure of popular folk lore. Symbolic of the frightening power of conscience, he also represents the world of radio drama more so than any other single character. He is an icon of justice, yes, but a frightening representation of Mystery itself. He leaves us wondering—What really lurks in the heart of The Shadow?

The Shadow radio transcription

SKY KING

Sky King began October 28, 1946, ABC, as a quarter-hour serial five times weekly, was re-designed with thirty minute episodes, complete, two times a week, three times a week on alternate weeks (trading places with Jack Armstrong weekdays) 1947, then regularly Tuesdays and Thursdays beginning 1948, and finally moved to MBS, 1950–1954.

Cast

Sky King	Roy Engel (1946-1947)
	Jack Lester (1947-1949)
	Earl Nightingale (1950-1953)
	Carlton KaDell (1954)
Clipper	Johnny Coons
	Jack Bivens
Penny	Beryl Vaughn
	Beverly Younger
Jim Bell	Cliff Soubier
Martha Bell	Viola Berwick
"Peter Pan" (girl in commercials):	Jean Mowry

Announcers: Mike Wallace, Pierre Andre

Others: Clarence Hartzel, Stanley Gordon, Norman Gottchak, Richard Thorne, Art Hern, Ken Nordine

Series Creators: Robert M. Burtt, Willfred G. Moore

Producer/Director/Chief Writer: Roy Windsor

Writers: Abe Burrows, others

Sponsor: Peter Pan Peanut Butter

Opening: Swooping airplane, roars up. Announcer, matching engine: "Skyyyyy...KING!"

Schyler "Sky" King was a family man, as he appeared in one of the last of the classic radio serials. After he returned from a stint as a Navy flier in World War II, he settled down on his Flying Crown ranch in the modern West (with a specific location near Grover, Arizona). The ranch seemed much like Tom Mix's TM-Bar with its horses and automobiles in the modern West, but to which was added a landing strip for Sky's airplane, the Songbird. But unlike Tom and his fellow hero, Captain Midnight, who concentrated purely on airplanes and flying, Sky was not merely a guardian to young wards, he was a full-fledged uncle. (So was the Lone Ranger an uncle to young Dan Reid, but more often in such programs the relationship was honorary. Kids did not seem to like the reality of a blood-tie father-figure interfering with their escape.) Sky's niece and nephew were Penny and Clipper King. Eventually, Penny became the more important character, perhaps a forerunner of women's liberation.

Part of such radio serials generally included some sort of a "grandfather figure." On *Sky King*, the "old-timer" was ranch foreman Jim Bell, combining elements of clowning and the wisdom of age played by Cliff Soubier, still appearing before the public in recent years as a lay minister, at the age of ninety. More unusual was a "grandmother figure," Jim's wife, Martha, gruff but warm-hearted.

The creators, Burtt and Moore, obviously thought a strong hero needed an equally strong adversary. On *Captain Midnight*, the Secret Squadron leader's nemesis was Ivan Shark, criminal and espionage mastermind. Sky King got Dr. Shade, a combination of The Shadow and the Phantom of the Opera. This sinister creature prowled his own castle built on the Arizona desert and plotted against Sky and his crew. But after World War II, kids were no longer prepared to follow a hero day after day, week after week fighting the same villain and seemingly getting nowhere. After he began the series, Dr. Shade reappeared every so often, but was never the eternal menace Ivan Shark was to that other aviator hero.

Other early adventures took Sky and his crew around the world to Europe and Asia in quarter-hour installments. But these exotic serials took Sky away from his ranch and the horses and Western locale that provided much of the appeal.

From the beginning, the program followed the accepted practice of offering premiums for Peter Pan inner-seals to entice listeners and to establish their number. The Signal Scope was a multifunctional item with whistle, reflecting mirror for message sending, magnifying glass, etc. The Mystery Picture ring had a small disc that, when turned, changed the picture from Sky King to one of him in disguise. This involved polarization and it has decayed over the years to where the ring is not known to survive in working condition. The radio series overlapped the TV version starring Kirby Grant and Gloria Winters in a restrained, well-crafted series superior in some ways to the radio show. Such items as the name and address Stamp Kit (which looked like an aspirin box with a rubber stamp in the lid and ink pad in the bottom) was offered by both radio and TV. Due to planned reruns after the offer was over, the TV show could not feature the premium in the story line itself. On the radio series, Penny could secretly stamp her name and address to leave Sky a clue when she was kidnapped.

With pressure from the vigorous infant, television, and from other competing quarter-hour radio serials, *Sky King* and another ABC serial, *Jack Armstrong*, struck a deal. They would present a half-hour complete story (as *The Lone Ranger* had been doing for decades, with very little imitation of its success for unexplainable reasons). They would split the time exactly even so one week one program would be on three times, but the next week only two. This proved confusing, so in a few years *Sky King* settled in permanently twice a week, Tuesdays and Thursdays.

An early half-hour Sky King involved the Sahara rescue of a prisoner from a band of hostile Arabs, something that would have been a mere incident in one of the continuing serials. Loose ends were left hanging. (Did anyone go back and capture the Arabs?) But soon, very complicated plots and event-filled stories were compressed into the half-hour. Eventually, the story would begin with the robbery of a Frontier Days stagecoach or a rustler-started cattle stampede, but it might take Sky King to the fog-shrouded streets of London or to a fight with a Polar Bear in the wild snow country of Alaska. He would be required to fly the prop-driven Songbird, or at times his jet, the Black Arrow. Penny and Clipper were on hand to spell him as copilot and Jim Bell would wish he was on a horse.

Toward the end of the series, Sky King captured and tamed a great Palomino stallion traveling with a wild horse band. His new horse was called Yellow Fury, and the stallion was called on, sometimes as only "Fury" from time to time, if not employed as often as the Songbird. Just before *Sky King* every Tuesday and Thursday on Mutual came Straight Arrow and his horse, a Palomino, called simply "Fury." Mutual never had as much money as the major networks. Perhaps it was economizing by having the two heroes ride the same horse.

Roy Windsor took up the writing and directing from the series creators. His radio scripts were the basis for the early episodes of the TV *Sky King*. After many other credits, he died in 1987, at the age of seventy-five.

First cast on radio was Roy Engel as the Flying Cowboy. Engel would work up real emotion on the air—and off it. He carried a revolver and

Sky King advertisement for the name and address stamping kit from 1950

sometimes would fire a shot in the air to warn off those who were less than polite to "Sky King."

After Engel went to Hollywood to become a successful character actor, Jack Lester became, in my opinion, the perfect Sky King. Born in Enid, Oklahoma, in cattle country, Jack learned to ride military style at the University of Oklahoma. All the great movie cowboys—Tom Mix, Tim McCoy—rode cavalry style, upright and level. (Cowboys on the range rode with elbows flapping, bouncing up and down.) After World War II, Jack Lester became an accomplished pilot in private life. The sincerity and conviction of his voice earned him many announcing and acting roles besides Sky King.

Announcing *Sky King* was Myron "Mike" Wallace—the newscaster of TV's *Sixty Minutes*. A man of many interests, Wallace had one in the stock market. Frequently, Wallace was on the phone to his broker. One day Wallace was still on the phone as *Sky King* went on the air, live. The only other person available who could do the announcing properly was "Sky" himself, Jack Lester. He did the commercial opening

for Peter Pan Peanut Butter, and keeping his voice higher than normal, set the scene for the story: "As we join them Sky is talking earnestly to Penny..." Then dropping to a more commanding baritone: "Penny, there's something mighty strange going on up on Lost Plateau..." Mike Wallace, chagrined, arrived about then.

"My biggest worry," Lester told me, "was that the sponsor was so cheap they would ask me to announce my own show all the time—for no extra money, of course. Maybe Mike thought of the same thing. He was on time after that."

Earl Nightingale played "Sky King" for a few years, appropriately named, (a bird name for a flier) although he became wealthier with a short program offering motivation and investment tips. Nightingale was frequently substituted for by one-time radio "Tarzan," Carlton KaDell, who eventually took over the leading role.

"The Mark of El Diablo," late in the series, was typical of the *Sky King* program. A black stallion was seemingly bringing death to the enemies of the devilish El Diablo, a masked figure who captured Penny and crusty old Jim

Kirby Grant as Sky King, TV. Courtesy Eddie Brandt's Saturday Matinee

Bell. The crook needed to know the whereabouts of a witness against him:

PENNY: Wait—I'll tell you where Zack Morely is...At a waterhole. It's near a strange

looking rock, pointing up like a finger. I'll take you there in the Songbird.

EL DIABLO: A waterhole. Now I'll find it without you.

JIM: It's Sky—he's coming!

SOUND EFFECTS: HOOFBEATS OF SEVERAL HORSES, HOLD UNDER

PENNY: And he's bringing all the ranchers with him.

EL DIABLO: He couldn't be!

PENNY: Sky—Sky, it's El Diablo!

JIM: On that black stallion, Sky!

SKY: I see him, and I'm going to see what's under that black mask!

EL DIABLO: No, you don't!

CLIPPER (coming on): Sky's bull-dogging him like a wild-eyed steer!

SKY: I've waited a long time for the pleasure of meeting you...

EL DIABLO: You won't get me!

SKY: And this is a really big pleasure! (exertion)

SOUND EFFECTS: TERRIFIC PUNCH, BODY FALLS

El Diablo, alias Link Higgins, used a horseshoe mounted on a club on his victims, putting the blame on the black stallion, a scheme to scare ranchers off mineral-rich land.

It was certain: "Once again, Sky King has won out in his constant fight for justice!"

SPACE PATROL

"High adventure in the wild, vast reaches of space..." was what *Space Patrol* promised. Fortunately, children have great imaginations. Radio had asked more of those imaginations, but early TV still called upon them. A bare wall decorated by a modernistic lamp from Sears became a Space Patrol station on Pluto. Beginning as a local afternoon television serial in Los Angeles, the program would be picked up by Ralston cereals for a national Saturday morning half hour on TV, and it would go from TV to radio (one of a handful of shows to do this) for an earlier hour Saturday morning broadcast. Fans were urged by closing announcements to also enjoy the program on the other medium. There were probably a few kids so obsessed by the new picture invention that they watched unmoving test patterns while their old radios gathered dust, but there were enough kids still waiting to get their first TV sets to keep the radio series going for more than a year.

Ralston was "the greatest premium believer in orbit" as authority Tom Tumbusch has observed. For two decades, the Ralston-Purina company had sponsored *Tom Mix* on radio, giving away hundreds of different items to his Straight Shooters. It considered putting the portrayer of Tom Mix on radio, Curley Bradley, into a TV show. Curley had been a real cowboy; he could ride and sing, and had some screen experience. But ultimately, the cereal company decided television was a new medium in a new world and they had ridden the trail long enough with a beloved, deceased silent film star. (The real Tom Mix had died in the seventh year of the radio series, but he was impersonated by Curley Bradley and earlier actors for another ten years.) Naturally, the giveaways changed from the wooden guns, spurs, arrowheads of Mix territory, to the outer space gadgets of the universe of *Space Patrol*.

Commander Buzz Corey (actor Ed Kemmer) was the lead in the Space Patrol series on both TV and radio. When the present writer talked to him a year or so ago, Kemmer hardly looked a decade older than when he roamed the spaceways forty years ago. He could tell me nothing new, and seemed cordial but exhausted from years of meeting eager fans. He still looked sad when the subject of his co-star, Lyn Osborn, the jovial young Cadet Happy came

The cast of TV's Space Patrol in the premier episode. Courtesy Eddie Brandt's Saturday Matinee.

up. Osborn had died from a brain tumor a few years after the program went off the air.

Buzz and Happy live forever in the memory of their viewers and listeners. Mike Moser, the creator and producer of the series, also died prematurely, but from his estate, kinescope recordings of the early television shows have survived and are occasionally rebroadcast and are offered on video cassettes. Many of the radio shows are in the hands of collectors and radio clubs like SPERDVAC of Los Angeles.

The television series was done "live" and reruns were not planned. In that way, the TV show could do what radio adventure serials had always done. *Space Patrol* could feature the current premium within the dramatic portion of the show. Filmed shows that were to be re-run for years did not want to play up a premium that would no longer be available in just a matter of weeks.

One multiple-episode series of *Space Patrol* on both TV and radio concerned Martian Totem Head masks that could be worn as a sort of space helmet with a special plastic visor, silvery from the outside, but transparent from the inside. These were supposed to be ancient artifacts found on Mars by the Space Patrol crew and by a rival band of criminals. Both sides wore the masks on various occasions, and there was a large altar built of a pile of masks. It was obvious that these ancient artifacts were all made of a floppy cardboard. They were a well-made premium, just not of some prehistoric magma.

The stories of Buzz, Happy, female associate Carol, reformed villains Tonga and Robbie Robertson (who became a major in the Space Patrol), and their adventures—often in opposition to the evil Prince Bacharatti rocketing out from Space Patrol headquarters on the man-made planet, Terra—were of the "space opera" variety, involving ray-gun battles and fist fights. Those hand-to-hand battles were done live, and often a punch would not narrowly miss as planned but actually connect. Kemmer complained that he would often have

to go out of the story climax and do a commercial for Hot Ralston splattered with his own blood from a cut lip.

By the last TV season in 1955, Nestle's Chocolate and Weather Bird Shoes had joined Ralston as sponsors. *Space Patrol* was one of the last live drama shows on television of any sort. More mature science fiction was now available. Cartoons would soon take over Saturday mornings. But it was a worthwhile effort which left behind memories, recordings, and premiums for its first fans like Andy Anderson, and for a new generation discovering it. "Smoke and rockets!" Cadet Happy might exclaim. As the century is about to turn, *Space Patrol* still blasts through "vast, wild reaches of interplanetary space."

SUPERMAN

Superman began in syndication in 1940 on radio two years after the first Superman comic book, *Action Comics* No.1, was published. It was the radio show, not the comic book, which first introduced such important elements as the copy boy, later cub reporter, Jimmy Olsen, as an important character, and the radioactive meteorite from Superman's original planet, Krypton—the element, Kryptonite—as the one poisonous substance that could rob him of his superhuman powers.

Clayton "Bud" Collier, radio commercial spokesman and actor, took the lead as another job in radio. He once said he really was not anxious to do it, but decided no one was likely to hear about him doing such a "silly" show. He spoke as Clark Kent in a high voice, then dropped to monumental depth and power when it became "A job for ... SUPERMAN!" Kent and the Man of Steel sounded different, yet it was apparent that both were the same man to the listener. The *Green Hornet* series somewhat lead the way in the '30s, because the racket-busting Hornet spoke in a gruff, menacing tone like a gangster, but as himself,

publisher Brit Reid, he sounded smooth and educated. None of the other men who have portrayed Superman on radio or in films or TV could duplicate this double voice.

Collier reported the cast pulled out all stops during rehearsals and sent the script "up" to get all the humorous elements out of their system, so they could do the live show dead serious. The character of Superman was so stern and lacking in humor, constant efforts were made to break Collier up on microphone—setting his script on fire, pulling his pants down, old radio stunts. But he never lost it.

He returned to voicing Superman in Saturday morning TV cartoons in the '60s, along with others of the radio cast including Jane Alexander ("Lois"). Collier had been in TV since the '50s as host of audience participation shows, *Beat the Clock* and *To Tell the Truth*. A circulatory problem would end his life in the '70s.

There was some evolution in the famous opening signature. On the first show of all it went:

ANNOUNCER: Faster than an airplane... More powerful than a locomotive... Impervious to bullets...

The only sound effect was the wind from Superman's flight. But in only a few episodes, the classic opening was fixed into place:

ANNOUNCER: Faster than a speeding bullet..
  (SOUND EFFECTS: Passing bullet.)
  More powerful than a locomotive...
  (SFX: Locomotive.)
  Able to leap tall buildings in a single bound...
(SFX: rushing wind, hold under)
MAN: Look—up in the sky!
WOMAN: It's a bird!
2ND MAN; It's a plane!
MAN: It's Superman!

The sound of Superman flying was a recording of shrieking wind combined with an artillery shell ripping through the air. By hand, the sound effects men could slow the "flying" record to indicate the Man of Steel diving down, stop the turntable to have him drop to earth. It was more than mere wind, and became one of the most readily identifiable sounds on the air.

From the beginning, Superman "came to Earth with powers and abilities far beyond those of mortal men" and he secretly was Clark Kent "mild mannered reporter for a great metropolitan newspaper." Even before television, as early as 1942, he was fighting for "Truth, Justice, and the American Way."

The first *Superman* episode was a dramatization of the last days of the planet Krypton where scientist Jor-El and his wife Lara sent their baby son, Kal-El, off the doomed world in a model prototype rocketship to Earth, which followed the comic strip origin. It was Episode Two that departed from the established origin, and condensed the classic version in a way that could only be described as "silly." Long time *Superman* scripter Jack Johnstone denied responsibility to me in 1987 for this episode. Superman grew to manhood on the interstellar flight; some sort of robotic equipment cared for him and educated him. As soon as he landed on Earth, his first job was to rescue an old man and a boy from a runaway trolley car. The family pair suggested their strange new friend get a job on a newspaper and call himself—chosen entirely at random—"Clark Kent." He followed both suggestions.

Early serial stories of the syndicated transcription series concerned a criminal who termed himself "the Wolf." His criminal plans were easy for Clark Kent to thwart. He only became the mighty Superman for a few fleeting moments, and tried to hide not only his secret identity but his very existence from the world.

Kent had managed to get a job on the great metropolitan newspaper, the *Daily Planet* fairly easily. Editor Perry White was loud and bossy, but really a pussy cat. Girl reporter Lois Lane seemed to hold him in complete contempt, but—No buts. She wasn't kidding. Only the office boy, would-be reporter Jimmy Olsen, seemed to have any respect for Kent.

The story heated up when the Wolf tried breaking out of prison and revealed he was working for an even bigger crook, the Yellow Mask. The sinister Mask had bigger plans—like blowing up the dam and drowning Dyerville if they did not pay his ransom. Lois and Clark investigated, and Superman stopped the explosion.

Early adventures took Clark Kent off to exotic locales—the Arctic, dark jungles, the South Seas. He met far fewer people in those forsaken climes than on the crime beat in Metropolis. That meant fewer actors to pay. Sometimes Clark only spoke with one or two others for a whole episode.

For example, around the fiftieth episode of the series, Clark Kent searched for the lost arctic explorer, Alonzo Craig, accompanied by only an old sea captain and a grizzled guide during the whole story. There was a little doubling of grunts and shouts from hostile natives. Superman eventually flew away with Craig, temporarily mad, serving as the tribal witch doctor, and returned him to Metropolis and his own mind.

In many of the stories, Jimmy Olsen was as important to Kent as Jack Armstrong was to Uncle Jim Fairfield. Jimmy traveled everywhere with Kent. Though as close as an uncle or foster father, Jimmy always politely referred to his companion in adventure as "Mr. Kent."

For example, the two were aboard the Clara M., the "last of the clipper ships" on a story. It was a classic sea story with a peg-legged villain named Pete, as well as a phantom presence on board known as "the Whistler" for the haunting melody he trilled. Despite wind and waves, storms and sails, men overboard and men in mutiny, stowaways and emergency operations on the high seas, Kent took care of the surgery with radio instruction from a doctor, and helped control a panicked sailor here and there. But of course, it took a number of appearances by the more-than-human Superman to make a few rescues from the sea, or to hold back a rioting crew. The last villain was clapped into irons about the time America was pulled into World War II, ending finally this type of sea tale forever.

On radio, Clark Kent was only "mild-mannered" in the spoken introduction to the program. He was courageous and resourceful and greatly admired by Jimmy who told him once he was "a lot like Superman." Only Lois ever accused him of being a coward. Apparently, the radio producer felt the audience would simply not understand why Kent could be timid at one moment, then heroic as Superman. On the air, he was a real man as Clark Kent, and he was a super man as Superman.

After the Japanese attack on Pearl Harbor on Dec. 7, 1941, Jimmy Olsen tried to enlist in the Navy but was turned down, because he was "only fourteen." Clark Kent received a secret visit and was awarded a commission in the Secret Service as an undercover officer. He would be called upon when needed. (In the comic books, he failed his army physical when he accidentally used his X-ray to look through the wall and read the wrong eye chart.)

For the duration of the war, Superman would combat enemy agents around the world. One of the most dangerous was Der Teufel ("The Devil" in German), a Nazi scientist who invented a gun employing atomic power, but must have generated an energy similar to that of Kryptonite. The Atomic Gun could hurt Superman, knock him out, but it was not strong enough to kill him.

To get away from a steady diet of war stories, Superman would take on solving seemingly supernatural mysteries.

A Ghost Car appeared and disappeared on the roads around a dude ranch out west. Radio performer Jackson Beck, long associated with the series as the impressive announcer as well as actor in various parts such as screechy-voiced copy boy Beanie (and still a prominent commercial spokesman in TV in the 1990s), first appeared on *Superman*, Program No. 317, February 18, 1942. He had an acting role as a South American gaucho, Alfredo. Superman proved he had a hand in the mystery of the "Ghost Car."

It was not until the appearance of Kellogg's Pep cereal as a sponsor that premiums became an important element in the *Superman* series.

Beck told us the story, but he turned the listeners over to announcer Dan McCullough who spoke of delicious, health-enhancing Kellogg's Pep wheat flakes—and the real reason for eating this knockoff of Wheaties: the

Pep (Superman) box

premium inside the box. That prize changed over the years from models of warplanes you could construct from balsa wood, and later from cardboard, to postwar metal buttons. Some had military insignias on them, but then came the most sought-after in-box premiums—the classic Pep comic buttons, a penny-sized pinback with one comic strip character on each: Superman, of course, and Flash Gordon, The Phantom, Dick Tracy, Little Orphan Annie, Moon Mullins, Harold Teen, the Little King, and many others. "The buttons are metal and will last a long time." They are still around in the hands of one-time listeners and collectors after forty years.

Besides in-box prizes, Superman also offered larger premiums that one had to send in a dime and Pep box top for. There was a toy walkie-talkie, based on the old tin cans connected by taut string formula. One could send in for a model of the rocket that brought Superman to earth, with a propeller driven by rubber band. The propeller was not authentic to the comic book version, and even kids knew that propellers would not function in airless space. It might have been necessary to make

the toy work, but the propeller was described in the story as part of the rocket.

Apparently, Kellogg's had to pay extra to use the name "Superman" on the premium toy itself. So the walkie-talkie and the rocket and various other premiums were blank. Only a very few premiums actually used the name or likeness of the Man of Steel. One of the most handsome was the "Superman Crusaders Ring" which bore that caption and an embossed portrait of Superman in what looked like solid silver. (The Crusaders worked for racial understanding and harmony on the series.)

This good-looking ring, while worth a few hundred dollars, should not be confused with the Superman Contest Ring offered by the comic book publisher which some "high roller" collectors ascribe fabulous value to, up to $120,000. (See "Introduction")

In 1945, Superman rescued an unconscious boy from an aimlessly drifting rowboat. The Man of Steel loosened the boy's clothing and found under his plain shirt a red vest with the letter "R" over the heart. "Great Scot," Superman murmured, recognizing the true identity of the boy. Announcer Beck asked the listeners if they knew who the boy was, and if they did, not to tell others and spoil the big surprise in the next episode. As a boy, I thought it over and came up with the answer. Robin! The boy companion to the mysterious Batman!

Regaining consciousness, Robin, in his civilian identity of Dick Grayson told Clark Kent of Batman disappearing after an armed attack on their house by men who mentioned one name—Zoltan. They found only one Zoltan in the phone book, the operator of a wax museum. At that strange place, they thought they had found Batman standing in the shadows— but it was only a wax figure of him.

Actually, it turned out to really be Batman, encased in Zoltan's wax formula that placed people in suspended animation. The museum operator had captured prominent scientists and made them into wax figures to be shipped to Nazi Germany to be used in their war effort. Superman put an end to that plot and freed Batman.

Superman Crusader's ring (1947). Values in Good, Fine, and Mint: 125, 188, 250.

For the first time, Superman met Batman on radio (and they had appeared together in only a few panels in the comics). It would not be the last. Batman became a regular on the *Superman* radio series, appearing in approximately every second serial story. Often he appeared alone, and his young partner, Robin, only joined him half of the time. The first Batman was Stacy Harris (a former Jack Armstrong). The actor most often heard was Matt Crowley (a former Buck Rogers and a future Mark Trail). The most famous radio Batman was Gary Merrill, who became a major movie star, Bette Davis' on and off screen husband. Other actors sometimes played the role for a few episodes. Young Ron Liss was the regular Robin.

After the wax museum and a rather routine mystery involving an amusement park, Batman and Robin played major parts in what was almost certainly the greatest serial of all in the more than twelve year run of the *Superman* radio series. Superman's greatest menace, Kryptonite (radioactive poison to him) became embodied in human form, the Atom Man. Superman faced death from the Atom Man for weeks and weeks, and at one time it looked as if he actually was dead. The Man of Steel was driven to his knees and then to the ground by bolts of green Kryptonite lightning

by the embodiment of evil, the Atom Man. "Is this the end of Superman? The end of Truth, Justice, and the American Way?"

The Atom Man would eventually destroy himself by his refusal to admit that even his great power was not strong enough to kill Superman. His Kryptonite powers could hurt Superman—knock him unconscious—but they could not take his life anymore than the valiant ideals for which he stood could be destroyed by the evil men of the world.

Other sinister people in league with the Atom Man made another effort to kill Superman. He was rendered unconscious by a piece of Kryptonite meteorite and placed inside a cyclotron atom-smasher where he would be disintegrated. But his friends Batman and Robin pulled him from the machine, and he recovered to capture the last of those who were menacing him.

There would be other fragments of Kryptonite showing up in years to come, in other adventures where Batman and Robin would lend heroic aid, and in others where Superman's friends, Lois Lane, Jimmy Olsen, editor Perry White, and Inspector Henderson, were threatened. But it was the triumph over the monstrous Atom Man and his henchmen that gave Superman his greatest triumph on radio.

TALES OF THE DIAMOND K WITH KEN MAYNARD

A very late entry into the kid adventure radio series, *Tales of the Diamond K* featured silent and talkie cowboy star, Ken Maynard, in the mid-50s on the regional Liberty radio network. Although Ken had made his last starring film in 1944, he was still known to some of the public from his appearances with small circuses, and to more from his old films on TV. Furthermore, the character of Nevada Smith in the book and movie *The Carpetbaggers* is based as much on Ken Maynard as anybody.

Ken's vocal abilities were never among his greatest talents, but there was a certain hominess in the way he simply told a story about the Old West or his own experiences exploring the Yucatan jungles like a favorite old uncle. There were no other actors, music, or sound effects—except a recorded whinny from his horse, Tarzan, at the opening and close. The program was fifteen minutes long.

The present writer knew Ken Maynard during his last years. He told me several stories that

Ken Maynard. Courtesy Eddie Brandt's Saturday Matinee.

would not have appeared on the radio show, including one account where he claimed he killed a man in self defense. He was a young fellow hopping a ride on a freight train in the early years of the twentieth century. A railroad policeman, a private bull, found Ken and attempted to throw him off the train. The freight was doing ninety miles an hour and Ken would have been killed for certain. The future star wound up kicking and stomping the bull, and eventually shoving him off the train instead. Around 1965, he told me "If that guy is still alive, I sure wouldn't want to see what he looks like today."

Ken was the source for a number of items from his personal collection, some scrapbooks, and one example of a premium offered on his radio show, a small 78 rpm record in which he tells a story similar to those he used on the air, but the record has an added feature in which he calls the listener who orders it by mail by the listener's own name. Unfortunately, he did not have one for "Jim" any longer and the one I got has him greeting "Buster." I don't know the details of the technology that allowed him to do this for every listener—for the sum of one dollar!

The record and a few other items were premiums of a sort, but because he never found a sponsor, they were low-priced items on which the aging cowboy hoped to turn a small profit.

Ken Maynard must not have made much money off the premiums from his show. I left him for the last time as he was sitting in his tiny house trailer in the San Fernando Valley.

TARZAN

Edgar Rice Burroughs himself produced his literary creation, Tarzan of the Apes, on radio in 1932. Much of the series has survived, hundreds of episodes, and today it seems primitive in the extreme. Jim Pierce, a screen Tarzan, played the lead, along with his wife and Burroughs' daughter, Joan Burroughs, as Jane. While they are as good as many others in the cast, the art of radio acting had not been perfected. Veteran radio performer Frank Nelson (the floor walker on *Jack Benny* with the big "YEEESSS!") did a number of the supporting roles. He was gifted with a set of tapes in recent years and after hearing himself threw them out.

The story line follows Burroughs' books, *Tarzan of the Apes* and *Return of Tarzan*, and on through the series. Tarzan's parents were shipwrecked in Africa, and the baby Tarzan was orphaned, and then raised by the Great Apes. He grew to manhood, met Jane, loved her, returned to civilization and his title, Lord Greystoke. But then he returned to the jungle, wishing to take Jane with him. He met many people, including the Priestess of La (the only other woman besides Jane he felt attraction to), cannibals, Arab slavers, Russian criminals, and many more.

The series was heavily promoted with many premiums, many of which are still sought after today.

In the 1950s, a modern series of half-hour Tarzan stories came to both local syndication and CBS Radio. Lamont Johnson now played the part, and Jane did not appear. The stories included such modern elements as one villain setting off a very low-yield atomic bomb in the jungle from which Tarzan barely escaped. The audience aimed for now was adult and no premiums were issued.

This Tarzan series was one of the last of any kind developed for the era of dramatic radio, and in a couple of years, this *Tarzan* and all stories on the air were gone. A number of *Tarzan* TV series were developed with varying formats, but after the early years in which other such shows offered giveaways.

TERRY AND THE PIRATES

The brilliant illustrative style of Milton Caniff assured the success of the *Terry and the Pirates* feature in the newspaper comics sections of the nation. Of course, on radio you could not see the distinctive characters Caniff had created, but the man was a writer as well as an artist and he had given his creations distinctive personalities. There was eager, adventurous, young Terry Lee and his unofficial guardian, the two-fisted man of action, Pat Ryan (played by Clayton Collier for a time, later radio's Superman). There were their Chinese allies, jug-eared, fast-talking Connie (short for Confucius), and the hulking giant, short on speech and intellect, Big Stoop. There was also their Oriental nemesis, the Dragon Lady, who was deadly but alluringly beautiful. "Dragon Lady" has become part of the American Language, and both young and old realize the term means a deadly but attractive woman.

In later years, during World War II, Terry was joined by American pilots, Col. Flip Corkin and Lt. Hot Shot Charlie and also by a mellowed Dragon Lady who now fought on the American side, against the Japanese invaders of her homeland, China.

For an early kid action series, Libby canned vegetables was an unusual sponsor. The sponsor must have theorized that if a good thriller could get fans of Tom Mix to eat the non-sugary Hot Ralston cereal, listeners of *Terry* could be convinced to eat their vegetables.

During World War II, the show was sponsored by Quaker Puffed Wheat and Puffed Rice. The stories involved spies and secret weapons, and Terry grew up fighting wartime enemies. Premiums were involved in the storyline. While still on for Libby, there was a "Terriscope," a cardboard and glass mirror periscope that was a big help to Terry and his friends on a certain adventure. One of the later Quaker premiums was a Gold Detector Ring which was instrumental in Terry locating a lost gold mine.

Although the series had been on for a decade, when afternoon thrillers began to convert to the complete-in-one-half-hour-episode, a format pioneered in the early afternoon by *Jack Armstrong*, the *Terry* series was discontinued. The Quaker company went to the master of the half-hour adventure, George W. Trendle, originator of the classic *Lone Ranger*. For Quaker, Trendle refurbished an old Mountie series he had, *Challenge of the Yukon* (later known as *Sergeant Preston of the Yukon*), and the sun set in the Far East for *Terry and the Pirates*—and all his Good Guy friends as well.

TOM MIX AND HIS RALSTON STRAIGHT SHOOTERS

Tom Mix began Sept. 25, 1933, three times weekly on NBC, fifteen minutes, five times weekly from 1936, off the air 1943, resumed June 7, 1944, a half-hour (not serial) three times weekly fall 1949 until it ended on June 23, 1950. It was revived in 1983 for a brief series.

Cast

Tom Mix (the greatest cowboy of them all)

Artells Dickson (New York, 1933)
Willard Waterman (one time, 1934)
Jack Ross (one time, 1935)

	Jack Holden (1935–1937)
	Russell Thorson (1938–1942)
	Curley Bradley (1944–1950, also 1983)
Wrangler	Percy Hemus (1933–1942)
Pecos Williams	Curley Bradley (1935–1942)
	Jim Harmon (1983)
Sheriff Mike Shaw	Hal Peary (1930s)
	Leo Curley (1944–1950)
	Jack Lester (1983)
Jane	Winifred Toomey (1930s)
	Jane Webb (1940s–1950)
	Virginia Gregg (1983)
Jimmy	Andy Donnelly
	George Gobel (1935)
	Hugh Rowlands
Wash	Vance McCune (1930s)
	Forrest Lewis (1940s–1950)
Doc Green	Forrest Lewis (1940s–1950)
	Les Tremayne (1983)

Straight Shooters (all of the above, and every kid in the world who believed in Tom Mix and his ideals of fair play and justice for all)

Amos Q. Snood	Sidney Ellstrom
Longbow Billy (a mountain man)	Willard Waterman (1947–1948)
Capitola (a maid)	Betty Lou Gerson
Sgt. Hank Smith (young serviceman)	Johnathon Hole (1947)
	Richard Gulla (1983)
Mary (Hank's sweetheart)	Barbara Gratz (1983)
The Great Dane (movie director)	Art Hern (1983)
Guest Star	Jock Mahoney (1983)

The Ranch Boys (singing trio, sang theme song/Ralston commercial, played parts in story): Jack Ross, Shorty Carson (later Ken Carson), Curley Bradley

Announcers: Don Gordon (1940–1950), Franklyn Ferguson, Les Griffith, Les Tremayne (1983)

Also in the cast 1930s–1950: Jack Lester, Art Hern, Olan Soule, Arthur Peterson, Jess Pugh, Carl Kroenke, DeWitt McBride, Patricia Dunlap, Jack Petruzzi

Series Creator: Charles Claggett

Producer/Directors: Clarence L. Menser (1930s–1942), Al Chance (1944–1947), Mary Afflick (1947–1950), Jim Harmon (1983)

Writers: Roland Martini (1930s), Charles Tazewell (1930s), George Lowther (1944–1950), Jim Harmon (1983)

Theme: To the tune of "When it's Round-Up Time in Texas (and the Bloom on the Sage)," but with commercial lyrics for Ralston cereals; by the Ranch Boys trio, then after 1944 by Curley Bradley

Tom Mix's history on the air began with a premium offer even before broadcasting began. Probably the foremost distributor of premiums on radio, the one which offered more to be rare and one-day valuable premiums, was in the game before the first episode. The story of Tom Mix on radio was told with the premiums the show offered. The *Tom Mix* series is the history of the radio premium in America.

The *Tom Mix* series started on radio in 1933 three times a week over NBC for a quarter hour. Before long, it would become a five day series,

Tom Mix *radio cast at Thanksgiving 1947 (Left to Right): Betty Lou Gerson (cook), Willard Waterman (Longbow Billy), Jane Webb (Jane), Curley Bradley (Tom Mix), Forrest Lewis (Wash Lee), Leo Curley (Sheriff Mike Shaw), Don Gordon (announcer).*

Monday through Friday. The new radio show was first broadcast from New York with a radio actor named Artells Dickson impersonating the great Western movie star, Tom Mix, in serialized adventures featuring his Wonder Horse, Tony, and his Straight Shooter pals including (we know from publicity shots) his weathered partner, the Old Wrangler, who narrated the stories, and Tom's young ward, Jane.

Dickson was said to be "much like Tom" in stalwart character, but looked unconvincing with a Western shirt and vest topping his tweed suit pants. He went on as simply Art Dickson to be the star of singing Western movie short subjects, following in a very minor way the path of the major star he portrayed. In a songbook he edited, Dickson admitted portraying Tom Mix on the radio was what he was most famous for, ten years after the fact.

The broadcast series was moved to Chicago, to be closer to Ralston's St. Louis headquarters after the first season, and Willard Waterman did the first broadcast. "I had to work with the little girl who played Jane, and the microphone was tilted down for her," Waterman told the present writer. "The ad agency told me I didn't 'dominate the scene' enough to be Tom Mix. I told them I had a contract. They told me to forget it if I wanted to continue working in the business. I forgot it."

The part of Mix was quickly reassigned to Jack Holden, the announcer on the *National Barn Dance* show. He had a sort of "country" accent, though not really Western. After several years, Russell Thorson, an announcer in Chicago, replaced Holden as Mix. Thorson had a great commanding voice, but free of any regional source. Of course, Tom Mix was becoming on radio more than a Western law man, but a hero for all seasons—sailing the high seas, flying airplanes, solving mysteries amid big city skyscrapers.

One of the earliest episodes involved Tom Mix being captured by the bad guys and imprisoned. His six-guns were taken, but they missed a wooden gun he had been working on to give to his young wards as a toy. He finished the gun and used it to bluff his way to free-

PREMIUM SPOTLIGHT

TOM MIX TELEGRAPH SETS

There were two different models of the Tom Mix Telegraph set: one about the size of the *Reader's Digest*, predominantly blue in color, and the other, smaller than a paperback book and red. Both had a "clicker" metal key and the Morse code printed on the cardboard box front, but the blue one was only a sounder. A recipient could pound out a message, and someone across the room could hear it and decode it. The red set, however, had a battery inside and if strung together by wire with another set, it could actually send a message from one house to another. These Tom Mix telegraphs, introduced in the 1930s, were the favorites of many.

In the storyline on the *Tom Mix* series, a railroad was being built in Tom's home town of Dobie. As usual, nothing ever went well for the owner of the TM-Bar ranch. Sinister forces were trying to stop the railroad for their own crooked ends. The unorthodox method was to have henchmen lie between the tracks, and as the train passed over them, cause a derailment by tampering with the tracks. Apparently these greedy underlings were willing to risk their own lives to accomplish their ends.

To get information on these acts of sabotage fast, Tom set up his own telegraph line, so he could communicate with his Straight Shooters, Wrangler, Pecos, and little Jane. Apparently, Tom had a special telegraph set that was in effect a radio telegraph. While waiting at the Dobie depot, the set in his back pocket began tapping out an urgent message from one of his Straight Shooters.

"Get a telegraph set just like Tom Mix' own," the radio announcer instructed listeners in the commercial. "Just send the blue seal from the pouring spout of a box of good ol' Hot Ralston, and ten cents in coin—no stamps please—to Tom Mix, Checkerboard Square, St. Louis, Missouri..."

Of course the set was not exactly like Tom Mix' own—it couldn't send messages through the air. Nearly half a million listeners in mid-1938 wrote in to get theirs and found that out. Perhaps because of some listener complaints, only a bit more than a year later in January of 1940, Ralston offered an "electric" battery telegraph. In those days, you could buy a set of battery-powered "Boy Scout" telegraph sets for several dollars, but at only a dime, the red telegraph was quite a bargain.

The red set, however, brought in just sixty thousand responses. It is possible listeners may have mistakenly thought this was only a repeat of the blue telegraph offer, and thinking they already had that, or anyway one much like it, did not send for the red set, the superior item. For that reason, the red set is more valuable and difficult to find for collectors today.

The original movie Tom Mix and Tony. This photo was offered as a premium in 1933 and 1983. 1983 Values in Good, Fine, and Mint: 5, 10, 15.

dom. The wooden gun was an important early premium offer.

Another storyline concerned the airplane Tom had taken to flying around his ranch. (A model of the plane was another premium offer.) The aircraft was forced down by a faltering engine and landed in the unburned center of a forest fire, ringed by flames. Tom could radio out his position but there was no way to reach him through the flames.

Young Jane and stalwart Pecos listened to Tom's radioed description of his trouble—a broken propeller blade. If a new aerial screw could be brought to him, he could fit it in place and take-off. Pecos looked grim. "We can't let Tom down. I can strap one of them propeller things to a horse and ride through the fire, to Tom."

"Oh, Pecos," Jane said, "no horse in the world would go through those flames."

"Tony would," Pecos said. "To get to Tom."

And Tony did go through the flames with Pecos on his back. The sound of the flames grew louder, but Tony's hoofbeats never faltered. On...on...to Tom.

"Tony! Pecos!" the ringing voice of Tom Mix carried over the sound of the forest fire.

Tony whinnied and nuzzled Tom, as the greatest of all Straight Shooters caught Pecos as he collapsed from the saddle. "We got through, Tom. We got through."

Tom and Pecos could mount the propeller and fly the plane out of the forest fire. But I can't remember how he got Tony out. Much of radio only exists in fading memory now. Many recordings and scripts have been preserved by dedicated hobbyists, but much more is gone forever.

Another sequence that survives in memory also concerns Tony. In one of the many hazardous feats he did for Tom, the Wonder Horse broke his leg. In those days, the only thing thought to be done for a horse with a broken limb was to end its pain. Tom prepared for the unthinkable. Tom Mix was going to have to shoot Tony. For this, Tom took a silver bullet that he and Tony had won together and loaded it into his six-shooter. (About this time, a smaller, sleeker wooden model of Tom's revolver was a premium.) Tom recalled the many things that

Tom Mix badge, six-gun, decoder, and other various Tom Mix items

he and Tony had lived through together...the times Tony had saved his life, and now all he could do to repay him was this—not enough.

Meanwhile, Jane and Pecos were in the TM-Bar ranch house, sunk in gloom, with the radio droning in the background. The results of a horse race were announced. The winner was a horse who had once had a broken leg, but who had been restored to racing fitness by a certain Eastern doctor. There was hope for Tony! The Straight Shooter pair rushed for Tony's stable. As they ran, a shot exploded.

Tom had fired, but the vision of the truest eye in the West was clouded. Tom Mix had missed his shot.

Tony survived the forest fire and he survived the broken leg, and went on to be Tom's faithful mount in a thousand more wonderful adventures.

The movie star Tom Mix died in a 1940 auto accident, but the show never missed a day, and

Tom Mix candy giveaway (this is not a radio premium)

Thorson continued in the lead role. I think children really did not understand that the real Tom Mix had died. He was still on radio, still the same voice, still alive. They forgot the news story of his death. The fictional stories of his continuing adventures was more compelling.

After the Second World War started, Tom Mix's radio adventures had him dealing with espionage, fighting enemy agents. Premiums featured Secret Manuals with various codes in them, and a decoder badge. The Master Mind, a spymaster, sought another secret message, a secret formula for a major new weapon. The formula had been given Tom to guard by the daughter of a scientist when she pinned a flower to his lapel.

The Master Mind's agents made an attempt to steal the flower from Pecos, who was carrying it to confuse the enemy. Kidnapped in a taxi, Pecos grabbed the steering wheel, causing the car to run off a bridge into the river below rather than give up the formula. He managed to get out the sinking car, but the flower was swept away—at least it was not in enemy hands.

The spies did not know the flower had been lost. They made another attempt to get it by kidnapping Wrangler to make Tom deliver the rosebud as ransom for his old partner. Of course, Tom would never sell out his country's security, even for the life of a friend. But he stalled them while he instigated a complex search for a source of the paper the ransom note had been written on. He even marshaled the forces of law and order with the skill of J. Edgar Hoover himself. After locating the address, he and the police closed in, and the enemies of America learned the hard way that their Lugers and daggers were no match for Tom Mix's six-guns.

Tom finally realized that the formula hadn't been lost after all. It had not been in the lost flower at all—it was engraved on the head of the pin that had fastened the flower to Tom's jacket. (At the time, there was a lot of publicity about how the Lord's Prayer could be engraved on the head of a pin.) Tom still had the pin in his lapel.

Other wartime adventures had Tom preventing traitorous Americans from dropping bombs from a plane on the Verdi River Powder Plant, a munitions factory, and exposing the scheme of using a phantom ship, a Flying Dutchman, to disguise the work of evil-doers (it

Tom Mix in Tom Mix Rides to the Rescue. *This is a "penny book," a tiny 2 x 3" book which was given away with candy and sold in stores for 3¢.*

was a movie projector throwing a ship's image on clouds of fog).

Tom Mix also had to deal with a mysterious man, the Black Cat, who was dressed like a cat and who could scale big city high-rises with feline ability. He was a villain, but he might be confused with a comic-book hero (there was a Black Cat in comics—but she was a heroine, definitely one of the "good guys"). If the radio series was beginning to resemble a comic book, perhaps it was because more premiums of the show were a series of comic books. In Book 6 of the comics run, Tom Mix fought a villain called the Cobra, even as the Cat was his enemy on the air.

The Black Cat used a trapeze to seeming magically come and go from high floors of skyscrapers. Tom Mix, once a circus man himself, figured out the Cat's scheme and apparently leaped to his death from a window. But the final episode revealed Tom had only dived out to grab the trapeze and followed the Black Cat

back to his lair across the way, and made him a prisoner.

When the radio series was first being planned in 1932, Tom Mix and Tony were magic names. Such silents as *The Great A & K Train Robbery* and *Riders of the Purple Sage* made those names, and there would be talkies ahead, *Destry Rides Again* in another year and eight more sound features for Universal, and in 1935 a fifteen chapter serial, *The Miracle Rider* from Mascot, called a mistake by critics, is now his most available screen appearance in video stores.

Mix first got into movies when the Selig Company came to Oklahoma and made *Life in the Great Southwest* on a ranch he had an interest in about 1909. He had a colorful career as a rodeo cowboy, law officer, and military man, one elaborated on by him and by others,

Pair of Tom Mix leather gloves—these were a store item, not a premium

such as film studio publicity agents. Unnecessarily. The truth was enough.

Tom Mix was a peace officer in the last days of the Wild West. Dewey, Oklahoma, has a museum dedicated to Tom Mix's work as a town marshal for the years around 1908. At the time of my first trip to Dewey about 1970, my taxi was driven by an old timer who remembered when "Tom Mix was the law in Dewey." He remembered Tom bringing in a horse thief with both men covered in blood from the contested arrest.

Mix was also "sheriff"—and unofficial mayor and court judge—of the railroad boom town of Le Hunt, Kansas, in 1905. It was said there was a killing one night in the town, and it would have been worse without Tom Mix being there.

In the mid-70s, Roy Rogers told me he thought "Tom Mix was the greatest guy who ever lived," and recalled how he and Tom

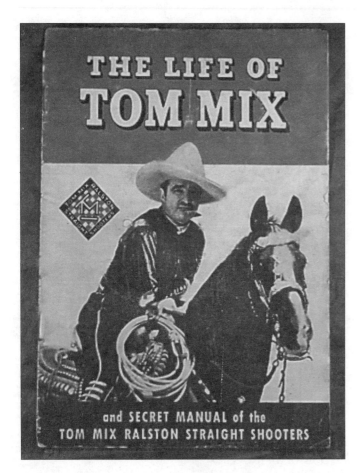

1941 Tom Mix "The Life of Tom Mix and Secret Manual of the Tom Mix Ralston Straight Shooters manual. Values in Good, Fine, and Mint: 40, 80, 160.

would go out horseback riding in the gray of morning in Griffith Park. Gene Autry also wanted Tom as a friend. Sidekick Pat Buttram told me "Autry worshipped Mix, but Mix didn't care that much for Autry. Oh, they were friends, they had horses together, but Mix did not appreciate singing Westerns."

Tom Mix was also making personal appearances in theatres and touring the country with the Sells Floto Circus. (In a few years, he would have his own Tom Mix Circus.)

He still had millions of fans—and one of the most prominent was William H. Danforth, president of Ralston-Purina, one of the largest processors of animal feed and cereals for the family breakfast table.

Charles E. Claggett, a copywriter for the Gardner Advertising Agency, suggested a way to win Danforth's approval was to sign up Tom Mix. According to legend, the screen and circus star signed an agreement on the back of an envelope which permitted the use of his name and likeness in advertising, and to be impersonated on radio.

As reported by Mix authorities Paul E. Mix and M.G. Norris, there was a later contract offering Tom Mix three payments of $5,000 over a period from 1935 to 1940 for use of his name and background on the radio series and for Sundays comics advertisements and premiums. After the final payment, Ralston would own such rights "forever." The final payment came only six months before Tom would die. If renegotiations with the heirs had been required, and possibly not agreed upon, the series would not have gone on for another ten years, and been briefly revived in 1982–83.

Despite Danforth's enthusiasm for Mix, some test of his continuing appeal seemed appropriate. A trial run of an advertisement in the Sunday comics came out, inviting youngsters to join Tom Mix's Straight Shooter Club. Ralston may have been happy with 25,000 answers, agency man Claggett once told me. They got half a million. "Boxtops buried the desk of Ralston president William H. Danforth."

The Tom Mix series began in 1933 and ran until 1942. The sponsors thought that due to the installation of permanent daylight savings time—called War Savings Time—children

A Tom Mix advertisement from 1936 for the Signature Ring

would stay outside longer and play, and not listen to their radio favorites. When the ratings of such shows as Jack Armstong did not falter, the people at Ralston realized their mistake, proceeded to put Tom Mix back on the air.

The important decision was who would play Tom. The Gardner Agency gave the role to Curley Bradley, who had been playing Pecos. To Curley, it was like a shoe dropping after years of waiting. As far back as 1935 in Hollywood, Ralston agency people spotted Bradley and considered him for playing Tom Mix.

Bradley was born in Coalgate, Oklahoma, on September 18, 1910, as Raymond George Courtney. While growing up, he played the guitar and sang with his family at fairs and dances. In between engagements he had worked as a cowboy along with his two brothers. As a youngster, he hid under the courthouse steps and saw some of the last of the old time shoot-outs between rivals on the fading frontier.

He was sixteen in 1926, six foot one and 175 pounds—apparently a full grown young man.

Traveling with musical groups and rodeos took him to Hollywood where he found work in the then still silent movies as a stuntman, riding in the films of Hoot Gibson, Buck Jones, and the foremost Western star of the period, Tom Mix. Curley rode in the gang of bad guys, then changed shirts and chased himself in the posse. He did running W horse falls, fights, and spills.

I asked him why he quit stunts. "I didn't like having one arm splinted up in the air, and a leg in a cast down here," Curley said, with gestures. "I liked singing. I didn't like being busted into little bits. I reckon there's no accounting for a man's taste."

Curley was friendly with most of the stars he worked with. He knew Tom Mix but according to him, Tom was always off training his horses or involved with his business managers about personal appearances and the like. He would engage in a bit of horseplay with the crew for an hour or so, but then he was off on business.

It was Buck Jones who has always around when somebody needed him. It was Buck who

Boys! Girls!
GET THESE GRAND PREMIUMS!

No. 17. Gold Ore Charm

Genuine Gold Ore from the old historical Comstock lode at Silver City, Nevada. Set in beautiful design. Suitable for watch fob or locket.

For one Ralston Wheat Cereal blue seal and 10c.

No. 18. Compass and Magnifying Glass

2-in-1 compass and magnifying glass made of metal with beautiful western design and TM Bar brand. Magnifying glass folds under compass.

For one Ralston Wheat Cereal blue seal and 10c.

No. 14. Telegraph Set

Electrical! Comes equipped with battery and International Code alphabet.

For one Ralston Wheat Cereal blue seal and 10c.

No. 5. Magnet

Fully magnetized—will pick up iron or steel objects. Fine quality steel. Horseshoe pattern.

For only one Ralston Wheat Cereal blue seal and 5c.

No. 4. Univex Candid Type Camera

Pocket size. No gadgets. Full year guarantee. Picture size is 1½"x1⅛". Can easily be enlarged to 3" x 4".

Camera for one Ralston Wheat Cereal blue seal and 25c.

Camera and one roll of film for one Ralston Wheat Cereal blue seal and 35c.

No. 6. Bracelet

A beautiful metal bracelet engraved with attractive Indian designs.

For one Ralston Wheat Cereal blue seal and 10c.

No. 7. The Ideal Pocket Webster Dictionary

A handy pocket size Webster Dictionary. Size 4" x 5¾". 378 pages, illustrated, self-pronouncing, completely new.

For one Ralston Wheat Cereal blue seal and 10c.

No. 8. This Beautiful Pen and Pencil!

Made of beautiful, highly polished plastic. Pen is self-filling, easy-writing, stainless steel, GOLD-PLATED point. Pencil has built-in eraser and special compartment for holding leads.

Get pen or pencil for one Ralston Wheat Cereal blue seal and 10c (both for two blue seals and 20c.)

COUPON ON PAGE 33 SHOWS HOW TO ORDER. ALSO MORE SWELL PREMIUMS ON PAGE 33.

C 3824-A—1-41   Printed in U. S. A.

Advertisement for various "Grand Premiums" from Ralston Wheat Cereal

90   •

had the kind, helpful personality of the Western hero that Tom Mix seemed to symbolize.

Curley Bradley preferred to be a singer, mostly with the trio the Ranch Boys. The group had been formed when some of the stunt riders were sitting around at the end of the day's work, and did what cowboys do around the campfire—told tall stories and sang songs. Three men began working together—Ken "Shorty" Carson, Jack Ross, and Curley. It was Ross' idea to call themselves the Ranch Boys and try to get work. Radio and recording work followed, and a few film appearances.

They eventually wound up in Chicago, appearing on the WLS *National Barn Dance* and on the *Tom Mix* program, singing the Ralston theme song/commercial and playing parts in the drama. It was Curley who earned the best part—Pecos Williams, Tom's right hand man.

In 1938, while the Mix show was on summer hiatus, the Ranch Boys went on a great adventure. Curley would talk about it for the rest of his life. The three men would ride from Hollywood back to their home in Chicago on horseback. No one had done such a ride in fifty years.

The three troubadours began the 2,875 mile ride on May 10, 1938. Their route would lead over old stagecoach pathways to San Francisco, and then over to Sacramento. They would go on to Carson City, Nevada, and up mountains,

Tom Mix Shredded Ralston box

Tom Mix Dixie Cup lid

across deserts and into Salt Lake City. Then it was up into the high country for Denver. They rode on to North Platte, Omaha, Council Bluffs, and then it was only one more bridge to cross over the Mississippi River and into Chicago.

At four thirty in the morning, the boys woke up to clean the horses, boil coffee, fry eggs, pack up the previous night's camp, and be in the saddle by six thirty. There was a driver and truck carrying relief horses. The Humane Society checked that the horses were not overworked.

Even in 1938, the motor age was here and the riders had to keep to the edge of the highways. They were imposing roads at the time, but today's massive freeways would probably make such a ride impossible. Most of the car and truck drivers back then were curious and well-mannered, but as the Ranch Boys made their way down the eastern slopes of California's Donner Pass one truck driver thought it would be fun to make his engine backfire to panic the horses. They reared and sideslipped, nearly taking Curley and his partners over the rim to meet death far below. But men who could ride well enough to make Tom Mix and

Buck Jones look good in the movies could handle their mounts even in this deadly situation. The Ranch Boys did eventually return to Chicago, to much adulation, and back to working on the *Tom Mix* series.

In 1944, the Gardner Agency approached Bradley and told him they were going to put *Tom Mix* back on the air, and he was going to be Tom—finally...fulfilling an offer made over a decade before.

In the time the show had been off the air, Percy Hemus had died, and with him died his character of the Old Wrangler. Mr. Danforth thought no one else could ever do that role as well and the part would be retired. Sheriff Mike Shaw had been around in the story for years, but now he was going to be elevated to the role of Tom's chief sidekick. Versatile actor Hal Perry had once played the part, but had moved to Hollywood to star as The Great Gildersleeve. One of those auditioning was an old vaudeville performer, square-jawed three hundred plus pounds Leo Curley. "I've only got five bucks in my pants, Curley. I'll buy the drinks if you put in a good word for me. I sure need this job."

Tom Mix glow-in-the-dark plastic compass and magnifying glass (1946). Values in Good, Fine, and Mint: 32, 65, 130.

Curley called into the control booth. "Hey, you know, I think this old fellow and I work together pretty good." Leo Curley got the job.

The new *Tom Mix* series began June 7, 1944, with Curley singing the theme (without the other Ranch Boys—the men had gone their own ways) in the best-remembered version:

> Shredded Ralston for your breakfast,
> Starts the day off shining bright,
> Gives you lots of cowboy energy
> With a flavor that's just right.
> It's delicious, And nutritious
> Bite size and ready to eat;
> Take a tip from Tom
> Go and tell your Mom
> Shredded Ralston can't be beat!

The cold cereal, Shredded Ralston (now known as Wheat Chex) became the usual sponsor of the radio series. Only during winter did "Tom" sing the praises of Hot Ralston:

> Hot Ralston for your breakfast,
> Start the day off shinning bright
> Gives you lots of cowboy energy
> With a flavor that's just right.
> It's delicious, And nutritious,
> Made of golden Western wheat,
> So take a tip from Tom
> Go and tell your Mom
> Hot Ralston can't be beat!

(There were variations over the years.)

Tom Mix Ralston boxes

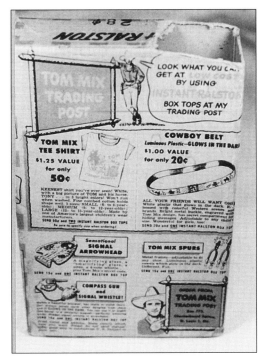

Tom Mix Ralston boxes

On the first revival episode, Tom Mix flew back from helping the war effort in Europe and met his old friends at the TM-Bar. The celebration was interrupted by the arrival of an Englishman at the ranch, one who was looking for Winston Churchill and who thought he might be up the fireplace chimney.

Winston Churchill was only the name of the rather silly Englishman's pet monkey, the next episode revealed—along with information about "The Mystery of the Vanishing Herd." Large numbers of cattle needed to feed a hungry nation in wartime were disappearing from the range. Behind the trouble was a Nazi spy and flying ace, the Iron Mask. In the final episode, in a borrowed Army fighter plane, Tom Mix swooped down on the nest of enemy agents and captured them all.

This story and the rest that would follow were by George Lowther, a gifted writer who had also scripted at times *Superman* and *Inner Sanctum*, and who would go on to write for *Captain Video* on TV. He once met a group from the show at an expensive restaurant—he entered with a pet duck on a leash.

Some of Lowther's style and characterization can be seen in the aftermath of the capture of the Iron Mask.

MIKE: One thing didn't...lead to another before you got back from England, Tom... It took you to find that gas was killing them steers and...that gas was spread by airplane.

TOM: Mike, I'm going to start preening my feathers like a peacock any minute now.

MIKE: No, you won't, Tom. You ain't no fancy dude with grand ideas. Sure, you've traveled. I reckon you've seen about all the world there is to see, sat down to chow with dukes and countesses, kings, and all that there sort of thing, but you're just natural and regular—like any other Westerner.

TOM: Let's say like any other American, Mike.

With Ralston returning and the war over, new premiums began to appear, like the Tom Mix Magnet Ring. According to a Sunday comics ad, Tom Mix lowered it on a string to grab the paper clip holding the stolen plans for the Atomic Bomb.

The series was very successful for four years, but it was time for a change in the fall of 1949. Other afternoon thrillers such as *Jack Armstrong* had converted from fifteen minute daily serials to a complete half-hour story several times a week, a format long followed by *The Lone Ranger*, providing a faster moving program to compete with TV for at least a little longer.

One of the half-hour stories was "The Invisible Rider" who seemed to be a transparent

The Tom Mix magic tiger-eye ring (1950) was the last Tom Mix ring offering. Values in Good, Fine, and Mint: 60, 125, 250.

Tom Mix *revival, circa 1983—Curley Bradley (Tom Mix) and actor-producer Jim Harmon.*

horseman, displaying only his gloves on the reins and his hat floating in air. The illusion was created by thin, stiff wires. His voice came from a radio in the saddlebags, giving the trained horse instructions on where to trot. Tom Mix once again employed a frequent theme of the series—solving a mystery involving a menace who seemed to have the power to make himself invisible.

As always in the *Mix* series, the premium offers for a boxtop, and later for a boxtop and ten cents (more later), played a large part in the stories. And in one of the very last offers, his glow-in-the-dark Tiger Eye ring would provide enough light for rescuers to spot him when he was tied hand and foot and tossed into a river.

With the ring, in a combination offer, came a toy TV set showing magnified still pictures of the *Tom Mix* cast and others. But when TV was one of the major interests of radio listeners, the end of this type of radio was not far off. After only one season of half-hour stories, after seventeen years over-all, *Tom Mix* went off the air.

So there came a final broadcast. "The end—yet only the beginning, Mike," Tom Mix said to trusted sheriff. "How many times will the figure of big, burly Mike Shaw stride across the imagination of some grown-up child?"

Then Tom rode Tony off into an echoing Valhalla, as Don Gordon said, "In the heart and the imagination of the world, Tom Mix rides on, and lives on, forever."

Tom Mix lived on in the imagination of many of us. Ralston received requests for the radio show to be revived long after that type of programming had disappeared. Finally, in 1982, a young Ralston executive named Steve Kendall decided to do something about this, and began a revival of Tom Mix on the Hot Ralston cereal box, offering new premiums, first a set of cereal bowls. The present writer became involved in the operation, and I wrote and edited a new miniature Tom Mix comic book to be offered in the cereal box itself, and I went on to write, produce, and appear in new radio episodes of Tom Mix with Curley Bradley back as Tom. (I played his sidekick, Pecos.) One of these episodes was on a set of premium recordings offered by Ralston.

As Charlie Chaplin made such silent films as *City Lights* long after the silent era was over, the foremost bestower of radio premiums, *Tom Mix and his Ralston Straight Shooters* presented loyal followers more premiums some thirty years after all the other great radio heroes had retired to Valhalla.

WILD BILL HICKOK

One of the rarest broadcasting formats is the program designed to appear on both TV and radio simultaneously. *Wild Bill Hickok* was one such series from 1951–1954. (*Martin Kane, Private Eye* with William Gargan, for a pipe tobacco company, was another TV-radio advertising vehicle, offering no premiums.) The *Hickok* series was designed after a Saturday afternoon "B" Western at the movie theatre, certainly not a biographical "A" picture about the famous pioneer. (In fact, two episodes of Hickok in various groupings were stuck together for some of the last of those Saturdays at the theatres, shown along with the last Gene Autry and Durango Kid features.)

Guy Madison as Wild Bill and Andy Devine as sidekick Jingles were in both the TV and radio series. *Wild Bill Hickok* was aired Saturday mornings on TV. The radio series was on at 5:30 P.M., on Mutual, on Monday, Wednesday, and Friday. The *Hickok* series was a far cry from the classic radio adventure serials. Devine was a fine radio actor, and Madison got by, but the stories were simplistic in the extreme. Perhaps the writers were given orders by the sponsor to make them so. While some cowboy heroes were involved in more mysteries than Westerns, with roots in literature and history, Hickok stories were mainly Westerns with the simplest of themes—Hickok was chasing a bandit leader who could not resist wearing shirts with loud colors and fancy designs. Occasionally a mystery theme was introduced, but again of threadbare design: a stagecoach seems to "disappear," but is actually pulled off the road into a cave opening covered by branches and tracks are swept away by tumbleweeds pulled by lariats. Many adult collectors who eagerly seek new episodes of several so-called juvenile series find that a single example of Hickok is enough.

The *Wild Bill Hickok* television series fared better and has been re-run in recent years. The TV show seems no better, but no worse, than similar movie and TV cowboys films, with many of the same familiar and loved performers like Raymond Hatton, Bud Osborne, and Devine himself.

The premiums offered were not of the quality of the TV series, and perhaps even below that of the radio program. The giveaways were mostly of paper—maps, trading cards, and the like—and a few in-box paper-thin metal badges. The Kellogg's Sugar Pops boxes with portraits of Wild Bill and Jingles would be more valuable that the premiums they offered.

One item, a "Bunkhouse Kit" with cut-outs of lariats, guns, etc., has been denied being a premium in some places because of a "$2.95" price printed on it. This is a "theoretical value" price, but the item was a giveaway of appliance dealers. In the 1950s, a realistic counter price for such a paper item would be 25 cents.

1937 Radio Orphan Annie Secret Society manual and decoder badge. Values in Good, Fine, and Mint: manual 25, 50, 100 and badge 30, 60, 100.

"Did ja ever taste anything so good as Ovaltine? And it's good for yuh, too…" Radio Orphan Annie Beetleware mug.

1941 advertisement for various Orphan Annie gifts.

One of Jim Harmon's "jewel cases."

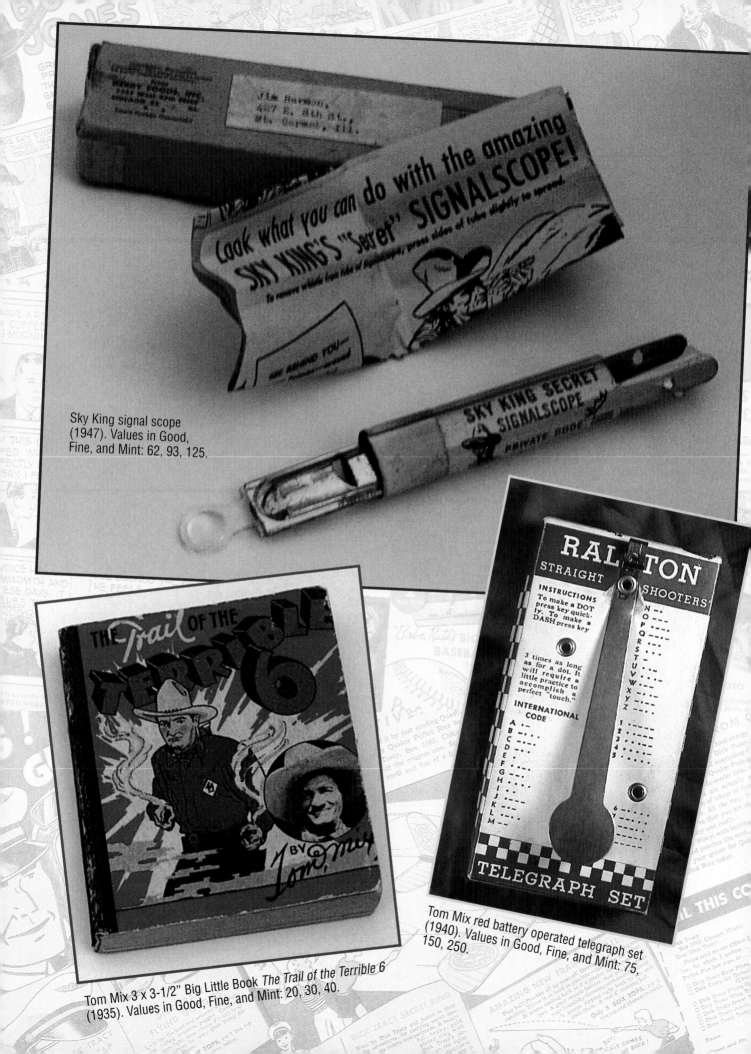

Sky King signal scope
(1947). Values in Good,
Fine, and Mint: 62, 93, 125.

Tom Mix 3 x 3-1/2" Big Little Book *The Trail of the Terrible 6*
(1935). Values in Good, Fine, and Mint: 20, 30, 40.

Tom Mix red battery operated telegraph set
(1940). Values in Good, Fine, and Mint: 75,
150, 250.

1938 advertisement for the Tom Mix Mystery Ring.

Superman Crusader's ring (1947). Values in Good, Fine, and Mint: 125, 188, 250.

Straight Arrow cards Book 1, 36 cards—"Straight Arrow's 72 Injun-uities" (1949). Values in Good, Fine, and Mint: 25, 50, 100.

Captain Midnight insignia shoulder patch (1934–44). Values in Good, Fine, and Mint: 15, 30, 50.

Captain Midnight Secret Squadron silver plastic code-o-graph badge (1957 TV). Values in Good, Fine, and Mint: 50, 100, 250.

"Ovaltine—The Heart of a Hearty Breakfast!" Captain Midnight Ovaltine mug offered on TV in the early 1950s.

Front view of Captain Midnight brass membership token (1940). Values in Good, Fine, and Mint: 8, 15, 30.

Captain Midnight code-o-graph mystery dial badge (1940). Values in Good, Fine, and Mint: 30, 60, 100.

Captain Midnight code-o-graph key-o-matic badge with key (1949). Values in Good, Fine, and Mint: 75, 150, 250.

Captain Midnight spy scope (1947). Values in Good, Fine, and Mint: 35, 70, 100.

Howdy Doody flip-up "Howdy for President" badge
(1947–55). Values in Good, Fine, and Mint: 15, 20, 25.

Captain Marvel "Captain Marvel Club" felt emblem
(1945). Values in Good, Fine, and Mint: 50, 100, 150.

Renfrew of the Mounted
cello pinback with photo
(1936–40). Values in
Good, Fine, and Mint: 8,
12, 16.

Howdy Doody string climber
(1947–55). Values in Good, Fine,
and Mint: 15, 30, 60.

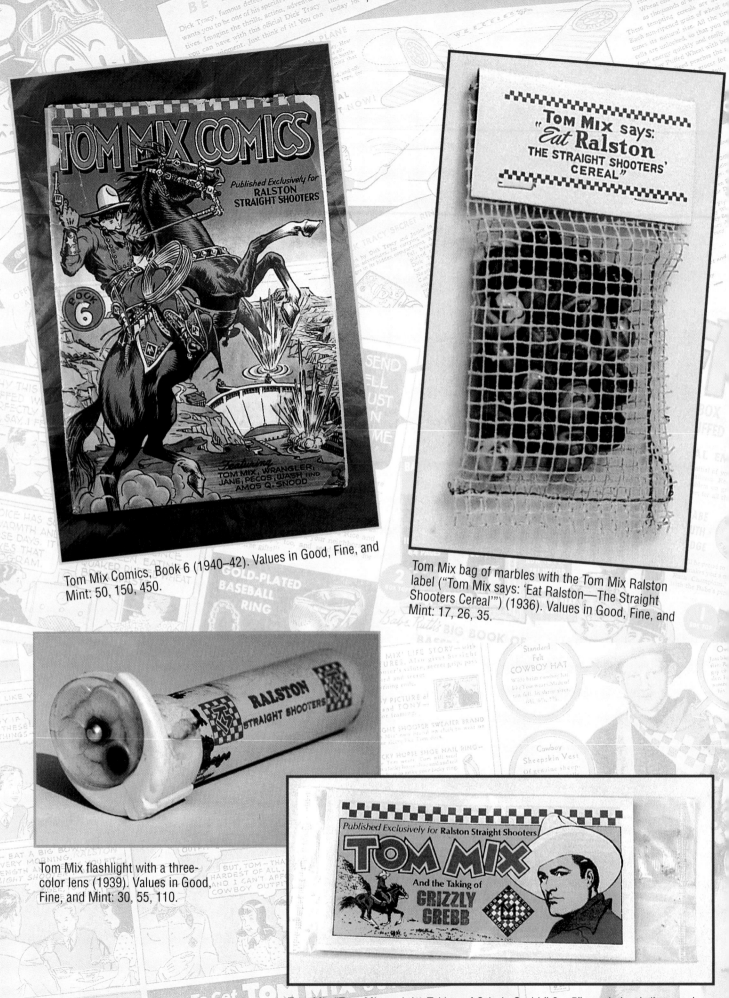

Tom Mix Comics, Book 6 (1940–42). Values in Good, Fine, and Mint: 50, 150, 450.

Tom Mix bag of marbles with the Tom Mix Ralston label ("Tom Mix says: 'Eat Ralston—The Straight Shooters Cereal'") (1936). Values in Good, Fine, and Mint: 17, 26, 35.

Tom Mix flashlight with a three-color lens (1939). Values in Good, Fine, and Mint: 30, 55, 110.

Tom Mix "Tom Mix and the Taking of Grizzly Grebb" 3 x 5" comic book (in cereal box), edited by Jim Harmon (1983). Values in Good, Fine, and Mint: 5, 10, 15.

Captain Video Rite-O-Lite gun kit (1950s). Values in Good, Fine, and Mint: 50, 100, 200.

SPACE MAP SHOWING RELATIVE SIZE & DISTANCE FROM SUN AT CENTER OF MAP. ROTATION OF PLANETS (WHEN VIEWED FROM [...] CLOCKWISE

NEPTUNE · URANUS · EARTH · SATURN · MERCURY · VENUS · MARS · JUPITER · PLUTO

Captain VIDEO®

SPECIAL OFFER

[...] YOU ORDER MORE
CAPTAIN VIDEO
SECRET RAY GUNS

Mail only 25c, and two Power House wrappers, to Power House, Box 863, New York 46, N. Y.

POWER HOUSE CANDY BAR

Power House, Box 863, New York 46, N. Y.

HERE'S YOUR
CAPTAIN VIDEO

Secret Ray Gun

COMPLETE WITH
BATTERY, AND BULB,
AND LUMA-GLO CARD
FOR WRITING
SECRET MESSAGES

• IT'S A POWER-PACKED FLASHLIGHT!
• IT'S A SECRET SIGNAL SENDER!
• IT WRITES SECRET MESSAGES THAT CAN BE READ ONLY IN THE DARK!

Sergeant Preston brass police whistle (shown without nylon cord) (1950). Values in Good, Fine, and Mint: 25, 38, 50.

A

ITEM	DATE	GOOD	FINE	MINT	SPONSOR
ADMIRAL BYRD					
Map of Antarctica	1934	10	20	50	Various local
Newspaper, South Pole Radio News #1	1934	10	20	50	Various local
Newspaper, South Pole Radio News #2	1934	10	20	50	Various local
Note from Admiral Byrd with map	1934	8	15	25	Various local
AMOS 'N' ANDY					
Check for $2, pictures of A&A on check	1936	375	650	950	Pepsodent
Figures, cardboard, standup (2), and folder	1930	20	40	60	Pepsodent

Amos 'N' Andy cardboard standup figures

ITEM	DATE	GOOD	FINE	MINT	SPONSOR

A 1935 Amos 'N' Andy advertisement featuring the map of Weber City

ITEM	DATE	GOOD	FINE	MINT	SPONSOR
Figures, cardboard (6)	1931	25	50	75	Pepsodent
Folder, "Story of Amos 'N' Andy"	1929	25	50	100	Pepsodent
Map of Weber City	1935	25	50	100	Pepsodent
Photo, Amos 'N' Andy	1929	10	20	35	Pepsodent
Puzzle	1931	20	40	60	Pepsodent
Script reprint, "Amos' Wedding," 12/25/35	1935	20	40	65	Pepsodent
Sheet music to Check and Doublecheck	1931	10	20	35	Pepsodent
Sheet music, "Perfect Song," orig. A&A theme	1935	10	20	35	Pepsodent
Standee of A&A	1948	40	80	160	Rexall

AUNT JENNY'S TRUE-LIFE STORIES

ITEM	DATE	GOOD	FINE	MINT	SPONSOR
Cookbooks, ea.	1945	10	20	35	Spry
Cooking utensil, ea.	1949	25	75	125	Spry
Recipes from Spry lids	1949	2	4	6	Spry

B

ITEM	DATE	GOOD	FINE	MINT	SPONSOR
BABE RUTH'S BOYS' CLUB					
Big Book of Baseball	1934	25	100	150	Quaker Cereals
Bracelet, charm	1934	40	80	125	Quaker Cereals
Button, membership, embossed	1934	10	30	90	Quaker Cereals
Button, pinback	1934	10	50	100	Quaker Cereals
Game, Ask Me	1934	20	40	65	Quaker Cereals
Ring, baseball design	1934	50	100	175	Quaker Cereals
Umpire's score keeper pad and photo	1934	25	50	75	Quaker Cereals

1935 Babe Ruth advertisement for various gifts

ITEM	DATE	GOOD	FINE	MINT	SPONSOR

BABY SNOOKS

ITEM	DATE	GOOD	FINE	MINT	SPONSOR
Dancing puppet	1949	50	100	175	Tums

BATMAN

ITEM	DATE	GOOD	FINE	MINT	SPONSOR
Batmask, movie serial premium	1943	400	500	1750	Columbia
Batplane punchout, movie serial premium	1943	500	1000	2000	Columbia
Buttons, pinback, TV, ea.	1966	5	10	20 7	
Card, Batman Club, movie serial premium	1943	15	30	75	Columbia
Card, infantile paralysis	1940s	20	40	65	Kellogg's
Card, membership, with code message	1966	100	200	400	
Coin holder for 10 coins	1966	20	40	65	
Coins, ea.	1966	5	10	15	
Poster set, Batman and Robin	1960s	30	60	100	Fact Publications
Printing set	1960s	30	60	100	

BLACK FLAME OF THE AMAZON

ITEM	DATE	GOOD	FINE	MINT	SPONSOR
Map of South America	Early 1930s	100	200	300	Mayrose Ham
Pinback, membership, tin litho	Early 1930s	10	20	35	HiSpeed Gasoline
Ring, compass	Early 1930s	75	200	375	HiSpeed Gasoline
Ruler, cardboard	Early 1930s	50	100	150	HiSpeed Gasoline

BOBBY BENSON

ITEM	DATE	GOOD	FINE	MINT	SPONSOR
Book: novel/comics, "Lost Herd"	1936	25	50	100	H O Company
Book: novel/comics, "Tunnel of Gold"	1936	25	50	100	H O Company
Bracelet, enamel	1932	60	120	250	H O Company
Button, H-Bar-O Rangers Club	1934	20	40	65	H O Company
Cereal bowl, 3 colors, ea.	1932	15	30	50	H O Company
Certificate, membership	1948	10	20	35	none
Code book	1932	25	50	75	H O Company
Code rule, cardboard decoder	1934	40	80	125	H O Company
Drinking glass, 3 colors, ea.	1932	8	15	30	H O Company
Game, circus: set of cards & booklet	1933	50	100	175	H O Company

ITEM	DATE	GOOD	FINE	MINT	SPONSOR

Bobby Benson H-Bar-O Rangers Club button

ITEM	DATE	GOOD	FINE	MINT	SPONSOR
Lariat, trick, humming	1948	25	50	75	none
Map	1932	25	50	75	H O Company
Photo, African scene production	1932	10	20	35	H O Company
Photo of Bobby	1948	10	20	35	none
Photos of Bobby, Polly, other cast members	1932	8	15	25	H O Company
Record, "Story of Bobby's Horse," Amigo, 45 & 78 rpm versions	1952	25	50	100	none
Tie clasp, enameled	1932	60	120	250	H O Company
1-1/2 cent money	1937	10	15	25	H O Company

BUCK JONES (HOOFBEATS)

ITEM	DATE	GOOD	FINE	MINT	SPONSOR
Badge, Jr. sheriff	1937	25	50	100	Grape Nuts Flakes
Manual, including premium catalog	1937	20	40	65	Grape Nuts Flakes
Pin, horseshoe	1937	25	50	100	Grape Nuts Flakes
Ring, club	1937	50	100	200	Grape Nuts Flakes
Ring, horseshoe	1937	50	100	200	Grape Nuts Flakes

BUCK ROGERS IN THE 25TH CENTURY

BADGES, EMBLEMS, AND PINS

ITEM	DATE	GOOD	FINE	MINT	SPONSOR
Badge, chief explorer	1935	40	80	175	Cream of Wheat
Badge, enameled	1934	40	60	100	Kellogg's
Badge, member, solar scout	1935	50	75	100	Cream of Wheat

1937 advertisement for the Buck Jones Club

ITEM	DATE	GOOD	FINE	MINT	SPONSOR
Badge, solar scout, spaceship commander	1936	50	75	100	Cream of Wheat
Badge, whistle, flight commander	1935	50	100	350	Cream of Wheat
Banner, flight commander	1935	50	100	350	Cream of Wheat
Button, 25th Century	1935	100	200	400	Cream of Wheat
Emblem, solar scout, weather	1935	2000	3000	4000	Cream of Wheat

APPAREL

ITEM	DATE	GOOD	FINE	MINT	SPONSOR
Handkerchief, Wilma	1935	125	250	375	Cream of Wheat
Helmet	1935	175	263	350	Cream of Wheat
Holster for disintegrator pistol	1935	75	300	500	Cream of Wheat
Uniform	1935	300	600	1500	Cream of Wheat

BOOKS, MANUALS, AND PAPER GOODS

ITEM	DATE	GOOD	FINE	MINT	SPONSOR
Big Little Book, "Buck Rogers in the 25th Century"	1933	50	75	125	Cocomalt
Big Little Book, "City of Floating Globes"	1935	75	150	350	Cocomalt

ITEM	DATE	GOOD	FINE	MINT	SPONSOR
Book, adventure, cut-out, uncut	1935	400	800	1200	Cocomalt
Book, origin story	1932-33	200	400	1500	Kellogg's
Chart, star explorer, unmarked	1935	15	30	50	Cream of Wheat
Folder, kite flying	1932	10	20	35	Kellogg's Pep
Games, Buck Roger's Interplanetary	1935	200	400	650	Cream of Wheat
Gun and helmet, paper, Buck or Wilma	1933-35	200	400	800	Cocomalt
Kit, space ranger, punch-out equipment, TV offer	1949	50	100	200	Sylvania
Manual, chief explorer	1935	75	150	250	Cream of Wheat
Manual, flight commander	1935	75	150	250	Cream of Wheat
Manual, solar scout	1935	75	150	250	Cream of Wheat
Map, solar	1933	200	400	800	Cocomalt
Match book	1940	8	15	25	Popcycle Pete
Picture, Buck and Wilma	1933	40	80	125	Cocomalt
Stationery, Flight commander	1935	30	60	75	Cream of Wheat

RINGS AND PENDANTS

ITEM	DATE	GOOD	FINE	MINT	SPONSOR
Pendant, Wilma	1935	40	60	100	Cream of Wheat
Ring, birthstone and initial (offered by others; price if accompanied by Buck Rogers papers)	1939	200	400	550	Popcycle Pete
Ring, repeller ray (seal ring)	1935	550	1800	3000	Cream of Wheat
Ring, Saturn, glow in dark, red stone	1945	150	300	550	Post Toasties
Ring of Saturn instruction sheet	1945	100	200	250	Post Toasties

TOYS

ITEM	DATE	GOOD	FINE	MINT	SPONSOR
Balloon globe of the world, unmarked	1935	20	40	65	Cream of Wheat
Compass, magnetic, unmarked	1935	15	30	50	Cream of Wheat
Disintegrator pistol	1935	50	200	400	Cream of Wheat
Films for projector	1935	15	30	50	Cream of Wheat
Flashlight, lite blaster	1935	50	100	150	Cream of Wheat
Invisible ink crystals, Dr. Huer's	1935	50	100	175	Cream of Wheat
Knife, solar scout	1935	300	600	1600	Cream of Wheat
Lead figures, painted, with folders, Buck, Wilma & Killer Kane, ea.	1933	20	40	75	Cocomalt
Lead figures, solid, unpainted: Buck, Wilma, Killer Kane, ea.	1935	30	60	120	Cream of Wheat
Movie projector, unmarked	1935	30	60	100	Cream of Wheat
Pencil box, red	1935	20	40	75	Cream of Wheat

ITEM	DATE	GOOD	FINE	MINT	SPONSOR
Printing set, 14 or 22 rubber stamps, box	1935	200	400	800	Cream of Wheat
Punch-O-Bag	1940s	20	40	100	Morton Salt
Rocket ship, whistling	1939	75	150	225	Muffets (in package)
Spaceship, dreadnought, balsa wood	1935	300	600	1200	Cream of Wheat
Spaceship (came in envelope)	1942	75	112	150	Morton Salt
Telescope, unmarked	1935	10	20	35	Cream of Wheat
NOTE: Satellite pioneers items are comic strip premiums. Misc. paper items, including application forms, premium listings, letters, etc., with Buck Roger's identification	1942	15	30	50	

BUFFALO BILL JR.

Ring, brass, buffalo on top, reads Jr.	1954	20	40	75	

Buffalo Bill Jr. brass ring, buffalo on top, reads "Jr."

Compass bullet	1954	10	20	50	

BUSTER BROWN

Bandanna	1947	25	50	100	Brown Shoe Co.
Card, membership	TV 1953	8	15	25	Brown Shoe Co.
Comics, Buster Brown Gang, #1	1945	60	190	600	Brown Shoe Co.
Comics, Buster Brown Gang, #2-43	1945-56	20	40	80	Brown Shoe Co.
Doll, rubber, Froggy's	1945	75	200	400	Brown Shoe Co.
Game, paddle ball	1947	10	15	25	Brown Shoe Co.
Mask, Froggy	1947	20	40	60	Brown Shoe Co.

Buster Brown Gang tab button featuring Midnight

ITEM	DATE	GOOD	FINE	MINT	SPONSOR
Periscope, secret agent	1947	20	40	65	Brown Shoe Co.
Ring/neckerchief slide	1947	30	60	150	Brown Shoe Co.
Tab, buttons (Buster and Tige, Froggy, Midnight, or Squeaky), ea.	1949	8	12	22	Brown Shoe Co.
Tablet, school	1946	8	12	22	Brown Shoe Co.

C

ITEM	DATE	GOOD	FINE	MINT	SPONSOR

CAPTAIN FRANK HAWKS

ITEM	DATE	GOOD	FINE	MINT	SPONSOR
Badges, propeller (member, lieutenant, and captain)	1935	20	40	65	Post's 40% Bran Flakes
Badges, wings (member, squadron leader, flight commander)	1936	20	40	65	Post's 40% Bran Flakes
Manual	1935	20	40	65	Post's 40% Bran Flakes
Manual	1937	20	40	65	Post's 40% Bran Flakes
Ring, air hawks	1937	125	188	250	Post's 40% Bran Flakes
Ring, scarab	1935	200	400	600	Post's 40% Bran Flakes
Ring, sky patrol	1935	125	188	250	Post's 40% Bran Flakes

CAPTAIN GALLANT

ITEM	DATE	GOOD	FINE	MINT	SPONSOR
Badge	1953	60	150	300	Heinz
Card, membership	1953	15	35	70	Heinz
Comic book	1953	8	15	25	Heinz
Letter	1953	30	60	125	Heinz
Medal, animal pictured	1953	25	50	85	Heinz
Medal, cross with "GRI" on it	1953	17	26	35	Heinz

CAPTAIN MARVEL

BUTTONS, EMBLEMS, AND PENNANTS

ITEM	DATE	GOOD	FINE	MINT	SPONSOR
Button, club membership, 5 styles	1941-48	45	90	135	Fawcett Publications
Buttons, comic (similar to Pep Buttons): Captain Marvel, Mary Marvel, Captain Marvel Jr., Billy Batson, Hoppy the Marvel Bunny, Ibis, Radar, Golden Arrow, Bulletman, and Nyoka, ea.	1945	30	75	150	Fawcett Publications
Buttons, comic, complete set	1945	400	800	1600	Fawcett Publications
Emblem, felt	1945	50	100	150	Fawcett Publications
Pennant, felt	1948	70	140	250	Fawcett Publications

ITEM	DATE	GOOD	FINE	MINT	SPONSOR

Capt. Marvel "Shazam" club membership button (Style 1)

Capt. Marvel "Shazam" club membership button (Style 2)

Capt. Marvel "Shazam" club membership button (Style 3)

Captain Marvel felt emblem

APPAREL

ITEM	DATE	GOOD	FINE	MINT	SPONSOR
Cap, beannie, felt	1945	75	150	300	Fawcett Publications
Cap, military style	1944	100	200	400	Fawcett Publications
Cap, skull	1946	80	160	320	Fawcett Publications
Sweatshirt	1948	50	100	200	Fawcett Publications

BOOKS, CARDS, PAPERS, AND PICTURES

ITEM	DATE	GOOD	FINE	MINT	SPONSOR
Associated items (not true premiums but collected as such):Toys, paper, cut and fold, in envelopes, mfg. by Reed & Associates, including Flying Marvel Family, Magic Eyes, Lightning Box,Buzz Bomb, Rocket Raider, Magic Picture, Ski Jump, etc. Also envelopes of iron-ons and tattoos.	1944-45	5	20	75	Fawcett Publications

Captain Marvel "The Good Humor Man" comic (left) and two Wheaties premium mini-comics

Item	Date	Good	Fine	Mint	Sponsor
Card, membership and code	1941-48	10	25	50	
Comics, "Captain Marvel Adventures" (Wheaties)	1947	60	150	Never found	Fawcett Publications
Comics, "Whiz Comics" (Wheaties)	1947	60	150	Never found	Fawcett Publications
Decoder, paper, dial	1943	50	100	300	Fawcett Publications
Letters from Captain Marvel, 3 styles, various colors	1941-48	12	24	50	Fawcett Publications
Paper forms, postcards, ads, greeting cards, etc.	1941-48	12	24	50	Fawcett Publications
Pictures, glow in dark (Capt. M, Mary M, Capt. M Jr., and Hoppy the Marvel Bunny)	1946	75	150	275	Fawcett Publications

TOYS

Item	Date	Good	Fine	Mint	Sponsor
Bean bags for tossing, Marvel insignias	1943	25	50	100	Fawcett Publications
Flute	1948	25	30	45	Fawcett Publications

ITEM	DATE	GOOD	FINE	MINT	SPONSOR

Captain Marvel whistle

ITEM	DATE	GOOD	FINE	MINT	SPONSOR
Key chain	1946	30	50	75	Fawcett Publications
Pen, Mary Marvel	1946	30	50	75	Fawcett Publications
Pencil clip	1946	10	20	35	Fawcett Publications
Statuettes, Capt. M, Mary M, Capt. M Jr., ea.	1947	2800	6000	9000	Fawcett Publications
Whistle, magic, full color picture of Captain M Both sides, ad inside	1943	25	38	50	American Seed Co.

CAPTAIN MIDNIGHT

BADGES, PINS AND TOKENS

ITEM	DATE	GOOD	FINE	MINT	SPONSOR
Badge, flight commander	1939	400	1000	2000	Ovaltine
Badge, code-o-graph, key-o-matic, with key	1949	75	150	250	Ovaltine
Badge, code-o-graph, magni-matic	1945	60	125	200	Ovaltine
Badge, code-o-graph, mirro-matic	1946	70	140	275	Ovaltine
Badge, code-o-graph, mystery dial	1941	30	60	100	Ovaltine
Badge, code-o-graph, photomatic, w/photo of CM	1942	88	132	275	Ovaltine

Captain Midnight weather-forecasting wings

ITEM	DATE	GOOD	FINE	MINT	SPONSOR

Captain Midnight 1940 code-o-graph mystery dial badge

Captain Midnight code-o-graph photomatic badge (with photo of Captain Midnight)

ITEM	DATE	GOOD	FINE	MINT	SPONSOR
Badge, code-o-graph, dial on side of police whistle	1947	50	100	200	Ovaltine
Badge, code-o-graph, gold, secret squadron, plastic	TV 1957	75	150	350	Ovaltine
Badge, code-o-graph, pocket piece, mirro-flash	1948	60	125	200	Ovaltine

Captain Midnight 1945 code-o-graph magni-matic badge

"Dial side" of the 1947 Captain Midnight code-o-graph (with the dial on the side of the police whistle)

Captain Midnight 1949 code-o-graph key-o-matic badge

ITEM	DATE	GOOD	FINE	MINT	SPONSOR

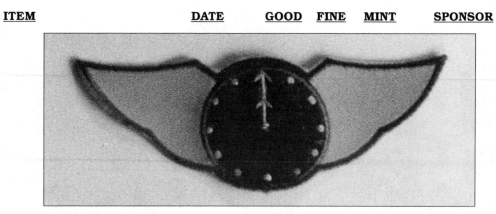

Captain Midnight patch, shoulder, insignia

ITEM	DATE	GOOD	FINE	MINT	SPONSOR
Badge, code-o-graph, silver, secret squadron, plastic	TV 1957	50	100	250	Ovaltine
Badge, flight wings, mystic magic weather forecasting	1939	20	30	50	Skelly Oil
Badge, flying cross, flight commander. Bounceback	1942	50	100	200	Ovaltine
Badge, loyalty, American flag	1940	75	150	300	Ovaltine
Patch, cloth, square	TV 1955-56	15	30	50	Ovaltine
Patch, cloth, square, 15th anniversary	1957	15	30	50	Ovaltine
Patch, shoulder, insignia	1943-44, 48-49	15	30	50	Ovaltine
Pin, school	1942	25	50	100	Ovaltine
Pin, service ribbon, unmarked	1944	55	110	225	Ovaltine
Token, membership, brass	1940	8	15	30	Skelly Oil

Back view of Captain Midnight brass membership token (1940). Values in Good, Fine, and Mint: 6, 8, 10.

1942 Captain Midnight Secret Squadron manual

1945 Captain Midnight Secret Squadron manual

1946 Captain Midnight Secret Squadron manual

1947 Captain Midnight Secret Squadron manual

1948 Captain Midnight Secret Squadron manual

1949 Captain Midnight Secret Squadron manual

ITEM	DATE	GOOD	FINE	MINT	SPONSOR
Token, reproduction. Repro has small "r" under "s" of Skelly.	1940	5	10	12	Skelly Oil

APPAREL

T-shirt	1987	12	25	35	Ovaltine

BOOKS AND PAPER ITEMS

ITEM	DATE	GOOD	FINE	MINT	SPONSOR
Book of tricks and riddles, 64 pages, 3 x 2	1939	20	35	70	Skelly Oil
Booklet, Story of US Marines, by CM	1942	15	30	60	Ovaltine
Card, membership	1939	20	40	80	Skelly Oil
Card, membership	1955-56	20	75	150	Ovaltine
Card, membership	1940-41	25	50	100	Skelly Oil
Certificate, flight commander. (Beware reproductions.)	1955-56	30	75	150	Ovaltine
Folder, detect-o-scope	1940-41	40	80	160	Ovaltine
Folder, insignia	1943	45	50	180	Ovaltine
Folder, service ribbon	1944	20	40	60	Ovaltine
Handbook, flight commander	TV 1957	75	150	300	Ovaltine
Handbook, flight commander. Bounceback. Came w/ flying cross	1942	60	125	250	Ovaltine
Letter from Chuck's dad	1939	20	35	75	Skelly Oil
Manual	1940-41	50	100	200	Ovaltine
Manual	1942	75	150	300	Ovaltine
Manual	1945	50	100	125	Ovaltine
Manual	1946	50	100	125	Ovaltine
Manual, first smaller size	1947	30	50	75	Ovaltine
Manual	1948	30	50	75	Ovaltine
Manual	1949	50	100	200	Ovaltine
Manual	TV 1955	110	225	450	Ovaltine
Manual	TV 1957	75	150	300	Ovaltine
Map, Chuck's treasure	1939	65	125	250	Skelly Oil
Map of America, airline	1940-41	175	350	700	Skelly Oil
Newspapers, flight patrol report, Vol. 1, No. 1-6.	1939-40	40	75	175	Skelly Oil
Photo	TV 1955-56	75	150	300	General Mills
Photo, Captain Midnight, Chuck and Patsy	1939	20	40	75	Skelly Oil
Photo, Chuck Ramsey	1939	20	40	75	Skelly Oil

ITEM	DATE	GOOD	FINE	MINT	SPONSOR
Photo, CM, treasure hunt rules on back	1939	40	80	175	Skelly Oil
Photo, CM wearing secret ring	1939	20	45	90	Skelly Oil
Stamp album of air heroes and 16 stamps	1939	25	50	100	Skelly Oil

RINGS AND WATCHES

ITEM	DATE	GOOD	FINE	MINT	SPONSOR
Ring, flight commander	1940-41	150	300	450	Ovaltine
Ring, initial printing	1948	150	300	525	Ovaltine
Ring, Marine Corps	1942	125	250	500	Ovaltine
Ring, mystic eye, detector. Same as ROA lookaround and LR defender.	1942	75	150	250	Ovaltine
Ring, mystic sun god	1946	750	1500	4500	Ovaltine
Ring, signet, flight commander	1957	500	1000	2000	Ovaltine
Ring, sliding secret compartment	1942	100	200	375	Ovaltine
Ring, whirlwind, whistling	1940-41	175	400	550	Ovaltine
Watch	1987	50	100	150	Ovaltine

Captain Midnight ring, initial printing

TOYS

ITEM	DATE	GOOD	FINE	MINT	SPONSOR
Airplane, aerial torpedo bombers (set)	1941	30	60	125	Ovaltine
Airplane model kit, Spartan bomber	1939	30	60	125	Skelly Oil
Blackout lite-ups (magic)	1942	125	250	500	Ovaltine
Decoder, plane puzzle, plastic, secret squadron	TV 1955-56	100	200	375	Ovaltine

ITEM	DATE	GOOD	FINE	MINT	SPONSOR
Detect-o-scope, five-way, w metal insert	1940-41	50	75	150	Ovaltine
Game, jumping bean, Ringo Jumpo	1939	75	150	300	Skelly Oil
Plane detector, complete with plane inserts	1942	300	600	1200	Ovaltine
Spy scope	1947	35	70	100	Ovaltine
Whistle, dog, 3-way, mystic	1942	25	50	100	Ovaltine

MUGS

ITEM	DATE	GOOD	FINE	MINT	SPONSOR
Mug, shake-up, 15th anniversary, red with blue top	1957	20	40	65	Ovaltine
Mug, shake-up, embossed, orange with blue top. Most desired.	1947	75	150	200	Ovaltine
Mug for hot Ovaltine	TV 1953	10	20	60	Ovaltine

Two Captain Midnight Ovaltine shake-up mugs. From left to right: red 15th anniversary mug with a blue top, and orange embossed mug with a blue top (this one is the most desired).

RECORDINGS AND MISCELLANEOUS

ITEM	DATE	GOOD	FINE	MINT	SPONSOR
Radio recordings, Longines Symphonette Society (plastic, thin as paper), ea.	1960s-70s	8	16	24	Ovaltine
Radio recordings, vinyl LP. Also sold in stores.	1960s-70s	10	20	35	Ovaltine
Surprise package	1940	25	38	50	Skelly Oil

ITEM	DATE	GOOD	FINE	MINT	SPONSOR

CAPTAIN TIM HEALY'S STAMP CLUB

ITEM	DATE	GOOD	FINE	MINT	SPONSOR
Package backs, "Know Your Stamps," ea.	1934	8	12	24	Kellogg's
Pin, club membership	1934	8	12	24	Kellogg's
Stamp album	1934	10	15	30	Kellogg's
Stamp album	1935	10	15	30	Kellogg's

CAPTAIN VIDEO

ITEM	DATE	GOOD	FINE	MINT	SPONSOR
Card, membership	1950	50	100	200	Powerhouse
Coder, mysto	1950s	75	150	350	Powerhouse
Gun, ray, space fleet	TV 1952	60	125	200	Powerhouse
Gun kit, Rite-o-Lite	1950s	50	100	200	Powerhouse
Pendant, plastic, glow-in-dark photo	1950s	350	750	1000	Powerhouse
Photo, Captain Video	1950s	10	20	35	Powerhouse
Ring, flying saucer	1950s	400	800	1500	Powerhouse
Ring, photo	1950s	100	200	375	Powerhouse
Ring, secret seal	1950s	100	300	600	Powerhouse
Rocket balloon, X-9	1950s	27	40	55	Powerhouse
Rocket launcher and ships	1950s	50	100	200	Powerhouse
Space men, plastic, 12 different, ea.	1950s	8	12	24	Came in Raisin Bran boxes
Tab, bread	1950s	5	10	20	Purity

CASEY, CRIME PHOTOGRAPHER

ITEM	DATE	GOOD	FINE	MINT	SPONSOR
Photo, cast	1947	20	30	50	Anchor-Hocking

CHANDU, THE MAGICIAN

ITEM	DATE	GOOD	FINE	MINT	SPONSOR
Booklet, card miracles	1934-35	15	30	50	White King
Magic trick, Buddha money	1934-35	20	25	30	White King
Magic trick, Chinese coin	1934-35	25	50	65	White King
Magic trick, Choco-Mint	1934-35	15	20	25	White King
Magic trick, galloping coin	1949	25	50	65	White King
Magic trick, Hindu cones	1934-35	25	50	65	White King
Magic trick, holiday trick	1934-35	25	50	65	White King
Magic trick, mysterious bottle trick #5	1934-35	25	50	65	White King
Magic trick, Svengali mind reading	1934-35	25	50	65	White King

ITEM	DATE	GOOD	FINE	MINT	SPONSOR
Magic tricks, boxed set, Chandu, White King of Magic. Has theoretic price of $2.50, but was free with purchase of two White King boxes.	1934-35	325	488	650	White King
Photo, Betty Regent	1934-35	10	20	30	White King
Photo, Bob Regent	1934-35	10	20	30	White King
Photo, Chandu in costume	1934-35	15	30	65	White King
Photo, Chandu (Gayne Whitman)	1934-35	10	20	30	White King
Photo, Dorothy Regent	1934-35	10	20	30	White King
Pinback, Chandu	1934-35	75	150	300	White King

CHARLIE McCARTHY

ITEM	DATE	GOOD	FINE	MINT	SPONSOR
Card, fan, personalized	1938	5	10	15	Chase & Sanborn
Dummy, cardboard, Charlie	1939	25	50	100	Chase & Sanborn
Dummy, cardboard, Mortimer Snerd	1939	50	100	200	Chase & Sanborn
Game, radio party, 21 cardboard figures	1938	42	63	85	Chase & Sanborn
Photo, Edgar and Charlie	1940	10	20	30	Chase & Sanborn
Ring	1940	50	100	200	Chase & Sanborn
Spoon, Charlie's likeness on handle	1939	5	10	15	Chase & Sanborn

CINNAMON BEAR

ITEM	DATE	GOOD	FINE	MINT	SPONSOR
Badge, Wieboldt's TV, complete with paper bear	1949	25	50	100	Weibolt's, other dept. stores
Bear, stuffed	1949	50	100	200	Weibolt's, other dept. stores
Coloring book, printed on newspaper	1947	20	40	75	Weibolt's, other dept. stores
Coloring book, repro on white bond paper	current	1	1	1	
Star, silver foil, with Paddy picture	c. 1940s	25	50	100	
Tape cassettes of entire series	current		15		
Tab (Weibolt's), rare	1949	100	250	500	Weibolt's

CISCO KID

BADGES, BUTTONS, AND TABS

ITEM	DATE	GOOD	FINE	MINT	SPONSOR
Badge, microphone shape, Coco Wheats Radio Club	1951-55	25	38	50	Coco Wheats
Badge, Western hat on chain	1951-55	17	26	35	Butternut Bread
Button, Rancher Club	1951-55	10	20	35	Butternut Bread
Button, Triple S Club	1951-55	10	20	35	Butternut Bread

ITEM	DATE	GOOD	FINE	MINT	SPONSOR
Tab, Cisco, five different colored hats	1951-55	10	20	30	Butternut Bread
Tab, Cisco, and Pancho	1951-55	10	45	20	Blue Seal Bread
Tab, Cisco, and Pancho	1951-55	10	20	30	Weber Bread

MASKS

ITEM	DATE	GOOD	FINE	MINT	SPONSOR
Mask, Cisco, radio face	1951-55	10	20	35	Butternut Bread
Mask, Cisco, TV face	1951-55	10	20	35	Butternut Bread
Mask, Pancho, radio face	1951-55	10	20	35	Butternut Bread
Mask, Pancho, TV face	1951-55	10	20	35	Butternut Bread

CARDS, PHOTOS, AND OTHER PAPER ITEMS

ITEM	DATE	GOOD	FINE	MINT	SPONSOR
Card, Rancher Club	1951-55	8	12	24	Tip-Top Bread
Certificate, Cisco Texas Citizenship	1951-55	8	12	24	Tip-Top Bread
Certificate, Rancher Club	1951-55	8	12	24	Tip-Top Bread
Club kit, Triple S	1951-55	25	50	100	Tip-Top Bread
Lariat, humming paper	1951-55	10	25	50	Tip-Top Bread
Letters, Triple S Club	1951-55	10	20	35	Tip-Top Bread
Manual, cattle brands	1951-55	20	30	50	Tip-Top Bread
Newsletter: "Name the Pony"	1951-55	8	12	16	Tip-Top Bread
Photo, Cisco, 8-1/2 x 11"	1951-55	5	8	15	Tip-Top Bread
Photo, Pancho, 8-1/2 x 11"	1951-55	5	8	15	Tip-Top Bread
Photo, Rancher Club	1951-55	5	8	15	Tip-Top Bread
Postcards, photo, 5 ea.	1951-55	4	6	10	Tip-Top Bread
Puzzle, illustrated envelope	1951-55	15	20	35	Tip-Top Bread

RINGS AND TOYS

ITEM	DATE	GOOD	FINE	MINT	SPONSOR
Ring, picture	1951-55	75	100	125	Tip-Top Bread
Ring, secret compartment, picture	1951-55	250	500	800	Tip-Top Bread
Game, "Range War"	1951-55	250	500	1200	Tip-Top Bread
Gun, cardboard, 7", clicker sounds when handle squeezed	1951-55	25	50	100	Harvest Bread

CLARA, LU & EM

ITEM	DATE	GOOD	FINE	MINT	SPONSOR
Puzzle	1936	5	10	15	

D

ITEM	DATE	GOOD	FINE	MINT	SPONSOR

DAVID HARDING

ITEM	DATE	GOOD	FINE	MINT	SPONSOR
Badge, junior agent	1949	37	56	75	Pepsi-Cola
Certificate, membership	1949	10	20	30	Pepsi-Cola
Match book	1949	5	10	20	Pepsi-Cola

DEATH VALLEY DAYS

ITEM	DATE	GOOD	FINE	MINT	SPONSOR
Booklet, Death Valley Tales as Told by the Old Ranger	1934	20	40	60	Borax, Boraxo
Booklet, High Spots of Death Valley Days, Vol. 1, No. 1	1939	20	40	60	Borax, Boraxo
Booklet, Old Ranger's Years of Death Valley	1933	20	40	60	Borax, Boraxo
Booklet, Story of Death Valley	1931	20	40	60	Borax, Boraxo
Booklet, Story of Death Valley	1932	20	40	60	Borax, Boraxo
Cowboy songs in Death Valley	1934	20	40	50	Borax, Boraxo
Jigsaw puzzle, 20 mule team	1933	15	30	65	Borax, Boraxo
Model, 20 mule team and wagon	1935	30	60	90	Borax, Boraxo
Model, 20 mule team and wagon (reissue)	1950	20	40	60	Borax, Boraxo
Model, 20 mule team and wagon (reissue)	1970s	15	30	60	Borax, Boraxo
Script in folder, "World's Biggest Job"	1935	15	30	50	Borax, Boraxo
Seed packets, Old Ranger's	1939	10	20	30	Borax, Boraxo

DETECTIVES BLACK AND BLUE

ITEM	DATE	GOOD	FINE	MINT	SPONSOR
Badge	1934	15	23	35	Folger's Coffee
Cap	1934	10	20	30	Folger's Coffee

DICK DARING

ITEM	DATE	GOOD	FINE	MINT	SPONSOR
Book: "Bag of Tricks"	1933-34	10	30	60	Quaker Oats

ITEM	DATE	GOOD	FINE	MINT	SPONSOR
Jigsaw puzzle and picture: city underground	1933-34	25	60	120	Quaker Oats
Jigsaw puzzle and picture: mountain underground	1933-34	25	60	120	Quaker Oats

DICK STEEL

ITEM	DATE	GOOD	FINE	MINT	SPONSOR
Badge, membership, brass	1930s	20	40	80	Educator Hammered Wheat Thinsies
Badge, membership, steel	1930s	100	200	300	Educator Hammered Wheat Thinsies
Instruction sheet and sample, "Start Your Own Newspaper"	1930s	75	125	200	Educator Hammered Wheat Thinsies
Manual, "Dick Steel's Secrets of Police Reporting"	1930s	75	150	300	Educator Hammered Wheat Thinsies
Photo, cast	1930s	5	10	15	Educator Hammered Wheat Thinsies
Premium offer sheet	1930s	5	10	15	Educator Hammered Wheat Thinsies
Whistle	1930s	50	100	200	Educator Hammered Wheat Thinsies

DICK TRACY

BADGES AND PINS

ITEM	DATE	GOOD	FINE	MINT	SPONSOR
Badge, air detective	1938	20	40	60	Quaker
Badge, belt, detective club, leather pouchback	1938	30	75	150	Quaker Rice
Badge, captain	1938	75	150	325	Quaker
Badge, crime stoppers	1960s	12	18	25	
Badge, detective, club, shield	1938	25	60	120	Quaker
Badge, detective, picture of Tracy and Junior	1938	20	30	50	Quaker
Badge, girls' division	1939	20	40	60	Quaker
Badge, inspector general	1938	175	375	800	Quaker
Badge, lieutenant	1938	40	80	200	Quaker
Badge, member, brass	1939	40	80	200	Quaker
Badge, member, second year	1939	40	80	200	Quaker

Dick Tracy Secret Service Patrol badges. From top left clockwise: Lieutenant, Captain, Inspector General, and Sergeant

ITEM	DATE	GOOD	FINE	MINT	SPONSOR
Badge, paper, from detective kit	1944	5	10	15	Tootsie Rolls
Badge, sergeant	1938	40	80	160	Quaker
Pin, bar, patrol leader	1938	15	30	60	Quaker
Pinback, member	1938	15	30	60	Quaker
Tab, detective club, crime detection folio (4), ea.	1942	20	40	120	Quaker
Wings, aviation	1938	40	80	160	Quaker

Dick Tracy brass member badge

ITEM	DATE	GOOD	FINE	MINT	SPONSOR

Dick Tracy member pinback

BOOKS, MANUALS, AND OTHER PAPER ITEMS

ITEM	DATE	GOOD	FINE	MINT	SPONSOR
Book, secret code, secret service patrol	1938	50	100	180	Quaker
Book: Family Fun	1938	50	100	180	Quaker
Cards, decoder, red and green, ea.	1944	8	12	24	
Certificate, from detective kit	1944	20	40	75	Quaker
Certificate for posting promotion stickers	1938	20	40	75	Quaker
Chart, wall, suspect, detective kit	1944	30	60	120	Tootsie Rolls
Code book, secret, secret service patrol	1938	40	80	160	Quaker
Decoder	1942	60	120	240	Quaker
Dial, secret code, detective kit	1944	80	160	325	Tootsie Rolls
Folio, detective club, crime detection	1942	20	40	60	Quaker
Kit, detective	1944	100	200	400	Tootsie Rolls
Kit, secret detecto	1938	60	120	240	Quaker
Manual, detective kit	1944	40	80	160	Tootsie Rolls
Manual and code book	1939	60	120	240	Quaker
Manual: Secret detective methods & magic tricks	1939	40	80	120	Quaker
Mystery sheets, set of 3	1942	15	30	60	
Notebook	1942	15	30	60	Quaker
Puzzle	1942	15	30	60	Quaker
Radio script, Vol. 1, "The Invisible Man"	1939	40	80	160	Quaker
Radio script, Vol. II, "The Ghost Ship"	1939	40	80	160	Quaker
Tape measure, detective kit	1944	5	8	12	Tootsie Rolls

ITEM	DATE	GOOD	FINE	MINT	SPONSOR

RINGS AND BRACELETS

ITEM	DATE	GOOD	FINE	MINT	SPONSOR
Bracelet, lucky bangle	1938	50	100	225	Quaker
Bracelet, wing	1938	150	350	700	Quaker
Ring, monogram	1939	200	500	1000	Quaker
Ring, hat, enameled	1938	100	200	300	Quaker
Ring, secret compartment	1938	100	250	400	Quaker

TOYS

ITEM	DATE	GOOD	FINE	MINT	SPONSOR
Flashlight, pocket	1939	25	50	100	Quaker
Gun, paper, pop	1942	20	40	60	Quaker
Gun, rubber band	1942	20	40	60	Quaker
Kit, detective, with wood decoder, pot metal badge	1961	10	20	35	
Pencil, siren code	1939	15	30	60	Quaker
Plane, flagship, rocket	1939	40	80	125	Quaker
Plane, siren	1938	35	70	150	Quaker
Telephones, private	1939	60	150	325	Quaker

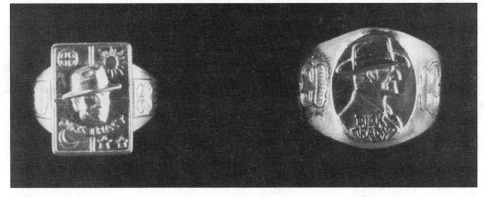

Dick Tracy rings. The ring at left is the secret compartment ring.

DOC SAVAGE

ITEM	DATE	GOOD	FINE	MINT	SPONSOR
Medal of honor	1936	1000	2000	4000	Doc Savage Magazine
Illustration, bust, color	1936	60	120	300	Doc Savage Magazine
Pin, membership, bronze	1936	60	125	250	Doc Savage Magazine
Illustration, reclining figure, color	1936	40	80	160	Doc Savage Magazine
Stamp, rubber, member's	1936	100	200	300	Doc Savage Magazine

ITEM	DATE	GOOD	FINE	MINT	SPONSOR

DON McNEILL'S BREAKFAST CLUB

ITEM	DATE	GOOD	FINE	MINT	SPONSOR
Album, breakfast club family	1942	10	20	35	Hormel
Badge, metal, Aunt Jemima	1942	30	60	125	Aunt Jemima Flour
Card, membership	1940s	8	12	16	Hormel
Don's Other Life	1944	8	12	16	Hormel
Folder, membership	1940s	5	10	15	Hormel
Kiddy party ideas	1940	5	8	12	Fritos
Twenty Years of Corn	1940s	10	20	35	Hormel
Twenty Years of Memory Time	1952	10	20	35	Hormel
Yearbook	1948	8	12	16	Hormel
Yearbook	1949	8	12	16	Hormel
Yearbook	1950	8	12	16	Hormel
Yearbook	1954	10	15	20	Hormel

DON WINSLOW OF THE NAVY

ITEM	DATE	GOOD	FINE	MINT	SPONSOR
Badge, honor	1942	60	120	250	Post
Book, magic slate, secret	1942	40	80	150	Post
Book, USN secret code, 16 pages	1935	40	80	150	Oxydol giveaway
Card, membership, for ring	1939	20	40	80	Kellogg's Wheat Krispies
Catapult bomber	1942	125	250	500	Post Toasties
Certificate, undercover deputy	1942	100	250	500	Post Toasties
Code sheet	1940	60	120	160	Kellogg's Wheat Krispies
Coin, good luck	1938	60	120	160	Kellogg's Wheat Krispies
Coloring, picture	1943-44	20	40	80	Red Goose Shoes
Creed, manual & membership card, squadron of peace	1939	10	30	125	Kellogg's Wheat Krispies
Creed, with cast photo	1942	75	150	250	Post Toasties
Decoder, torpedo, gold	1942	600	1800	3500	Post Toasties
Periscope	1939	75	150	300	Kellogg's Wheat Krispies
Photo, Don and Red	1940	10	20	30	Kellogg's Wheat Krispies
Pin, ensign	1939	400	800	1250	Kellogg's Wheat Krispies
Pin, lieutenant commander	1939	250	700	1400	Kellogg's Wheat Krispies
Ring, member, serial number on top	1939	250	700	1400	Kellogg's Wheat Krispies
Stamp, rubber, anchor with listener's initials	1940	40	80	150	Kellogg's Wheat Krispies

ITEM	DATE	GOOD	FINE	MINT	SPONSOR

DOROTHY HART

BADGES AND PINS

ITEM	DATE	GOOD	FINE	MINT	SPONSOR
Badge, membership only Arrow Soap Flakes	1937-38	10	20	30	Sunbrite Cleanser & Quick
Badge, supervisor Arrow Soap Flakes	1937-38	10	20	30	Sunbrite Cleanser & Quick
Button alone Arrow Soap Flakes	1937-38	7	15	25	Sunbrite Cleanser & Quick
Patch, official armband Arrow Soap Flakes	1937-38	5	10	15	Sunbrite Cleanser & Quick
Pin, graduate, Jr. nurse Arrow Soap Flakes	1937-38	8	16	24	Sunbrite Cleanser & Quick

APPAREL AND GROOMING

ITEM	DATE	GOOD	FINE	MINT	SPONSOR
Brush and comb set Arrow Soap Flakes	1937-38	8	16	24	Sunbrite Cleanser & Quick
Handbrush Arrow Soap Flakes	1937-38	8	16	24	Sunbrite Cleanser & Quick
Handkerchief Arrow Soap Flakes	1937-38	8	16	24	Sunbrite Cleanser & Quick
Toothbrush Arrow Soap Flakes	1937-38	3	6	9	Sunbrite Cleanser & Quick
Towel, hand Arrow Soap Flakes	1937-38	3	6	9	Sunbrite Cleanser & Quick
Uniform, official, including Jr. nurse corps badge and compass Arrow Soap Flakes	1937-38	80	160	225	Sunbrite Cleanser & Quick

PAPER ITEMS

ITEM	DATE	GOOD	FINE	MINT	SPONSOR
Catalog, 1937-38 Arrow Soap Flakes	1937-38	10	20	30	Sunbrite Cleanser & Quick
Notebook Arrow Soap Flakes	1937-38	8	16	24	Sunbrite Cleanser & Quick
Pictures: Dorothy, Aunt Jane, Pat, Sa-Ca-Ja-Wea, cast, ea. Arrow Soap Flakes	1937-38	4	8	12	Sunbrite Cleanser & Quick

RINGS AND BRACELETS

ITEM	DATE	GOOD	FINE	MINT	SPONSOR
Ring Arrow Soap Flakes	1937-38	35	70	87	Sunbrite Cleanser & Quick

ITEM	DATE	GOOD	FINE	MINT	SPONSOR
Wristlet, identification Arrow Soap Flakes	1937-38	24	75	125	Sunbrite Cleanser & Quick

TOYS

Cabinet, first aid Arrow Soap Flakes	1937-38	15	25	35	Sunbrite Cleanser & Quick
Doll, Dorothy Hart Arrow Soap Flakes	1937-38	20	30	50	Sunbrite Cleanser & Quick
Kit, first aid Arrow Soap Flakes	1937-38	20	30	50	Sunbrite Cleanser & Quick
Kit, sewing Arrow Soap Flakes	1937-38	8	16	24	Sunbrite Cleanser & Quick
Official service set tary	1937-38	10	20	25	Unguentine, complimen
Official service set: nurse's chart, button, bandaids Arrow Soap Flakes	1937-38	10	20	25	Sunbrite Cleanser & Quick

DUFFY'S TAVERN

Duffy's first reader	1945	15	30	35	Pabst Blue Ribbon Beer
Photo, Archie	1944	4	8	16	Pabst Blue Ribbon Beer

E

ITEM	DATE	GOOD	FINE	MINT	SPONSOR
ED WYNN					
Face mask	1933	50	100	150	Texaco
EDDIE CANTOR					
Book of magic	1935	10	20	30	Pebeco Toothpaste
Comics, Cantor's	1935	30	60	120	Pebeco Toothpaste
Master card mysteries	1935	10	20	30	Pebeco Toothpaste
Photo album of Eddie	1932	10	20	30	Chase & Sanborn Coffee
Photo album of Eddie	1933	10	20	30	Chase & Sanborn Coffee
Photo album of Eddie	1934	10	20	30	Chase & Sanborn Coffee
Pin, magic club	1935	15	30	75	Salthepatica
Secrets of master magic	1935	10	20	30	Salthepatica
ELLERY QUEEN					
Pinback, Ellery Queen Club Member	1939	20	30	40	Bromo-Seltzer

F

ITEM	DATE	GOOD	FINE	MINT	SPONSOR

FIBBER McGEE & MOLLY

ITEM	DATE	GOOD	FINE	MINT	SPONSOR
Badge, weather forecaster, litmus paper (rare)	1940s	35	75	125	Johnson's Wax
Photo, cast	1941	30	50	70	Johnson's Wax
Recipe folder, Pet Milk	1953	3	6	9	Pet
Spinner, Fibber	1936	100	200	550	Johnson's Wax
Spinner, Molly	1936	100	200	550	Johnson's Wax

FLASH GORDON

ITEM	DATE	GOOD	FINE	MINT	SPONSOR
Ring	1949	35	50	75	Post Toasties Corn Flakes

FLYING FAMILY - THE HUTCHINSONS

ITEM	DATE	GOOD	FINE	MINT	SPONSOR
Book: History of Notable Flights and Flyers	1932	8	12	16	Cocomalt
Folder, flight commander offer	1932	8	12	16	Cocomalt
Jigsaw puzzle and illustrated envelope	1932	10	15	20	Cocomalt
Pin, club, flight commander	1932	30	40	50	Cocomalt
Pin, membership, flying club	1932	30	40	50	Cocomalt

FRANK BUCK

ITEM	DATE	GOOD	FINE	MINT	SPONSOR
Game, Blackflag Jungle	1934-38	30	60	75	Pepsodent
Handbook, adventure club	1934-38	15	30	50	Pepsodent
Knife, ivory	1939	50	100	150	Ivory Soap--special prom tion
Lariat	1934-38	25	50	75	Pepsodent
Lucky piece	1934-38	10	20	35	Pepsodent
Map and game, "Bring 'Em Back Alive"	1934-38	50	100	150	Pepsodent or Scott's Emulsion
Neckerchief, jungle	1934-38	20	40	60	Pepsodent

ITEM	DATE	GOOD	FINE	MINT	SPONSOR
Pinback, adventure club	1934-38	10	20	40	Pepsodent
Ring, black leopard (double for "World's Fair")	1934-38	750	1500	3200	Pepsodent
Ring, ivory, initial	1939	100	200	400	Ivory Soap--special promotion
Watch, explorer's sun, Post WWII, offered by Jack Armstrong	1949	48	72	95	Wheaties

FRED ALLEN

Book, donut	1934	8	12	16	Probably offered in stores

FU MANCHU

Button	1934	80	150	220	Various local
Key puzzle	1934	40	80	120	Various local

G

ITEM	DATE	GOOD	FINE	MINT	SPONSOR

G-MAN

ITEM	DATE	GOOD	FINE	MINT	SPONSOR
Badge	1933-35	15	20	30	Post
Badge, stud (fits button hole)	1933-35	4	8	12	Post
Ring, signet, official	1933-35	40	80	125	Post
Ring, signet, tiny (for small child)	1933-35	6	12	16	Post

GABBY HAYES

ITEM	DATE	GOOD	FINE	MINT	SPONSOR
Antique cars, set	1950s	50	80	160	Quaker
Clipper ship, inside bottle	TV 1952-53	10	20	30	Quaker
Comic books, set of 5	TV 1952-53	100	200	300	Quaker
Movie viewer	TV 1952-53	75	150	200	Quaker
Ring, shooting cannon	TV 1951	75	150	300	Quaker
Western gun collection:3 pistols, 3 rifles, solid, non-working	TV 1951	37	56	80	Quaker
Western wagon collection	TV 1952-53	30	40	65	Quaker

GANGBUSTERS

ITEM	DATE	GOOD	FINE	MINT	SPONSOR
Badge, Phillips H. Lord, blue and gold litho	1936	15	30	60	Sloan's Liniment
Game, "Stop, Thief"	1938	20	40	60	Sloan's Liniment
Pin	1936	30	40	60	Sloan's Liniment

GENE AUTRY

ITEM	DATE	GOOD	FINE	MINT	SPONSOR
Bread end seal map/poster, complete	1940	30	60	120	
Flying A Wings	1949	10	20	30	
Photo (pre-network)	1938	10	20	30	Wrigley's
Photo	1946	8	16	24	Wrigley's
Photo and letter, Flying A (Wood Mfg)	1949	8	16	24	Wrigley's

ITEM	DATE	GOOD	FINE	MINT	SPONSOR
Premium comics (5), ea.	1950	6	12	15	
Ring, American Eagle (Dell)	1950	150	300	750	Dell Comics subscriptions one year
Ring, American flag	1950	25	50	125	Dell Comics subscriptions one year
Ring, Flying A horseshoe nail (says "Gene Autry")	1949	35	60	85	Store item

GOLDBERGS

Puzzle	1930s	20	30	40	

GREEN HORNET

Card, membership	1936	45	90	180	local
Photo, captioned G. H.	1936	30	60	100	local
Photo, Britt Reid, 8 x 10"	1936	80	160	275	local
Photo, Kato	1936	80	160	275	local
Photo, Lenore Case	1936	40	80	120	local
Photo, Mike Axford	1936	40	80	120	local
Photo postcard	1936	40	80	120	local
Postcard to order Michigan network photos	1936	80	160	275	Golden Jersey Dairy
Ring, seal, green and orange plastic	1966	20	30	40	local
Ring, secret compartment, glow-in-the dark, seal	1949	350	750	1750	General Mills

Green Hornet secret compartment glow-in-the-dark seal ring

NOTICE!

HOW TO SIGNAL WITH THIS GREEN HORNET RING

HOW TO LEAVE GREEN HORNET SEAL

To leave official seal of the Green Hornet, follow these easy instructions:

Select some soft material, such as paper and press it down on top of ring. Do not press ring down on soft material for pressing too hard in this manner may damage swinging shutter mechanism.

SECRET MONEY COMPARTMENT

SWINGING SHUTTER

GREEN HORNET SEAL

SECRET SIGNAL RADIATOR

ADJUSTABLE FINGER BAND

This sheet came with the Green Hornet secret compartment glow-in-the-dark seal ring. The sheet alone is worth $500 in mint.

H

ITEM	DATE	GOOD	FINE	MINT	SPONSOR
HERMIT'S CAVE					
Folder	1940	30	60	150	Olga Coal
HOBBY LOBBY					
Charm	1939	30	60	150	
HOP HARRIGAN					
Bomber, super-fortress model	1944	250	500	1000	
Card, membership	1942	10	20	50	
Flight wings	1942	15	30	50	
Para-plane, cardboard, parachute drops CB water canister	1949	200	400	600	
Patch, flying club	1944	20	50	90	
Patch, observation corps	1944	20	50	90	
Ring, compass, unmarked	1949	50	100	175	
Ring, sun dial, unmarked	1948	50	100	175	
Viewer with film stills from movie serial. Radio offer.	1945	200	300	375	

HOPALONG CASSIDY

BADGES, BUTTONS, AND TABS

Badge, tin, giveaway	1950s	17	26	35	Post Raisin Bran
Button, membership, Bar 20 foreman	1950s	75	145	275	Savings club sponsor
Button, membership, bronc buster level	1950s	25	35	45	Savings club sponsor
Button, membership, bulldogger level	1950s	25	35	45	Savings club sponsor
Button, membership, straw boss level	1950s	75	145	275	Savings club sponsor
Button, membership, teller	1950s	25	35	45	Savings club sponsor

ITEM	DATE	GOOD	FINE	MINT	SPONSOR
Button, membership, tenderfoot savings level	1950s	25	35	45	Savings club sponsor
Button, membership, tenderfoot savings level, small size	1950s	30	50	75	Savings club sponsor
Button, membership, trail boss level	1950s	25	35	45	Savings club sponsor
Button, membership, wrangler	1950s	25	35	45	Savings club sponsor
Buttons, Harmony Farms & similar	1950s	25	35	45	Milk sponsor
Tabs, Hoppy	1950s	25	35	45	Cereal sponsor
Tabs, Western hero other than Hoppy	1950s	20	30	40	Cereal sponsor
Tokens, various	1950s	10	20	30	Savings club sponsor

CARTONS, PHOTOS, AND OTHER PAPER ITEMS

ITEM	DATE	GOOD	FINE	MINT	SPONSOR
Book cover	1950s	3	6	12	Bread sponsor
Bread end seals, ea.	1950s	2	4	6	Bread sponsor
Cards, western collector, set of 36, set	1950s	190	380	750	Cereal sponsor
Cartons, milk, various sizes	1950s	2	4	6	Milk sponsor
Certificate, member	1950s	8	16	24	Savings club sponsor
Comic book, premium	1950s	20	30	95	Cereal sponsor
End seal hang up album	1950s	15	30	40	Bread sponsor
Letter and envelope	1950s	8	16	24	Savings club sponsor
Mailer, club invitation	1950s	8	16	24	Savings club sponsor
Photo, 8-1/2 x 11", color, ea.	1950s	5	8	12	Bread sponsor
Photo, postcard size, color, ea.	1950s	5	8	12	Bread sponsor
Photo, wallet size, color, ea.	1950s	5	8	12	Bread sponsor
Poster	1950s	15	30	40	Sunny Spread
Premium folder	1950s	8	12	24	Savings club sponsor
Radio show announcement, in pack	1950s	5	8	12	Cereal sponsor

RINGS

ITEM	DATE	GOOD	FINE	MINT	SPONSOR
Ring, compass, Bar 20	1950s	50	80	250	
Ring, face	1950s	40	75	175	
delete line - duplicate listing		60	120	200	

MISCELLANEOUS

ITEM	DATE	GOOD	FINE	MINT	SPONSOR
Bank, plastic	1950s	20	40	80	Savings club sponsor
Wallet	1950s	20	35	50	Savings club sponsor

HOWDY DOODY

BADGES

ITEM	DATE	GOOD	FINE	MINT	SPONSOR
Badge, flip-up, "Howdy for President"	1947-55	15	20	25	Poll-Parrot Shoes

ITEM	DATE	GOOD	FINE	MINT	SPONSOR
Badge, paper, flip-up	1947-55	10	20	40	Wonder Bread

RINGS AND KEYCHAINS

ITEM	DATE	GOOD	FINE	MINT	SPONSOR
Book, Jumble Joy	1955	30	60	100	Poll-Parrot Shoes
Coloring book	1947-55	20	40	100	Poll-Parrot Shoes
Coloring book, Christmas	1947-55	20	40	100	Poll-Parrot Shoes
Comic, "Howdy Doody's Comic Circus Animals"	1947-55	30	60	100	Poll-Parrot Shoes
Comic, "Twin-Pop Jackpot of Fun"	1947-55	10	20	40	Poll-Parrot Shoes
Comic books	1947-55	10	20	40	Poll-Parrot Shoes
Cook book	1952	10	20	40	Welch's
Newspaper, No. 1	5/1/1950	50	100	200	Poll-Parrot Shoes
Album, American history end seals	1947-55	8	12	16	Wonder Bread
Breadend seals, ea.	1947-55	5	8	16	Wonder Bread
Frozen desert bags, ea.	1947-55	3	8	16	Royal
Label with Howdy	1947-55	6	12	24	Welch's
Package back, coloring cards, ea.	1947-55	3	4	5	Royal
Package back, trading cards, ea.	1947-55	3	4	5	Royal
Cards, divider, Canadian, ea.	1947-55	3	6	9	Nabisco
Hat, paper	1947-55	8	16	24	Wonder Bread
Magic kit	1947-55	15	30	45	Mars
Masks	1947-55	6	12	16	Royal
Masks, face, 3-D, 6 characters, ea.	1947-55	15	30	60	Poll-Parrot Shoes
Masks	1946-55	10	20	50	Wheaties
Prize Doodle list	1947-55	5	8	12	

PUPPETS, FIGURES, AND CLIMBERS

ITEM	DATE	GOOD	FINE	MINT	SPONSOR
Dangle dandies	1947-55	8	16	24	Kellogg's Corn Flakes
Figure, cardboard, Howdy, 8" high	1947-55	40	60	80	Wonder Bread
Figure, cardboard, Princess Winterfallsummerspring, 14" high	1947-55	30	40	50	Wonder Bread
Puppet	1947-55	15	30	40	Wonder Bread
Puppet, animated, Clarabell	1947-55	20	40	80	Mars
Puppet, dancing princess, movable joints, 13" high	1947-55	20	40	75	Snickers
Puppet, Howdy, cardboard, 15" high	1947-55	37	56	75	Mars
Puppets, ea.	1947-55	15	30	45	Wonder Bread
Puppets, ea.	1947-55	10	20	35	Poll-Parrot Shoes
Stand-up	1947-55	10	20	40	Palmolive
String climber, Howdy, Clarabell, ea.	1947-55	15	30	60	Welch's

ITEM	DATE	GOOD	FINE	MINT	SPONSOR
RINGS AND KEYCHAINS					
Keychain, flicks from Howdy to Poll Parrot, 3D	1950s	30	40	60	Poll-Parrot Shoes
Ring, flasher	1947-55	30	60	75	Poll-Parrot Shoes
Ring, flashlight, Howdy Doody face	1950s	80	120	240	Poll-Parrot Shoes
Ring, flicks from Howdy to Poll Parrot	1947-55	30	60	75	Poll-Parrot Shoes
Ring, horn, Clarabell	1947-55	70	120	225	Poll-Parrot Shoes
TOYS					
Periscope	1947-55	100	200	400	Colgate
TV viewer, miniature	1947-55	50	100	175	Colgate
KITCHEN ITEMS					
Jar lid with Howdy	1947-55	5	10	15	Welch's
Jelly jar/glasses, ea.	1947-55	8	16	24	Welch's
Bottle cap, juice, with Howdy	1947-55	3	6	12	Welch's
Mug, drinking	1947-55	20	40	80	Ovaltine
Mug, shake-up	1947-55	25	50	90	Ovaltine

HOWIE WING

ITEM	DATE	GOOD	FINE	MINT	SPONSOR
Card, membership	Early 1930s	5	8	12	Kellogg's
Certificate, membership	Early 1930s	5	8	12	Kellogg's
Chart, adventures on the Canadian lakes	Early 1930s	20	30	45	Kellogg's
Chart, flying guide, Cadet Aviation Corps	Early 1930s	20	30	45	Kellogg's
Coin, aluminum, good luck	Early 1930s	20	40	100	Kellogg's
Decoder, Mystery Lodge	Early 1930s	30	40	60	Kellogg's
Gun, rubber band	Early 1930s	10	20	30	Kellogg's
Handbook	Early 1930s	20	30	45	Kellogg's
Kits, model airplanes, ea.	Early 1930s	10	20	30	Kellogg's
Movie viewer	Early 1930s	20	40	60	Kellogg's
Newspapers, Cadet Aviation Corps., ea.	Early 1930s	10	20	30	Kellogg's
Ring, weather forecast	Early 1930s	150	300	450	Kellogg's
Shirt, official flying	Early 1930s	20	30	45	Kellogg's
Ventriloquist's dummy, Typhoon Tootel	Early 1930s	30	40	120	Kellogg's
Wings	Early 1930s	10	20	30	Kellogg's

ITEM	DATE	GOOD	FINE	MINT	SPONSORI
I LOVE A MYSTERY					
Photo, Jack, Doc, and Reggie	c. 1940	50	70	95	Fleishmann's Yeast
INSPECTOR POST					
Badge, captain	1932-33	20	30	60	General Foods, Post
Badge, detective	1932-33	20	30	60	General Foods, Post
Badge, lieutenant	1932-33	20	30	60	General Foods, Post
Badge, sergeant	1932-33	20	30	60	General Foods, Post
Case book, Inspector Post	1932-33	15	20	30	General Foods, Post
Manual #1, detective	1932-33	15	20	30	General Foods, Post
Manual #2, detective sergeant	1932-33	15	20	30	General Foods, Post
Manual #3, lieutenant	1932-33	15	12	30	General Foods, Post
Manual #4, captain	1932-33	15	12	30	General Foods, Post

J

ITEM	DATE	GOOD	FINE	MINT	SPONSOR

JACK ARMSTRONG

BADGES, BANNERS, AND PATCHES

ITEM	DATE	GOOD	FINE	MINT	SPONSOR
Badge, whistle, captain, listening squad	1940	500	1000	1500	Wheaties
Badge, whistle, lieutenant, listening	1940	250	400	800	Wheaties
Banner, WAFC	1942	50	100	200	Wheaties
Identification tag, GI (included with Cub Pilot News #3)	1945-46	25	50	100	Wheaties
Patch, cloth, Future Champions of America	1943	10	20	30	Wheaties
Transfer ensemble, Cub Pilot Corps	1945-46	20	30	50	Wheaties

APPAREL

ITEM	DATE	GOOD	FINE	MINT	SPONSOR
Belt, champion	1940s	80	160	350	Wheaties (bounceback)
Cap, baseball	1934	20	35	50	Wheaties
Goggles, Army	1947	10	20	30	Wheaties
Neckerchief, sports	1940s	10	20	30	Wheaties (bounceback)
Safety belt, blackout, luminous	1941	45	95	120	Wheaties/General Mills
Sun glasses	1947	10	20	30	Wheaties (bounceback)

BOOKS, MANUALS, AND OTHER PAPER ITEMS

ITEM	DATE	GOOD	FINE	MINT	SPONSOR
Book, picture, Jack Armstrong	1941	20	35	60	Wheaties
Book, scrapbook, baseball	1936	30	40	50	Wheaties (bounceback)
Book, Six Man Football	1938	10	15	20	Wheaties
Booklet, charm	1937	10	15	20	Wheaties
Booklet, flip movie, Babe Ruth, How to Hit a Home Run	1933	100	200	400	Wheaties
Booklet, Oriental stamp offer	1936	15	30	45	Wheaties
Booklets, Library of Sports, 18, ea.	1943	5	8	15	Wheaties
Books, library of sports, 20, ea.	1945-46	4	6	8	Wheaties
Comic Book, "Captain Marvel," 6 x 8", 32 pages	1948	80	300	never found	Wheaties

ITEM	DATE	GOOD	FINE	MINT	SPONSOR
Comic book, "Flash Comics," 6 x 8", 32 pages	1948	80	300 never found		Wheaties
Comic book, "Funny Stuff," miniature, 6 x 8", 32 pages	1948	40	200 never found		Wheaties
Comic book, "Whiz," miniature, 6 x 8", 32 pages	1948	80	300 never found		Wheaties
Magazine subscription, *American Boy Magazine*	1938	10	20	30	Wheaties
Manual, from "Write a Fighter Corps"	1942	25	40	60	Wheaties
Manual, patches and transfer stars, future champion	1943	25	40	60	Wheaties
Manual, "How to Fly," from preflight training kit	1945-46	8	14	20	Wheaties
Newspaper, Cub Pilot Corps, Vol. 1, No. 1	1945-46	10	15	35	Wheaties
Newspaper, Cub Pilot Corps, Vol. 1, No. 2, learn to fly contest	1945-46	10	15	35	Wheaties
Newspaper, Cub Pilot Corps, Vol. 1, No. 3	1945-46	10	15	35	Wheaties
Newspaper, Tru-Flite, Vol. 1, No. 1	1944	10	20	40	Wheaties
Newspaper, Tru-Flite, Vol. 1, No. 2	1944	10	20	40	Wheaties

STAMPS

ITEM	DATE	GOOD	FINE	MINT	SPONSOR
Stamp collection offers	1935	15	30	45	Wheaties
Stamp offer, treasure hunter (unsorted stamps)	1939	15	20	30	Wheaties
Folder, stamp offer	1934	15	20	30	Wheaties
Postage stamps, 200	1948	20	30	40	Wheaties

KITS

ITEM	DATE	GOOD	FINE	MINT	SPONSOR
Kit, fingerprint	1939	20	40	60	Wheaties (bounceback)
Kit, first aid, junior ace	1939	25	50	100	Wheaties
Kit, listening squad	1940	100	200	375	Wheaties
Kit, sound effects	1941	50	75	200	Wheaties
Kit, "Write a Fighter Corp," with manual, stars, stencil, etc.	1942	100	200	300	Wheaties
Kit, training, cub pilot corps	1945	100	200	300	Wheaties

MISC. PAPER ITEMS

ITEM	DATE	GOOD	FINE	MINT	SPONSOR
Envelope, store	1945-46	8	12	16	Wheaties
Card, whistle ring code	1938	20	30	50	Wheaties

ITEM	DATE	GOOD	FINE	MINT	SPONSOR
Certificate, listening squad	1940	20	30	40	
Folio, baseball	1940s	20	30	40	Wheaties (bounceback)
Lie detector (trial offer)	1942	100	200	400	Wheaties (bounceback)
Offer, Indian arrowhead	1935	30	60	90	Wheaties
Stationery	1937	20	40	60	Wheaties

PACKAGE BACKS

ITEM	DATE	GOOD	FINE	MINT	SPONSOR
Package back, No. 1, "Jack Rescues Castaway Crew"	1938	20	30	40	Wheaties
Package back No. 2, "Tibetan Magic Mystifies Jack"	1938	20	30	40	Wheaties
Package back No. 3, "Jack Finds Phantom Submarine Hideout"	1938	20	30	40	Wheaties
Package back No. 4, "Escape in the Flying Fortress"	1938	20	30	40	Wheaties
Package back No. 5, "Attacked by an Enraged Tibetan Eagle"	1938	20	30	40	Wheaties
Package back No. 6, "Discovery of Ill-fated Treasure Ship"	1938	20	30	40	Wheaties
Photo, from package back, Betty playing golf	1935	30	40	45	Wheaties
Photo, from package back, Jack playing baseball	1935	40	50	55	Wheaties
Any complete box with any of the above nine photos	1934-38	75	150	300	Wheaties

PHOTOS (Glossy, By Mail)

ITEM	DATE	GOOD	FINE	MINT	SPONSOR
Photo, Betty	1934	10	20	30	Wheaties
Photo, Hockey players	1935	6	15	20	Wheaties
Photo, Jack	1934	20	35	75	Wheaties
Photo, Jack, Betty and Arrow Champ	1934	15	30	45	Wheaties
Photo, Jack Armstrong on his horse, Blackster	1934	15	30	45	Wheaties
Photo, Johnny Weismuller	1933	30	75	150	Wheaties
Photos, Baseball World Series 1934, autographed	1934	10	20	30	Wheaties

RINGS AND BRACELETS

ITEM	DATE	GOOD	FINE	MINT	SPONSOR
Wrist band, Strongheart (movie dog)	1938	40	60	120	Wheaties (bounceback)
Bracelet, Betty's luminous gardenia	1940	150	300	600	Wheaties
Sun watch, Frank Buck explorer	1948	30	65	100	Wheaties
Ring, dragon's eye, crocodile design, green stone	1940	200	400	800	Wheaties

ITEM	DATE	GOOD	FINE	MINT	SPONSOR
Whistling ring, Egyptian	1937	30	65	110	Wheaties
Brooch, luminous gardenia	1940	75	200	400	Wheaties
Ring, baseball	1938	150	300	600	Wheaties

TOYS

ITEM	DATE	GOOD	FINE	MINT	SPONSOR
Answer box, magic	1940	40	80	160	Wheaties
Baseball pencil, 100th anniversary	1939	20	35	100	Wheaties (bounceback)
Baseball pencil, bakelite	1939	25	50	100	Wheaties
Baseball pencil, luminous	1940	35	75	100	Wheaties
Baseball pencil, wooden	1943	20	35	50	Wheaties (bounceback)
Bat, baseball	1937	75	150	300	Wheaties (bounceback)
Bombsight, secret, with 3 bombs	1942	125	250	600	Wheaties
Compass, wrist	1937	40	75	125	Wheaties
Distance finder, heliograph	1937	25	50	100	Wheaties
Flashlight, safety signal light kit	1939	30	60	120	Wheaties
Flashlights, sentinel first aid kit	1939	100	200	400	Wheaties
Flashlights, torpedo, 3 (red, black, blue, red), ea.	1939	15	30	60	Wheaties
Game, Big ten football, Wheaties package backs, ea.	1936	10	20	35	Wheaties
Game, dragon talisman map, spinner, and game pieces	1936	100	200	400	Wheaties

Jack Armstrong "Frank Buck" explorer sun watch

ITEM	DATE	GOOD	FINE	MINT	SPONSOR

Jack Armstrong magic answer box

ITEM	DATE	GOOD	FINE	MINT	SPONSOR
Golf ball	1947	20	30	45	Wheaties (bounceback)
Grid-o-scope (football premium)	1939	20	35	60	Wheaties
Grip developer, unmarked	1933	10	15	20	Wheaties
Gun, propeller plane, shooting (Daisy)	1933	35	75	150	Wheaties
Hike-o-meter	1939	25	50	100	Wheaties
Hike-o-meter, blue rim	1938	25	50	100	Wheaties

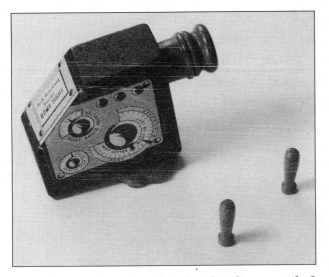

Jack Armstrong secret bombsight shown with 2 bombs

Jack Armstrong Hike-o-meter pedometer

ITEM	DATE	GOOD	FINE	MINT	SPONSOR

Jack Armstrong catapult plane

ITEM	DATE	GOOD	FINE	MINT	SPONSOR
Hike-o-meter, sports figures on rim	1934	25	50	100	Wheaties
Light kit, safety signal	1939	30	60	75	Wheaties
Mirror, emergency signaling	1939	20	25	30	Wheaties
Moviescope viewer	1937	30	65	100	Wheaties
Parachute ball	1947	50	100	150	Wheaties
Pedometer, silver aluminum rim	1939	20	50	100	Wheaties
Pencil, whistling	1939	30	60	120	Wheaties (bounceback)
Pistol flashlight	1941	50	100	150	Wheaties
Plane, catapult	1939	35	40	75	Wheaties
Rock crystal	1935	10	20	30	Wheaties
Rocket chute	1939	50	100	200	Wheaties
Signal mirror, Navy	1947	50	100	150	Wheaties
Talisman, bronze, from dragon game	1936	25	50	75	Wheaties
Telescope, explorer	1937	20	35	50	Wheaties
Viewer with African filmstrip	1937	50	80	120	Wheaties
Water pistol	1933	75	150	300	Wheaties
Weathercaster	1939	30	40	50	Wheaties (bounceback)

ITEM	DATE	GOOD	FINE	MINT	SPONSOR

The first Jack Armstrong advertisement (September 24, 1933) features a free shooting plane

ITEM	DATE	GOOD	FINE	MINT	SPONSOR
Wee gyro	1934	30	60	150	Wheaties
Whistle, crocodile	1941	1200	3000	5000	Wheaties

Jack Armstrong explorer telescope

MODELS

ITEM	DATE	GOOD	FINE	MINT	SPONSOR
Airplanes of WWII, set of 10, light pasteboard, to be assembled	1945-46	50	100	200	Wheaties
Model airplanes, Tru-Flite, Fairey Fulmar and Heinkel He.113	1944	15	20	30	Wheaties

ITEM	DATE	GOOD	FINE	MINT	SPONSOR
Model airplanes, Tru-Flite, American Bell P-39 "Airacobra"					
"Airacobra" and Russian IL-2 Slormovik	1944	15	20	30	Wheaties
Model airplanes, Tru-Flite, Curtis Flying Tiger P-40 and					
and Mitsubishi Zero	1944	15	20	30	Wheaties
Model airplanes, Tru-Flite, Thunderbolt P-47 and Russian					
Yaki-26	1944	15	20	30	Wheaties
Model airplanes, Tru-Flite, P40 and Zero	1943	20	40	60	Wheaties
Model airplanes, Tru-Flite, Supermarine spitfire V and					
and Focke Wulf 190	1944	15	20	30	Wheaties
Model airplanes, Tru-Flite, Gruman Hellcat FGF and					
and Japanese Nakajima	1944	15	20	30	Wheaties
Model airplanes, Tru-Flite set, Mustang fighter and AICHI					
dive bomber	1944	15	20	30	Wheaties
Airplane, Sky Ranger	1940	50	100	200	Wheaties
Model, preflight trainer, from preflight training kit	1945-46	50	100	200	Wheaties
Model ship, sloop	1943	15	35	50	Wheaties

UTENSILS

ITEM	DATE	GOOD	FINE	MINT	SPONSOR
Bon-bon dish	1934	20	40	95	Wheaties (bounceback)
Bowl, Breakfast of Champions	1937	20	35	60	Wheaties
Dish, Shirley Temple	1935	30	60	120	Wheaties
Mug, Shirley Temple	1935	30	60	120	Wheaties
Spoon, Christmas	1933	10	20	30	Wheaties
Sugar and creamer set	1934	15	25	40	Wheaties

RECORDINGS

ITEM	DATE	GOOD	FINE	MINT	SPONSOR
Record, Radio Broadcast	1973	8	16	38	Wheaties

JACK BENNY

ITEM	DATE	GOOD	FINE	MINT	SPONSOR
Book, Jell-O recipes	1937	5	8	12	Jell-O

JIMMIE ALLEN

PATCHES, PINS, AND TRANSFERS

Item	DATE	GOOD	FINE	MINT	SPONSOR
Patch	1936	10	20	45	Weather Bird
Pin, airplane	1934	10	20	45	Skelly Oil
Transfer (Jimmie Allen)	1935	30	50	80	Skelly Oil
Wings, cadet, die-cut airplane	Late 1930s	15	30	55	Skelly Oil
Various: Skelly Oil, Town Talk Bread, Hi-Speed, Blue Flash, Richfield, Cleo Cole					
Wings, flying cadet, bronze	Late 1930s	20	30	40	Rainbo Gas, Certified

PUBLICATIONS

Item	DATE	GOOD	FINE	MINT	SPONSOR
Album	1935	25	50	100	Skelly Oil
Album, stamps	1934	20	25	30	Skelly Oil
Book, air battles	1934	15	30	45	Skelly Oil
Manual, weather bird	1936	30	40	50	Weather Bird
Newspapers, club, 12 issues, ea.	1935	10	20	40	Skelly Oil

PHOTOS

Item	DATE	GOOD	FINE	MINT	SPONSOR
Photo, action	1934	10	20	30	Skelly Oil
Photo, Jimmie Allen, different poses	1934	10	20	30	Skelly Oil
Photo, Speed Robertson, different poses	1934	10	20	30	Skelly Oil

PAPER TOYS, CARDS, AND OTHER ITEMS

Item	DATE	GOOD	FINE	MINT	SPONSOR
Airplane, Speed Robertson's Blue Flash, paper	1934	30	45	90	Skelly Oil

Jimmie Allen bronze wings, flying cadet

ITEM	DATE	GOOD	FINE	MINT	SPONSOR
Blotter	1936-39	10	20	30	Skelly Oil
Card, membership	1934	20	40	80	Skelly Oil
Certificate	1934	15	30	45	Skelly Oil
Chart, flying maneuvers	1934	15	30	45	Skelly Oil
Flying lessons, 5 total, ea.	1934	10	15	20	Skelly Oil
Pilot's creed	1934	10	20	30	Skelly Oil
Roadmaps, various states, brands	Various	10	20	30	Various sponsors, various dates

BRACELETS

ITEM	DATE	GOOD	FINE	MINT	SPONSOR
Bracelet	1935	100	250	500	Kansas City air races
Bracelet, ID	1935	15	30	60	Richfield, Weather Bird
Shoes and others					

TOYS

ITEM	DATE	GOOD	FINE	MINT	SPONSOR
Knife	1936	30	60	150	Skelly Oil
Log cabin	1934	20	30	45	

JOE E. BROWN

ITEM	DATE	GOOD	FINE	MINT	SPONSOR
Pin	1936	10	15	20	

K

ITEM	DATE	GOOD	FINE	MINT	SPONSOR
KATE SMITH					
Recipe books	1938-42	3	8	12	Grape-Nuts
Recipe mailers, monthly, ea.	1938-42	5	8	12	Grape-Nuts
KUKLA, FRAN, AND OLLIE (TV)					
Newspaper, Kuklapolitan Courier, ea.	1949	15	30	75	
Yearbook, Kuklapolitan Courier	1950	30	60	100	

L

ITEM	DATE	GOOD	FINE	MINT	SPONSOR
LASSIE (TV)					
Photo membership folder	1953	75	100	150	
Photo, color, Robert Bray	1953	30	60	90	
Ring	1953	60	125	190	
LIGHTNING JIM					
Badge, membership	1930s	30	60	90	Meadow Gold Dairy
Card, membership	1930s	15	30	60	Meadow Gold Dairy
Photo	1930s	10	20	40	Meadow Gold Dairy

LITTLE ORPHAN ANNIE (RADIO ORPHAN ANNIE)

BADGES, EMBLEMS, AND PINS

Badge, decoder	1936	25	50	79	Ovaltine

Decoders were all the rage as radio premiums. This is the 1936 offering from the Orphan Annie show.

ITEM	DATE	GOOD	FINE	MINT	SPONSOR

Radio Orphan Annie mysto-snapper membership badge with read and white stripes

ITEM	DATE	GOOD	FINE	MINT	SPONSOR
Badge, decoder	1937	30	60	100	Ovaltine
Badge, decoder	1938	30	60	110	Ovaltine
Badge, decoder	1939	30	60	110	Ovaltine
Badge, decoder	1940	40	80	140	Ovaltine
Badge, membership, mysto-snapper, red and white stripes	1942	25	50	100	Quaker
Badge, membership, mysto-snapper, Canadian union jack	1941	30	40	120	Quaker
Badge, signaler, tri-tone	1941	25	50	100	Quaker
Button, Annie	1930	200	400	800	Ovaltine
Button, Annie and Joe Corntassel	1931	125	300	600	Ovaltine
Button, Joe	1930	100	200	500	Ovaltine
Button, pinback, LOA, member Funny Frosty's Club	Mid 1930s	21	32	42	Frosty's
Button card	1930	35	70	100	Ovaltine
Coins, foreign	1937	25	38	50	Ovaltine
Emblem, captain, glow wings	1941	75	150	400	Quaker
Lucky piece	1934	15	25	50	Ovaltine
Pin, Associated membership	1934	15	22	50	Ovaltine

ITEM	DATE	GOOD	FINE	MINT	SPONSOR
Pin, code, captain, Safety Guard Magic Glowbird	1941	75	150	400	Ovaltine
Pin, code, captain, secret compartment	1939	30	65	100	Ovaltine
Pin, decoder	1935	25	50	100	Ovaltine
Pin, decoder, speedomatic	1940	35	75	150	Ovaltine
Pin, decoder, sunburst	1937	20	40	100	Ovaltine
Pin, decoder, telematic	1938	22	45	90	Ovaltine
Pin, decoder, round	1935	20	40	100	Ovaltine
Pin, school	1938	15	30	75	Ovaltine
Pin, secret society	1934	25	38	50	Ovaltine
Pin, secret society, bronze	1934	10	15	30	Ovaltine
Pin, silver star	1934	48	72	95	Ovaltine
Tag, identification bracelet	1939	35	70	85	Ovaltine
Transfer pictures, magic	1935	50	100	250	Ovaltine

BOOKS AND MAGAZINES

ITEM	DATE	GOOD	FINE	MINT	SPONSOR
Adventure books, 6, ea.	1934	12	25	35	Ovaltine
Book, recipe	1941	15	30	40	Quaker
Book, Snow White cutouts (Whitman) (Double for red cover)	1938	200	400	600	Ovaltine
Book about dogs	1936	20	40	60	Ovaltine

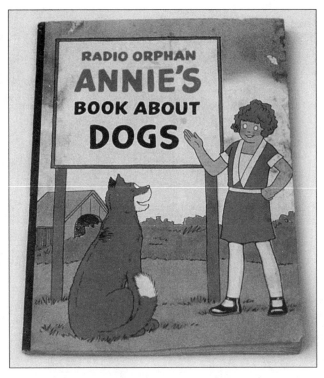

Radio Orphan Annie's Book About Dogs

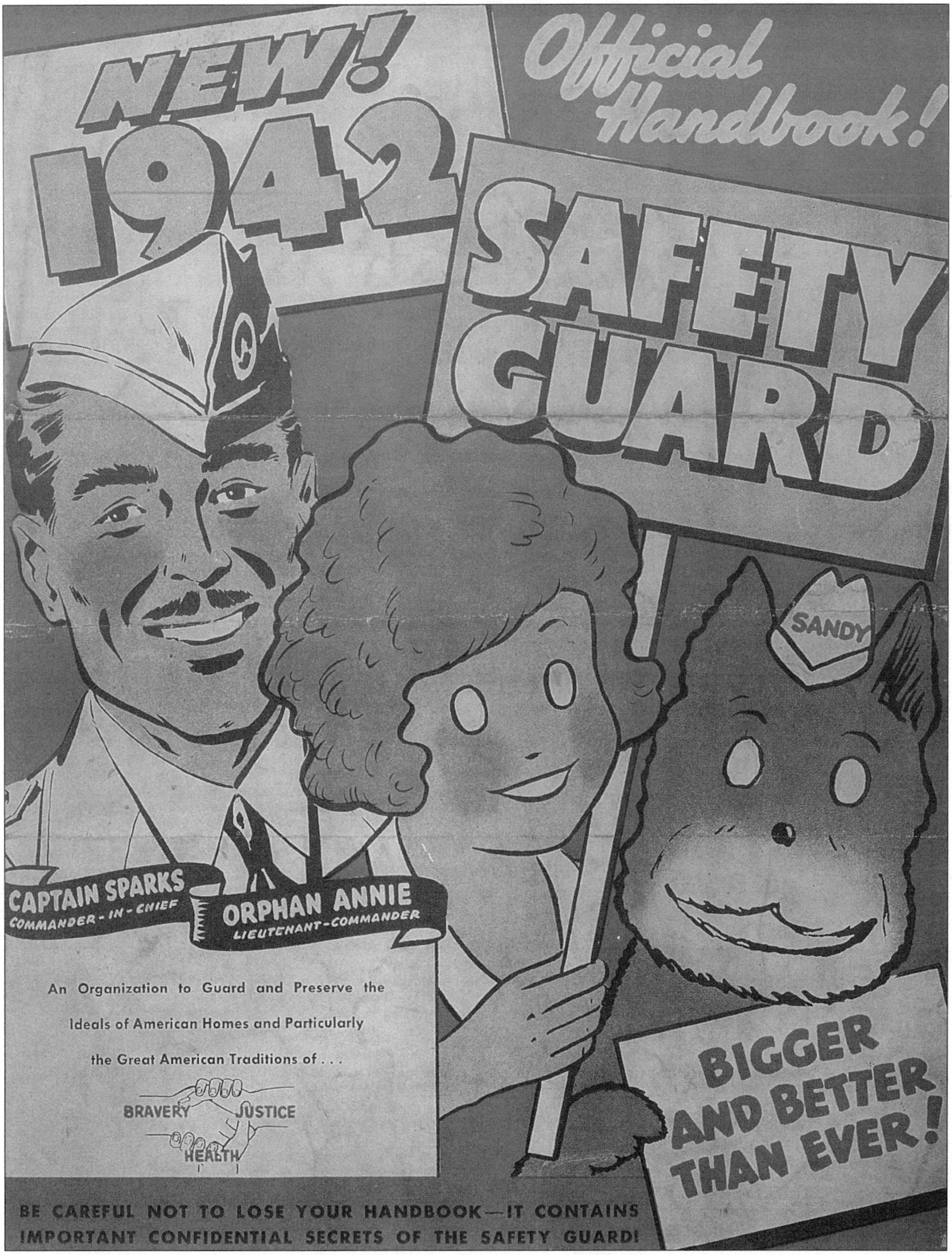

A Quaker Cereals Orphan Annie manual (1942)

1937 Radio Orphan Annie Secret Society manual

Radio Orphan Annie decoder, whirl-o-matic, paper board

ITEM	DATE	GOOD	FINE	MINT	SPONSOR
Comic book, "Sparkies," Book 1	1941	27	55	110	Quaker
Comic book, "Sparkies," Book 2	1941	25	50	75	Quaker
Comic book, "Sparkies," Book 3	1941	22	45	70	Quaker
Decoder, slideomatic, paper	1941	53	105	210	Quaker
Decoder, whirl-o-matic, paper board	1942	50	100	200	Quaker
Goofy Gazettes, 3, ea.	1939	12	25	50	Ovaltine
Handbook, Safety Guard	1941	75	150	200	Quaker
Handbook, Safety Guard	1942	80	175	300	Ovaltine
Manual	1934	62	93	125	Ovaltine
Manual	1935	27	55	80	Ovaltine
Manual	1936	20	45	60	Ovaltine
Manual	1937	25	50	100	Ovaltine
Manual	1938	35	75	125	Ovaltine
Manual	1939	35	70	100	Ovaltine
Manual	1940	45	90	150	Ovaltine
Manual, code, captain	1940	35	75	150	Ovaltine
Manual, secret, captain	1941	35	75	300	Quaker
Manual, Silver Star	1934	15	30	60	Ovaltine
Manual, Silver Star	1935	15	30	60	Ovaltine
Manual, Silver Star	1936	20	40	75	Ovaltine

Radio Orphan Annie Secret Society manual (1938) "5th Anniversary Year—Bigger and Better Than Ever!"

ITEM	DATE	GOOD	FINE	MINT	SPONSOR
Manual, Silver Star	1937	15	30	40	Ovaltine
Manual, Silver Star	1938	12	25	35	Ovaltine
Manual, "How to Fly"	1942	18	35	70	Quaker
Sheet music	1930	10	15	20	Ovaltine

APPAREL

ITEM	DATE	GOOD	FINE	MINT	SPONSOR
Bandanna	1934	20	40	80	Ovaltine
Belt and Buckle, code captain	1940	75	150	300	Ovaltine
Cap, Secret Guard insignia	1941	35	75	150	Quaker
Mask, Annie	1933	50	75	100	Ovaltine
Outfit, Secret Guard nurse	1941	75	150	300	Quaker

GAMES AND KITS

ITEM	DATE	GOOD	FINE	MINT	SPONSOR
Game, treasure hunt	1933	75	150	300	Ovaltine
Kit, detecto, Secret Guard	1941	30	60	120	Quaker
Package: whirl-o-matic decoder, whistle badge, booklet, and order blanks	1942	150	300	600	Quaker

CARDS, LETTERS, AND ENCLOSURES

ITEM	DATE	GOOD	FINE	MINT	SPONSOR
Card, membership	1941	10	15	20	Quaker
Card, membership	1942	10	15	20	Quaker
Christmas card set	1937	20	35	75	Ovaltine
Commission, captain	1941	15	30	60	Quaker
Commission, captain	1942	20	35	75	Quaker
Contest letter/winners list	1934	5	10	15	Ovaltine
Enclosure, game instructions, came with shake-up mug	1930-31	17	26	35	Ovaltine
Foreign coin folder	1937	20	35	75	Ovaltine
Mailer, election	1930	20	35	60	Ovaltine
Map, Simons Corners	1936	25	55	110	Ovaltine

PHOTOS

ITEM	DATE	GOOD	FINE	MINT	SPONSOR
Annie full figure (Shirley Bell)	1932	20	30	40	Ovaltine
Annie, face (Shirley Bell)	1932	20	30	40	Ovaltine
Joe (Allan Baruck)	1932	15	25	35	Ovaltine
Photo frame, silver plates, engraved "To my best friend"	1938	30	60	75	Ovaltine

ITEM	DATE	GOOD	FINE	MINT	SPONSOR

PAPER TOYS

ITEM	DATE	GOOD	FINE	MINT	SPONSOR
Circus action show	1936	100	250	500	Ovaltine
Cockpit, aviation training, Captain Sparks/Orphan Annie	1941	100	250	500	Quaker
Glassips	1936	100	250	500	Ovaltine
Goofy circus	1939	160	325	750	Ovaltine
Puzzle, Tucker County race	1933	20	40	60	Ovaltine
Scribbler, 2 or 3 versions	1941	30	60	120	Quaker
Shadowettes, 6	1938	60	150	300	Ovaltine
Stamps, photo	1938	15	30	45	Ovaltine
Stationery set, talking	1937	60	125	250	Ovaltine

RINGS, BRACELETS, AND WATCHES

ITEM	DATE	GOOD	FINE	MINT	SPONSOR
Bracelet, identification disc	1934	37	56	75	Ovaltine
Bracelet, identification tag	1939	15	30	50	Ovaltine
Necklace, metal figure of Annie on metal chain	1936	60	125	250	Ovaltine
Ring, altascope (fewer than 15 known)	1942	2500	8000	24000	Quaker
Ring, Annie's face	1934	27	55	110	Ovaltine
Ring, birthstone	1936	100	200	400	Ovaltine
Ring, initial, Secret Guard	1941	1300	2600	6000	Quaker
Ring, magnifying, Secret Guard	1941	1250	2300	4750	Quaker
Ring, mystic eye (lookaround)	1939	100	250	500	Ovaltine
Ring, secret compartment, silver star, triple mystery	1938	500	750	1500	Ovaltine
Ring, secret message, Silver Star	1937	95	190	375	Ovaltine
Ring, signet, two initials	1937	60	120	240	Ovaltine
Ring, silver star, crossed keys on star	1936	125	250	500	Ovaltine

TOYS

ITEM	DATE	GOOD	FINE	MINT	SPONSOR
Airplane, folding wing, Wright Pursuit Not found. Estimated price.	1941	500	1000	2000	Quaker
Compass, secret Egyptian, and sundial	1938	48	72	95	Ovaltine
Decoder, mysto-matic	1939	30	60	125	Ovaltine
Penlight, secret guard	1941	65	130	260	Quaker
Skates, roller	1938	50	100	200	Ovaltine
Stamp, rubber, Secret Guard	1941	20	100	200	Quaker
Whistle, dog, 3-way, Sandy's head	1940	60	120	250	Quaker

ITEM	DATE	GOOD	FINE	MINT	SPONSOR

Radio Orphan Annie secret Egyptian sundial compass

ITEM	DATE	GOOD	FINE	MINT	SPONSOR
Whistle, dog, 3-way, Annie's head	1941	75	150	300	Quaker

MUGS

ITEM	DATE	GOOD	FINE	MINT	SPONSOR
50th Annie-Versary	1982-83	15	30	65	Ovaltine
Beetleware, Annie and Sandy running	1935	20	35	75	Ovaltine
Beetleware, Annie and Sandy standing	1933	25	50	100	Ovaltine
Ceramic cup with handle, Annie alone	1932	20	40	75	Ovaltine
Shake-up, white, Annie and Sandy full length	1930	25	50	100	Ovaltine
Shake-up, white, Annie and Sandy heads	1935	27	55	110	Ovaltine
Shake-up, green	1940	40	80	160	Ovaltine
Shake-up, movie, has scenes from film	1982-83	8	16	32	Ovaltine
Shake-up, radio and film, drawing of Annie, says "Annie 1932"	1983	15	25	50	Ovaltine
Shake-up (Annie dances with milk bottle)	1938	50	105	150	Ovaltine
Shake-up, brown	1939	45	90	185	Ovaltine
Uncle Wiggily	1930-31	20	30	45	Ovaltine
Uncle Wiggily with Ovaltine sign on house	1930-31	25	40	55	Ovaltine

LONE RANGER

BADGES, PINS, AND TOKENS

ITEM	DATE	GOOD	FINE	MINT	SPONSOR
Badge, brass star, Republic Serial	1938	62	150	350	Republic
Badge, chief scout, red, blue and gold	Early 1940s	75	112	150	Silvercup Bread
Badge, deputy, secret compartment	1949	30	60	85	Cheerios
Badge, membership, Safety Scout	1934-38	15	30	45	Silvercup Bread
Badge, Miami Maid Safety Club	1937	15	30	45	Miami Maid
Badge, Safety Club	1938	22	33	45	Bond Bread
Omit this line-dup item		22	33	45	
Badge, Victory Corps	1942	32	48	65	Kix
Badges, membership, Safety Club, various brands	1938-40	15	20	40	Bond Bread, Butternut, Silvercup, etc.
Lucky piece, advertises 17th anniversary	1933-50	50	100	200	Cheerios
Pin, military, unmarked	1942	10	20	30	Cheerios
Pin, Silver, Hi-yo	1938	20	30	60	Bond Bread
Pinback, Safety Club	1934-38	25	50	75	Merita
Pinback, war bonds	1943-46	5	12	20	Kix
Tab	1969	10	15	20	Good Food Guys/LR Restaurant
Tab, victory corps	1942	20	25	32	Cheerioats
Token, good luck	1938-40	8	12	16	Bond Bread

APPAREL

ITEM	DATE	GOOD	FINE	MINT	SPONSOR
Bandanna	1949	15	30	45	Kix
Belt, glow-in-the dark	1951	75	112	150	Kix
Belt, leather, Texas cattleman's, Lone Ranger scenes	1941	30	45	90	Kix
Belt, safety, glo-in-dark	1941	30	45	60	Kix
Belt, Texas cattleman, scenes tooled into genuine leather	1941	30	60	90	Kix
Belt, Tonto's, beaded leather	1952	30	60	90	Kix
Billfold	1942	25	50	85	Kix
Mask	1934-38	20	40	60	Merita
Mask	1943-46	15	35	55	Kix
Mask, black. Promotes personal appearance by LR and Silver.					

ITEM	DATE	GOOD	FINE	MINT	SPONSOR
About last radio prem.	1953 or 4	25	38	50	Cheerios/Wheaties
Neckerchief for shirt or mask	1949-50	15	30	45	Cheerios
Polo shirt with hi-yo Silver design	1941	15	30	50	Cheerios
Tonto head dress and beadset	1964	8	12	16	Lone Ranger Restaurant

KITS

ITEM	DATE	GOOD	FINE	MINT	SPONSOR
Kit, movie membership	1957-82	15	30	60	Cheerios
Kit, Safety Club: letter, photo, and card	1950	40	40	60	Merita
Kit, Jr. deputy: card, tin badge, and plastic mask	1951-56	15	25	35	Cheerios/Wheaties

BOOKS AND MAGAZINES

ITEM	DATE	GOOD	FINE	MINT	SPONSOR
Album, victory battles of 1942-45	1945	60	150	300	Kix
Book, Christmas, safety club	1938	20	30	50	May Co.
Book, coloring	1951	20	30	40	Merita
Book, "Lone Ranger and Tonto Health and Safety"	1955	20	30	40	Merita
Book, "Lone Ranger Ranch Fun"	1955	15	30	35	Cheerios
Booklet, "How Lone Ranger Captured Silver," 7 ch.	1934	25	50	100	Bond Bread
Comics, giveaway, "His Mask and How He Met Tonto"	1951-56	10	15	20	Bond Bread
Comics, "First LR"	1938	700	2000	4000	Ice cream cone
Comics, giveaway, "How to be a Lone Ranger"	1954	10	15	20	Merita
Comics, giveaway, "Story of Silver"	1951-56	10	15	20	Cheerios
Comics, "Legend of Lone Ranger"	1969	10	15	20	Good Food Guys/Lone Ranger Restaurant
Manual, secret writing	1938-40	20	30	50	Bond Bread
Manual, Victory Corps	1942	20	40	50	Kix
News, Safety Club, Vol. 1, No. 1 to No. 6	1939, AUG, start	40	80	190	Bond Bread

CERTIFICATES, LETTERS, AND MEMBERSHIP CARDS

ITEM	DATE	GOOD	FINE	MINT	SPONSOR
Card, membership, war bonds	1943-46	20	40	60	Kix
Certificate, Safety Club	1938-40	25	50	100	Kix
Charter, Deputy Club	1951-56	25	50	100	Kix
Commission, chief scout	1934-38	20	40	60	Kix
Decoder, paper	1943-46	35	75	125	Weber's Bread
Folder, secret, deputy	1949	15	22	28	Cheerios

ITEM	DATE	GOOD	FINE	MINT	SPONSOR
Pledge letter, Safety Club	1934-38	10	20	35	Bond Bread
Portfolio, secret, National Defenders	1941	20	45	75	Kix
Tattoo decals	1944	50	100	200	Kix

PHOTOGRAPHS

ITEM	DATE	GOOD	FINE	MINT	SPONSOR
Photo	1941	20	30	50	Kix
Photo	1938-40	20	30	50	Kix
Photo, color	1938-40	20	30	50	Silvercup
Photo, four color	1938-40	25	50	60	Kix
Photo, Lone Ranger	1934-38	15	30	65	Kix
Photo, Tonto	1934-38	30	40	65	Kix
Photo, Michigan network	1933	20	40	75	local sponsor

CARDS AND LETTERS

ITEM	DATE	GOOD	FINE	MINT	SPONSOR
Letters, Safety Club, many different, ea.	1938-40	20	30	40	Bond Bread
Postcard	1938-40	20	40	50	Bond Bread
Postcard, chief scout, first degree	1934-38	30	60	120	Bond Bread
Postcard, chief scout, second degree	1934-38	30	60	120	Bond Bread
Postcard, chief scout, third degree	1934-38	45	90	180	Bond Bread
Postcard, chief scout, fourth degree	1934-38	20	60	240	Bond Bread

Part of the Lone Ranger Frontier Town still on the Cheerios box

ITEM	DATE	GOOD	FINE	MINT	SPONSOR

Part of the Lone Ranger Frontier Town set

ITEM	DATE	GOOD	FINE	MINT	SPONSOR
Postcard, contest, color	1954	20	30	40	Cheerios

BOXES AND BACKS

ITEM	DATE	GOOD	FINE	MINT	SPONSOR
Airbase cereal box, complete	1943	60	150	300	Kix
Airbase - sheet map	1943	50	100	299	Kix
Box backs, mystery, 10 ea.	1951-56	30	40	50	Wheaties and Kix
Coloring contest drawing from package back, ea.	1951	30	40	50	Kix
Frontier Town, full set		2000	3000	4000	Cheerios
Frontier Town, Northeast section	1948	125	250	500	Cheerios
Frontier Town, Northwest section	1948	125	250	500	Cheerios
Frontier Town, Southeast section	1948	125	250	500	Cheerios
Frontier Town, Southwest section	1948	125	250	500	Cheerios
Frontier Town, package backs, 9 total, ea.	1948	20	40	75	Cheerios

MISC. PAPER ITEMS

ITEM	DATE	GOOD	FINE	MINT	SPONSOR
Blotter	1938	5	10	15	Bond Bread
Cut-outs (Brace Beemer image)	1951-56	40	60	100	Merita
Flyer, introduction	1941	10	15	20	Kix
Map of the old West	1957-82	20	30	50	Wheaties
Posters, life size, LR & Tonto, ea.	1957-82	100	200	300	Wheaties

An advertisement for the Lone Ranger's Atomic Bomb Ring (1945)

Poster, "Win Silver's Colt"	1941	50	150	250	Bond Bread
Recipes, Ho Ling's	1938-40	20	30	40	Bond Bread
Safety Club, LR hunt map	1938-40	50	75	100	Bond Bread
Stationery set, 8 different, Victory Corp	1942	40	80	120	Kix

RINGS AND BRACELETS

Bracelet, charm	1938	250	500	1000	local

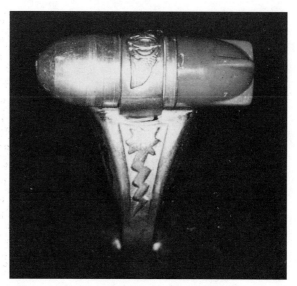

The Lone Ranger Atom Bomb ring

ITEM	DATE	GOOD	FINE	MINT	SPONSOR

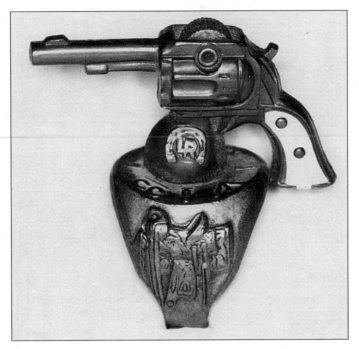

The Long Ranger plastic and metal six-shooter gun ring. The flint sparks when the wheel is turned.

ITEM	DATE	GOOD	FINE	MINT	SPONSOR
Bracelet, Lone Ranger	1938	350	700	1500	local
Ring, atom bomb	1947	40	80	125	Kix
Ring, flashlight	1948	30	60	95	Kix
Ring, movie film, w/8 mm Marine Corps film	1940	47	70	95	Cheerios
Ring, National Defenders (lookaround), military	1941	30	60	95	Cheerioats
Ring, photos of LR and Silver, military insignia	1942	200	400	600	Kix
Ring, picture of LR	1938	600	1500	3200	
Ring, picture of Tonto	1938	500	1250	3800	
Ring, silver saddle, with 16 mm film scenes	1952	62	93	125	Cheerios
Ring, six-shooter gun, plastic and metal, flint sparks when wheel turned	1947	75	112	150	Kix
Ring, weather, color square stone on top w litmus paper. No markings to identify as LR.	1938	32	48	65	Silver Cup Bread

HOW TO USE

the secret invisible ink that comes with this Lone Ranger "Silver Bullet"

Large White Tablet makes secret invisible ink. Dissolve in one tablespoon water. Use this ink to write secret messages, codes, passwords! Writing is invisible until you apply special developer.

Small Red Tablet is special developer. Dissolve tablet in two tablespoons water. Brush or wipe over secret writing and it will appear as if by magic!

These two tablets are absolutely non-toxic.

— **SPECIAL NOTICE!** —

Inside "Silver Bullet" is small metal ring. Attach this to small hole in rim of bullet. Provides a way to pin to clothes to avoid losing.

GIVE THIS

Good Turn Coupon

TO A FRIEND

It Will Help Speed Delivery!

FILL OUT and **mail** **AT ONCE!**

TO GENERAL MILLS, INC., DEPT. 180
MINNEAPOLIS 2, MINNESOTA

I am enclosing 15c and one Cheerios box-top. Please send me one Cheerios Lone Ranger "Silver Bullet", complete with built-in compass and secret invisible ink tablets.

(Print your name here)

(Print your address here)

(Town) *(Zone)* *(State)*

This enclosure came with the Lone Ranger's silver bullet with compass and secret compartment

Lone Ranger Hike-o-meter pedometer

TOYS

ITEM	DATE	GOOD	FINE	MINT	SPONSOR
Blackout kit, glow in the dark material, glow in dark pledge to flag, glow in the dark armband, plus instruction	1942	48	72	95	Kix
Bullet, silver, 45-caliber, secret compartment	1941	15	25	35	Kix
Bullet, silver, with compass and secret compartment	1947	35	70	100	Kix
Bullet, solid silver, Safety Club	1942	20	35	85	Kix
Gun, flashlight, secret compartment in handle	1949-50	25	55	90	Cheerios
Gun, rubber band, 6 different targets, cardboard	1938	100	200	450	Morton Salt
Gun, Victory Corp	1942	35	70	100	Kix
Hike-O-Meter	1951-56	20	30	45	Wheaties

A 1947 advertisement for the official Lone Ranger Pedometer

1940 advertisement for the Lone Ranger's Danger-Warning Siren

ITEM	DATE	GOOD	FINE	MINT	SPONSOR
Initial stamper, branding iron, unmarked	1951-56	20	30	50	Wheaties
Movie ranch wild west town plastic figures, 22 pieces	1957-82	150	350	500	Wheaties
Pedometer, aluminum rim	1948	30	60	90	Cheerios
Pistol, clicker, black (movie giveaway)	1939	50	100	200	Republic
Revolver, rapidfire	1957-82	20	30	50	Wheaties
Warning siren, national defenders	1941	30	70	125	Kix

LUM AND ABNER

ITEM	DATE	GOOD	FINE	MINT	SPONSOR
Badge, walkin' weather prophet	1936	15	30	50	
Button, "Let's 'lect Lum"	1936	10	20	30	
Family almanac	1936	8	12	16	
Family almanac	1937	8	12	16	
Family almanac	1938	8	12	16	
Malt maker	1936	35	65	150	Horlick
Newspaper, Pine Ridge News	1933	10	20	30	
Photo, Lum and Abner in and out of makeup	1937	8	12	16	

*"Let's 'lect Lum Edwards for President" button
(in poor condition)*

M

ITEM	DATE	GOOD	FINE	MINT	SPONSOR

MA PERKINS

ITEM	DATE	GOOD	FINE	MINT	SPONSOR
Book, recipe	1942	8	12	16	Oxydol
Photo	1938	8	12	16	Oxydol
Seed packets, ea.	1939	5	8	12	Oxydol

MAJOR BOWES

ITEM	DATE	GOOD	FINE	MINT	SPONSOR
Microphone, wood, with decal	1936	40	60	100	Chase & Sanborn
Newspapers, various years	1930s	5	8	12	Chase & Sanborn
Winners folders, various years	1930s	5	8	12	Chase & Sanborn

MANDRAKE THE MAGICIAN

ITEM	DATE	GOOD	FINE	MINT	SPONSOR
Card, membership	1940	20	40	60	Tastee Bread
Card, message	1940-42	10	20	30	Tastee Bread
Pin, magic club	1934	50	100	175	Tastee Bread
Pinback, magic club	1934	50	100	175	Tastee Bread
Sheet of special magic tricks	1934	10	20	30	Tastee Bread

MELVIN PURVIS, G-MAN & JR. G-MAN CORPS.

BADGES

ITEM	DATE	GOOD	FINE	MINT	SPONSOR
Badge, captain, secret operations, Law and Order Patrol	1937	30	50	100	Post Cereals
Badge, chief operative, Jr. G-man corps	1936	20	35	75	Post Cereals
Badge, girls' division, Jr. G-man corps	1936	20	35	60	Post Cereals
Badge, girls' division, secret operator	1937	15	30	55	Post Cereals
Badge, lieutenant, Law & Order Patrol, secret operator	Mid 1930s	30	50	100	Post Cereals
Badge, Law & Order Patrol, secret operator	Late 1930s	15	530	60	Post Cereals

ITEM	DATE	GOOD	FINE	MINT	SPONSOR
Badge, roving operative, Jr. G-man corps	1936	20	40	75	Post Cereals

PAPER AND MISCELLANEOUS ITEMS

ITEM	DATE	GOOD	FINE	MINT	SPONSOR
Wallet and card, official identification, Law and Order Patrol	1937	30	60	125	Post Cereals
Certification of appointment, captain, Law and Order Patrol	1937	10	15	20	Post Cereals
Commission, chief operative, Jr. G-Man Corps	1936	30	60	125	Post Cereals
Commission, roving operative, Jr. G-Man Corps	1936	10	15	20	Post Cereals
Identification card, Jr. G-Man Corps	1936	20	30	60	Post Cereals
Manual, secret operator, Law and Order Patrol	1937	20	40	60	Post Cereals
Manual, instructions, Jr. G-Man Corps	1936	20	40	60	Post Cereals
Notebook, secret operator, Law and Order Patrol	1937	25	50	75	Post Cereals
Pass, inner district, Law and Order Patrol	1937	20	30	60	Post Cereals
Photo, autographed by MP, Law and Order Patrol	1937	25	50	75	Post Cereals

RINGS AND STUDS

ITEM	DATE	GOOD	FINE	MINT	SPONSOR
Key ring, secret operator, Law and Order Patrol	1937	20	30	60	Post Cereals
Ring, Jr. G-Man Corps	1936	25	50	100	Post Cereals
Ring, Jr. G-Man, tiny for small child	1936	20	30	60	Post Cereals
Ring, Law and Order Patrol	1937	50	100	200	Post Cereals
Stud for buttonhole, Jr. G-Man, gold or silver	1936	20	30	40	Post Cereals

TOYS

ITEM	DATE	GOOD	FINE	MINT	SPONSOR
Fingerprint set, Jr. G-man Corps	1936	15	30	45	Post Cereals
Fingerprint detection tape and card, Law and Order Patrol	1937	20	30	60	Post Cereals
Flashlight pistol, Jr. G-Man Corps	1936	15	20	30	Post Cereals
Knife, Melvin Purvis, Law and Order Patrol	1937	25	50	100	Post Cereals

ITEM	DATE	GOOD	FINE	MINT	SPONSOR
Magnifying glass and handwriting study, Secret Operators, Law Order Patrol	1937	15	30	45	Post Cereals
Pen and pencil combination, Law and Order Patrol	1937	150	450	800	Post Cereals
Pencil, Law and Order Patrol	1937	50	100	200	Post Cereals
Shoulder holster, Law and Order Patrol	1937	25	50	100	Post Cereals

MICKEY MOUSE

ITEM	DATE	GOOD	FINE	MINT	SPONSOR
Mickey and Donald's Race to Treasure Island, 12 x 25"	1939	88	132	175	Standard Oil Giveaway
Mickey and Donald's Race to Treasure Island, US map, full color, 20 X 27" 1939		300	450	600	Calco giveaway, with stamps
Button, pinback, Mickey Mouse Club, copyright 1928-30 by W E Disney	1928-30	50	75	100	
Map, Mickey Mouse Globe Trotters, 38 x 20"	1937	325	488	650	NBC Bread
Map, Mickey Mouse Globe Trotters, 28 x 22", w/ all pictures pasted on	1937	325	488	650	NBC Bread
Map, Mickey Mouse Globe Trotters Map	1930s	325	488	650	Pevely Milk premium
Money, Official. MM cones dollar bills, denom. is "1," ea.	1930s	10	15	20	
Playboard, 9" high, MM		25	38	50	Comics giveaway

N

ITEM	DATE	GOOD	FINE	MINT	SPONSOR
NICK CARTER					
Badge, membership	1936	60	120	250	Nick Carter Magazine
Card, membership	1936	20	30	45	Nick Carter Magazine
Fingerprint kit	1936	39	75	125	Nick Carter Magazine

O

ITEM	DATE	GOOD	FINE	MINT	SPONSOR
OG, SON OF FIRE					
Figures, monsters and dinosaurs, ea.	1935	25	50	100	Libby Foods
Figures: Og, Ru, Nada, Black Caveman, ea.	1935	30	75	150	Libby Foods
Map	1935	100	200	400	Libby Foods
ONE MAN'S FAMILY					
Album, Barbour family	1951	10	15	20	Tender Leaf Tea
Book, "Fanny Barbour's Memory"	1940	12	24	36	Tender Leaf Tea
Booklet, "Father Barbour's This I Give..."	1953	10	15	20	Tender Leaf Tea
Booklet, history of Barbour family	1935	12	15	20	Tender Leaf Tea
Booklet, "I Believe in America"	1941	10	15	20	Tender Leaf Tea
Booklet, "One Man's Family Looks at Life"	1938	15	20	30	Tender Leaf Tea
Cookbook, 20th Anniversary souvenir	1952	10	15	20	Tender Leaf Tea
Diary, Teddy Barbour	1937	12	24	36	Tender Leaf Tea
Scrapbook, Barbour family	1946	10	15	20	Tender Leaf Tea
Scrapbook, Jack Barbour	1936	20	25	30	Tender Leaf Tea

P

ITEM	DATE	GOOD	FINE	MINT	SPONSOR
PHANTOM PILOT PATROL					
Badge, membership	1938	25	50	75	Langendorf Bread
POPEYE					
Pin, cloisonné, Olive Oyl	1937	20	30	60	Wheatena
Pin, cloisonné, POPEYE	1937	20	30	60	Wheatena
Pin, cloisonné, Wimpy	1937	20	30	60	Wheatena
Pin on card, ea.	1937	35	75	100	

Q

ITEM	DATE	GOOD	FINE	MINT	SPONSOR

QUIZ KIDS

Postcards	1949-52	3	6	9	

R

ITEM	DATE	GOOD	FINE	MINT	SPONSOR
RED RYDER					
Arrowhead, plastic, Daisy	1942-45	40	80	164	Langendorf
Decoder, rodeomatic, paper	1942-45	150	350	700	Langendorf
Decoder, sliding, paper	1941	100	200	500	Langendorf
Membership kit, decoder, super book of comics	1941	500	1200	3500	
Pin, member	1942-45	30	60	90	Langendorf
Pin, pony contest	1942-45	20	30	75	Langendorf
Pinback, Little Beaver	1942-45	15	22	45	Langendorf
Pinback, Red Ryder	1942-45	15	22	45	Langendorf
Token, good luck	1942-45	8	12	16	JCPenney
RENFREW OF THE MOUNTED					
Booklet, Around the Campfire with Carol and David	1936-40	10	20	39	Wonder Bread
Handbook for his friends	1936-40	20	30	49	Wonder Bread
Map of Wonder Valley	1936-40	30	80	150	Wonder Bread
Photo, Renfrew	1936-40	8	12	16	Wonder Bread
Pinback, cello, photo	1936-40	8	12	16	Wonder Bread
RIN TIN TIN					

PATCHES AND PINS

ITEM	DATE	GOOD	FINE	MINT	SPONSOR
Patches, paper, 7: Rusty, Major Swanson, Lt. Rip Masters, Cochise, Fort Apache, TTT, and 1 other, ea.	1954-56	8	10	12	Nabisco
Pennant, from membership kit	1954-56	75	150	225	Nabisco
Pin, pot metal, membership, from membership kit	1954-56	25	40	60	Nabisco

ITEM	DATE	GOOD	FINE	MINT	SPONSOR
Pin, rifle	1954-56	15	30	45	Nabisco
Pinback, name the puppy	1954-56	10	15	25	Nabisco

APPAREL

Beanie	1954-56	30	60	110	Nabisco
Belt, cavalry, from membership kit	1954-56	20	40	80	Nabisco
Hat, cavalry, from membership kit	1954-56	50	100	175	Nabisco
Sweatshirt	1954-56	30	50	100	Nabisco
T-shirt	1954-56	25	45	90	Nabisco

CARDS, PHOTOS, AND OTHER PAPER ITEMS

Ad cards, ea.	1954-56	4	8	10	Nabisco Shreaded Wheat
Card, club membership, from membership kit	1954-56	10	30	50	Nabisco
Photo and letter, cast, from membership kit	1954-56	20	30	40	Nabisco
Punchouts	1954-56	120	180	240	Nabisco

RINGS

Ring, plastic	TV 1950s	15	22	30	Nabisco
Ring, plastic, Rip Masters	1950s	17	26	35	Nabisco
Rings, plastic, ea.	1954-56	10	15	20	Nabisco

TOYS

Bugle, cavalry, from membership kit	1954-56	20	40	80	Nabisco
Dinosaur set, plastic	1954(radio-TV)	48	72	95	Nabisco
Figures, plastic, Fort Apache	1960	50	75	125	Nabisco
Game, "Ball-in-the-hole" (sealed coin-size games of Rinty, Rip Masters, Fort Apache, etc.), ea.	1954-56	9	13	18	Nabisco
Gun and holster, cavalry	1954-56	125	260	550	Nabisco
Stuffed dog, Rinty	1954-56	80	160	325	Nabisco
Televiewer, stero, from membership kit	1954-56	40	75	150	Nabisco
Totem poles, 8, ea.	1954-56	8	12	16	Nabisco
Wonderscope (telescope-microscope-compass)	1954(radio-tv)	30	45	60	Nabisco

UTENSILS

Canteen	1954-56	10	20	35	Nabisco
Mess kit, mug and bowl, from membership kit	1954-56	25	50	75	Nabisco

ITEM	DATE	GOOD	FINE	MINT	SPONSOR

ROCKY JONES

ITEM	DATE	GOOD	FINE	MINT	SPONSOR
Code card	c. 1953	20	50	100	Silvercup Bread
Pinback, membership	c. 1953	10	15	25	Silvercup Bread

ROOTIE KAZOOTIE

ITEM	DATE	GOOD	FINE	MINT	SPONSOR
Card, membership	Early TV	10	20	40	
Ring, Rootie Kazootie lucky spot	Early TV	200	500	800	
Ring, Rootie Kazootie television	Early TV	75	130	260	

ROY ROGERS

BADGES, COINS, MEDALS AND PINS

ITEM	DATE	GOOD	FINE	MINT	SPONSOR
Badge, signal, with mirror, secret compartment and whistle	1950	45	90	175	Quaker
Coin, lucky, large, Rider's Club	1952	10	20	35	Post
Coin, lucky, small, Rider's Club	1952	10	20	35	Post
Medals, western, 27, ea.	1953-55	6	15	30	Post Raisin Bran
Pinback set, 15, ea.	1953-55	6	15	30	Post
Tab, Rider's Club	1952	20	40	60	Post

PAPER ITEMS

ITEM	DATE	GOOD	FINE	MINT	SPONSOR
Ad, family contest	1953-55	10	20	30	Post
Ad, win trip to Hollywood contest	1949	10	20	30	Quaker
Ad for Rider's Club	1952	10	20	30	Post
Bang gun	1953-55	8	15	25	Post
Card, club, Rider's Club	1952	20	40	80	Post
Cards, pop-out, 36, ea.	1953-55	8	15	24	Post
Comic book, Rider's Club	1952	40	80	175	Post
Lariat, humming	1951	15	25	40	Quaker
Photo, 3-D and glasses, ea.	1953-55	10	15	20	Post
Photo, color, Roy and Trigger, Rider's Club	1952	8	12	25	Post
Postcard, contest	1948	5	10	15	Quaker Oats

RINGS

ITEM	DATE	GOOD	FINE	MINT	SPONSOR
Ring, Branding Iron	1948	65	125	250	Quaker

ITEM	DATE	GOOD	FINE	MINT	SPONSOR

Roy Rogers sterling silver signed saddle ring

ITEM	DATE	GOOD	FINE	MINT	SPONSOR
Ring, microscope	1947	35	75	150	Quaker Oats
Ring, Roy Rogers, 12, ea.	1953-55	20	40	80	Post
Ring, silver hat	1948	225	450	800	Quaker
Ring, saddle, sterling silver, signed	1948	200	400	600	Post

TOYS

ITEM	DATE	GOOD	FINE	MINT	SPONSOR
Double R Bar Ranch set	1953-55	100	200	400	Post
Paint by numbers set	1950s	30	55	110	Post

UTENSILS

ITEM	DATE	GOOD	FINE	MINT	SPONSOR
Mug, plastic, Toby, Quaker man	1950	20	40	80	Quaker
Mug, plastic Toby, Roy, face	1950	10	20	30	Quaker

S

ITEM	DATE	GOOD	FINE	MINT	SPONSOR

SCOOP WARD

ITEM	DATE	GOOD	FINE	MINT	SPONSOR
Badge, official reporter, news of youth	1930s	10	15	20	Ward's Soft Bun Bread

SECKATARY HAWKINS

ITEM	DATE	GOOD	FINE	MINT	SPONSOR
Button, membership	1932	9	12	16	Ralston
Coin, good luck	1932	30	60	120	Ralston
Comic strip reprint booklet, "The Red Runners"	1932	40	80	125	Ralston
Novel, paperback, Ghost of Lake Tapaho	1932	40	80	160	Ralston
Spinner, fair and square	1932	20	40	80	Ralston

SECRET THREE, THE

ITEM	DATE	GOOD	FINE	MINT	SPONSOR
Badge	1930	50	100	200	Three Minute Oats Cereal
Chevron, lieutenant's special	1930	40	80	160	Three Minute Oats Cereal
Equipment list	1930	15	30	60	Three Minute Oats Cereal
Handbook	1930	50	100	200	Three Minute Oats Cereal

SERGEANT PRESTON

ITEM	DATE	GOOD	FINE	MINT	SPONSOR
Button, membership, cello (double for tin)	1956	400	1000	2000	Quaker Puffed Rice and Wheat
Goggles, Trail, complete cereal box	1952	75	150	300	Quaker Puffed Rice and Wheat
T-shirt (not found, price est.)	1956	500	750	1000	Quaker Puffed Rice and Wheat

CARDS, COMICS, AND OTHER PAPER ITEMS

ITEM	DATE	GOOD	FINE	MINT	SPONSOR
Cards, dog, ea.	1949	3	5	8	Quaker Puffed Rice and Wheat

ITEM		DATE	GOOD	FINE	MINT	SPONSOR

A Sgt. Preston advertisement for Dog Picture Cards (1947)

ITEM	DATE	GOOD	FINE	MINT	SPONSOR
Cards, Yukon adventure story, 36 pc. set, ea. card	1950	5	7	15	Quaker Puffed Rice and Wheat
Cards, Yukon adventure story, 36 pc. set, ea. card	1956	5	7	15	Quaker Puffed Rice and Wheat
Cars, antique, 5 pieces	1954	50	80	175	Quaker Puffed Rice and Wheat
Postcard, contest	1950	10	20	25	Quaker Puffed Rice and Wheat
Comics, pocket, "How He Became a Sergeant"	1956	10	20	40	Quaker Puffed Rice and Wheat
Comics, pocket, "How He Found Yukon King"	1956	10	20	40	Quaker Puffed Rice and Wheat
Comics, pocket, "How Yukon King Saved Him From the Wolves"	1956	10	20	40	Quaker Puffed Rice and Wheat
Deed, Yukon land, 1 square inch	1955	15	25	50	Quaker Puffed Rice and Wheat
Map, color, Yukon Territory	1955	30	60	100	Quaker Puffed Rice and Wheat

ITEM	DATE	GOOD	FINE	MINT	SPONSOR
Photo, 8-1/2 x 11", black and white	1949	15	30	60	Quaker Puffed Rice and Wheat
Photo, postcard size, black and white	1949	15	30	50	Quaker Puffed Rice and Wheat
Photo, color, Richard Simmons	1956	15	35	75	Quaker Puffed Rice and Wheat
Poster, contest winner	1950	200	400	800	Quaker Puffed Rice and Wheat

PACKAGE BACKS AND BOXES

ITEM	DATE	GOOD	FINE	MINT	SPONSOR
Package back, adventure game, "Dog Sled Race"	1949	10	20	30	Quaker Puffed Rice and Wheat
Package back, adventure game, "SP Gets His Man"	1949	10	20	30	Quaker Puffed Rice and Wheat
Package back, adventure game, "Great Yukon River Race"	1949	10	20	30	Quaker Puffed Rice and Wheat
Package back, Yukon scenes to color (3), ea.	1952	10	20	30	Quaker Puffed Rice and Wheat
Package box, adv. game, "Great Yukon River Race," complete	1949	100	150	300	Quaker Puffed Rice and Wheat
Package box, adventure game, "SP Gets His Man," complete	1949	100	150	300	Quaker Puffed Rice and Wheat
Package box, adv. game, "Dog Sled Race," complete	1949	100	150	300	Quaker Puffed Rice and Wheat
Package box, complete, Yukon scenes to color (3), ea.	1952	100	200	300	Quaker Puffed Rice and Wheat
Yukon trail, cb models, 59 total from 8 boxes	1949	240	475	950	Quaker Puffed Rice and Wheat
Package box, "Yukon Trail," complete, ea.	1949	75	150	300	Quaker Puffed Rice and Wheat

TOYS

ITEM	DATE	GOOD	FINE	MINT	SPONSOR
Western gun collection, 5 pieces, ea.	1952	25	50	100	Quaker Puffed Rice and Wheat

ITEM	DATE	GOOD	FINE	MINT	SPONSOR
Detector, gold ore	1952	52	105	210	Quaker Puffed Rice and Wheat
Distance finder	1955	20	40	80	Quaker Puffed Rice and Wheat
Firefighting set	1940s	37	56	75	Quaker Puffed Rice and Wheat
Flashlight, signal	1949	25	50	100	Quaker Puffed Rice and Wheat
Knife, skinning	1954	100	200	300	Quaker Puffed Rice and Wheat
Land pouch, Klondike	1955	75	150	300	Quaker Puffed Rice and Wheat
Pedometer	1952	20	40	65	Quaker Puffed Rice and Wheat

Sergeant Preston pedometer

ITEM	DATE	GOOD	FINE	MINT	SPONSOR
Stove, camp, prospector's, unmarked	1954	75	150	300	Quaker Puffed Rice and Wheat
Tent, camp, prospector's, unmarked	1954	200	400	800	Quaker Puffed Rice and Wheat
Trail Kit, 10-in-1, electric	1956	250	375	500	Quaker Puffed Rice and Wheat
Trophy, North American big game set, ea.	1954	20	40	80	Quaker Puffed Rice and Wheat
Viewer, movie	1954	50	100	200	Quaker Puffed Rice and Wheat

ITEM	DATE	GOOD	FINE	MINT	SPONSOR
Western wagons, 5 pieces, ea.	1954	20	40	60	Quaker Puffed Rice and Wheat
Whistle, police, with nylon cord, brass	1950	25	38	50	Quaker Puffed Rice and Wheat

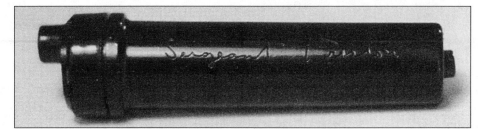

Sergeant Preston signal flashlight

VINYL RECORDS

ITEM	DATE	GOOD	FINE	MINT	SPONSOR
Record, "Case of the Indian Rebellion" (78 or 45 rpm)	1954	20	40	60	Quaker Puffed Rice and Wheat
Record, "Case of the Orphan Dog"	1954	20	40	60	Quaker Puffed Rice and Wheat
Record, "Challenge of the Yukon/Maple Leaf Forever"	1952	20	40	60	Quaker Puffed Rice and Wheat
Record, "How Preston Became a Sergeant"	1952	20	40	60	Quaker Puffed Rice and Wheat
Totem Pole Collection	1952	42	85	200	Quaker Puffed Rice and Wheat

THE SHADOW

ITEM	DATE	GOOD	FINE	MINT	SPONSOR
Ink blotter, several designs	1941	10	25	35	Blue Coal

The Shadow "It's So Easy To Heat with 'blue coal'" ink blotter

ITEM	DATE	GOOD	FINE	MINT	SPONSOR

The Shadow glow-in-the-dark blue coal ring

ITEM	DATE	GOOD	FINE	MINT	SPONSOR
Match book	1941	15	30	45	Blue Coal
Photo, actor Frank Readick in mask	1937	75	150	275	Blue Coal
Ring, glow in dark, blue coal jewel on white ring	1941	375	562	750	Blue Coal
Ring, same as JA crocodile, black stone (paper must validate)	1947	350	750	1100	Carey Salt

SHERLOCK HOLMES

ITEM	DATE	GOOD	FINE	MINT	SPONSOR
Book, hb, SH stories, Leigh Lovell as Watson on frontispiece	1933	15	25	40	George Washington Coffee
Book, hb, SH stories, Richard Gordon as SH on frontispiece	1933	15	25	40	George Washington Coffee
Map of Sherlock Holmes' London	1936	100	200	400	George Washington Coffee

SINGING LADY

ITEM	DATE	GOOD	FINE	MINT	SPONSOR
Book, Mother Goose story	1932-34	15	30	60	Kellogg's
Book, nursery songs and rhymes	1932-34	10	15	30	Kellogg's
Booklet, party kit	1936	20	40	80	Kellogg's
Mother Goose Film Booklet, Little Bo-Peep	1935	10	15	30	Kellogg's
Mother Goose Film Booklet, Old King Cole	1935	10	15	30	Kellogg's

ITEM	DATE	GOOD	FINE	MINT	SPONSOR
Mother Goose Film Booklet, Song Book	1935	10	15	30	Kellogg's
Mother Goose Film Booklet, The Old Woman in the Shoe	1935	10	15	30	Kellogg's
Mother Goose Film Booklet, Tommy Tucker's Birthday Party	1935	10	15	30	Kellogg's
Package backs, Mother Goose, ea.	1932-34	5	10	15	Kellogg's
Punch-out circus	1936	75	160	320	Kellogg's

SKIPPY

ITEM	DATE	GOOD	FINE	MINT	SPONSOR
Badge, captain Magnesia Toothpaste	1931-34	20	40	75	Wheaties or Phillips' Dental
Button, pinback, S.S.S.S. captain, all celluloid Magnesia Toothpaste	1930s	15	20	30	Wheaties or Phillips' Dental
Pinback, Racers' Club Magnesia Toothpaste	1931-34	20	35	75	Wheaties or Phillips' Dental
Big Little Book, "Story of Skippy" Toothpaste	1934	15	30	60	Phillips' Dental Magnesia
Card, Christmas Magnesia Toothpaste	1931-34	8	12	16	Wheaties or Phillips' Dental
Card, score and captain application	1931-34	150	300	600	Wheaties
Cards, activity, 12, ea.	1933	10	20	30	Wheaties
Certificate, life membership Magnesia Toothpaste	1931-34	20	40	60	Wheaties or Phillips' Dental
Club code, mystic circle Magnesia Toothpaste	1931-34	15	30	40	Wheaties or Phillips' Dental
Comics, "Skippy's Own Book of Comics," first comic of one character. (39 copies exist) Magnesia Toothpaste	1934	600	2000	3000	Wheaties or Phillips' Dental
Folder, secret code Magnesia Toothpaste	1931-34	20	40	60	Wheaties or Phillips' Dental
Picture Magnesia Toothpaste	1931-34	10	20	30	Wheaties or Phillips' Dental
Pledge, secret Magnesia Toothpaste	1931-34	20	40	60	Wheaties or Phillips' Dental
Compass Magnesia Toothpaste	1931-34	20	40	60	Wheaties or Phillips' Dental
Bowl, Beetleware, Skippy Magnesia Toothpaste	1931-34	10	15	20	Wheaties or Phillips' Dental
Bowl, cereal, ceramic, Skippy Magnesia Toothpaste	1931-34	100	200	300	Wheaties or Phillips' Dental

ITEM	DATE	GOOD	FINE	MINT	SPONSOR
Bowl, cereal, ceramic, Snooky Magnesia Toothpaste	1931-34	70	125	275	Wheaties or Phillips' Dental

SKY BIRDS

ITEM	DATE	GOOD	FINE	MINT	SPONSOR
Ring, propeller, brass and silver. (Gum premium, often considered to be a radio premium)	1930s	10	12	25	Goudey Gum premium

SKY KING

ITEM	DATE	GOOD	FINE	MINT	SPONSOR
Pinback, safety	1953	10	12	25	
Postcard	1953	10	20	40	Nabisco
Postcard, color photo of Sky	1953	8	16	24	Nabisco
Punch-out Admiral TV studio, Sky King, Peter Pan characters	1953	30	60	95	Admiral TV

RINGS

ITEM	DATE	GOOD	FINE	MINT	SPONSOR
Ring, Aztec Indian	1953	250	500	1000	Peter Pan Peanut Butter
Ring, kaleidoscope (prototype only)	1950				(Never offered)
Ring, Navajo Indian	1953	88	132	175	Peter Pan Peanut Butter
Ring, electronic television	1953	88	132	175	Peter Pan Peanut Butter
Ring, magni-glo writing	1953	32	65	130	Peter Pan Peanut Butter
Ring, magni-glo	1953	88	132	175	Peter Pan Peanut Butter
Ring, mystery picture, no picture	1953	30	60	100	Peter Pan Peanut Butter
Ring, mystery picture (rare complete)	1953	350	700	1000	Peter Pan Peanut Butter

Sky King teleblinker ring

ITEM	DATE	GOOD	FINE	MINT	SPONSOR
Ring, radar signal	1953	40	80	160	Peter Pan Peanut Butter
Ring, teleblinker	1950	88	132	175	Peter Pan Peanut Butter

TOYS

Address stamping kit	1950	30	45	60	Peter Pan Peanut Butter
Microscope, detecto	1950	47	72	95	Peter Pan Peanut Butter
Signal scope	1947	62	93	125	Peter Pan Peanut Butter
Statues, small plastic: Sky King, Penny, Sky King's horse, Sky King's plane The Songbird, Nabisco giveaways, ea.	1950s	15	22	30	Wheat Honey, Rice Honey
Writer, spy-detecto	1949	62	93	125	Peter Pan Peanut Butter

SPACE PATROL

Badge, plastic	1950-55	80	175	350	Ralston
Belt, code, jet glow, decoder	1951	125	188	250	Ralston
Buckle only	1950-55	60	80	160	Ralston
Space helmet	1954	162	243	325	Ralston
Goggles	1950-55	47	72	95	Ralston

BOOKS, CARDS, AND PAPER ITEMS

Book, coloring	1950-55	25	45	90	Ralston
Card, membership	1950-55	25	50	100	Ralston
Card, Ralston rocket	1950-55	30	60	120	Ralston
Cards, trading, 40, ea.	1950-55	10	20	35	Ralston
Catalog, premiums	1950-55	30	60	125	Ralston
Catalog, toys	1950-55	25	50	75	Ralston
Chart of universe	1950-55	50	100	200	Ralston
Flyer, blood donor, special mission	1950-55	25	75	150	Ralston
Handbook	1950-55	40	80	120	Ralston
Handbook, reprint	1950-55	3	5	6	Ralston
Photo	1950-55	30	60	90	Ralston
Pictures, magic, space, 24, ea.	1950-55	10	20	35	Ralston

RINGS

Ring, hydrogen ray gun	1950-55	75	150	300	Ralston
Ring, plastic	1950-55	300	750	1500	Ralston
Ring, printing with ink pad	1950-55	150	300	600	Ralston
Ring, with secret powder compartment	1950-55	125	188	250	Ralston
Ring, telescope-microscope-decoder	1954	125	250	500	Ralston

ITEM	DATE	GOOD	FINE	MINT	SPONSOR
TOYS					
Binoculars	1950-55	100	150	200	Ralston
Cockpit, control panel	1950-55	500	1500	2500	Nestles
Coin album, interplanetary	1950-55	50	100	150	Ralston
Coins, 4 values of moon, Saturn and Terra. Gold, blue, and	1950-55				
black. ea.	1950-55	8	12	18	Ralston
Coins, silver (same as others)	1950-55	10	15	25	Ralston
Diplomatic pouch, contains money, stamps, etc.	1950-55	125	188	250	Ralston
Gun, cosmic smoke, long barrel, green	1950-55	90	180	320	Ralston
Gun, cosmic smoke, short barrel, red	1950-55	90	180	320	Ralston
Lunar fleet base	1950-55	400	900	3000	Ralston
Microscope	1950-55	95	190	375	Ralston
Periscope	1950-55	95	150	450	Ralston
Project-o-scope	1950-55	100	200	400	Ralston
Rocket launcher, cosmic	1950-55	100	200	400	Ralston
Rocket ship balloon in envelope	1950-55	50	100	200	Ralston
Space ship	1950-55	88	132	175	Ralston
Space-O-Phone	1952	88	132	175	Ralston
Totem head, Martian	1950-55	100	200	400	Ralston

SPEED GIBSON

ITEM	DATE	GOOD	FINE	MINT	SPONSOR
Badge, flying police	1938	20	40	80	Dreikorn's Bread
Badge, member, plezol, red	1938	10	20	40	Plezol Bread

Speed Gibson green secret police badge

ITEM	DATE	GOOD	FINE	MINT	SPONSOR
Badge, secret police, green	1938	10	20	40	various local sponsors
Book, code	1938	35	75	150	various local sponsors
Game, "Great Clue Hunt" map	1938	80	175	350	various local sponsors
Newspaper, Wings	1938	25	50	100	various local sponsors
Rocket gyro, shooting	1938	40	80	175	various local sponsors
Shield, flying police	1938	20	40	80	various local sponsors

THE SPIDER

Card, membership	1936	50	100	200	Spider Magazine
Ring	1936	1650	4500	9500	Spider Magazine

STRAIGHT ARROW

Bandanna	1949	40	60	100	Nabisco
Headband, Comanche, with tribe card and sign language instructions	1949	50	100	200	Nabisco
Patch, shoulder, tribal	1950	20	30	40	Nabisco

MANUALS AND PAPER ITEMS

Cards, Injun-Nuity, Book 1, 36 cards	1949	25	50	100	Nabisco
Cards, Injun-Nuity, Book 2, 36 cards	1950	25	50	100	Nabisco
Cards, Injun-Nuity, Book 3, 36 cards	1951	15	50	100	Nabisco
Cards, Injun-Nuity, Book 4, 36 cards	1952	25	50	100	Nabisco
Manual, "Secrets of Indian Lore and Know How" (Books 1 and 2)	1950	15	30	45	Nabisco

BRACELETS, RINGS, AND TIE CLASPS

Bracelet, plastic with gold arrowhead and cowry shell	1950	38	75	150	Nabisco
Ring, face	early 1950s	48	72	95	
Ring, gold arrow	1949	35	70	135	Nabisco
Ring, gold nugget, picture, with picture intact	1950	70	140	275	Nabisco
Ring, magic cave, reissue, new art, customer's photos	1988	20	30	40	
Tie clasp, arrow	1950	100	150	300	Nabisco

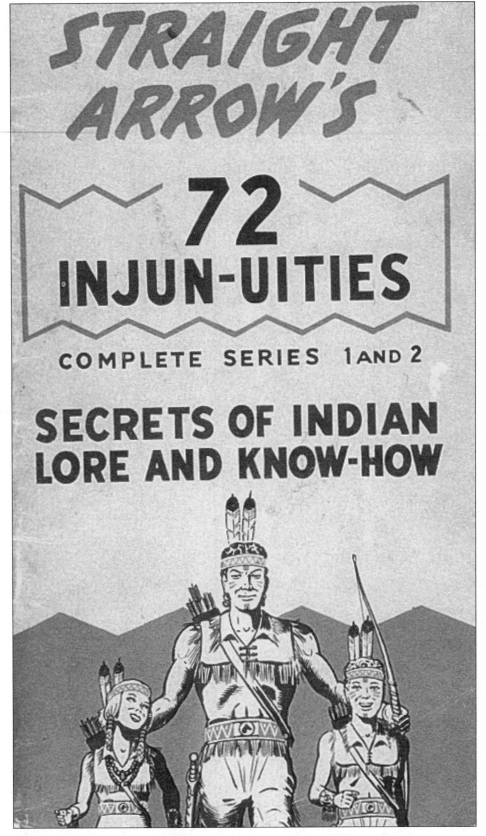

The Complete Series 1 and 2 of Straight Arrow's 72 Injun-uities

ITEM	DATE	GOOD	FINE	MINT	SPONSOR

Straight Arrow gold nugget ring with picture

TOYS

ITEM	DATE	GOOD	FINE	MINT	SPONSOR
Arrowhead, rite-a-lite	1951	160	375	950	Nabisco
Game, target, lithographed tin target board, 10 x 14"	1950	50	100	200	National Biscuit Co.
Puppets, props and scripts for a show	1952	20	30	40	Nabisco
puzzles, 12 dif., ea.	1949	15	30	40	Nabisco
Tom-tom and beater	1949	655	175	275	Nabisco

SUPER CIRCUS

ITEM	DATE	GOOD	FINE	MINT	SPONSOR
Book, Fourth Anniversary	1952	20	40	80	
Button, Mary Hartline	1950s	10	15	20	
Doll, Mary Hartline	1950s	40	80	160	
Photo, postcard size with autographs on reverse	1950s	15	25	50	
Puppets, Mary and Cliffy	1950s	35	75	150	
Side show	1950s	15	30	45	
Snicker Shack	1950s	8	16	24	

SUPERMAN

BUTTONS, BADGES, PINS, AND INSIGNIAS

ITEM	DATE	GOOD	FINE	MINT	SPONSOR
Badge	1940	600	1500	2500	GUM, INC.
Badge, Superman Tim	1942-50	30	40	50	TO-LEE GUM

ITEM	DATE	GOOD	FINE	MINT	SPONSOR
Button (alternate SM logo)	1939	30	65	120	Action Comics
Button, Action Comics	1938-42	30	60	90	Action Comics
Button, cello	1938-42	22	45	60	Action Comics
Button, membership, Superman Tim	1942-50	15	20	25	Tim Club
Button, Superman Tim membership, Tim's head in circle	1942-50	15	20	25	Tim Club
Button, pinback, Supermen of America, 1-3/8	1942-50	32	48	65	Tim Club
Button, Superman of America	1942-50	30	40	50	Tim Club
Button, Superman with white shirt	1938-42	300	600	1000	DC Comics
Button or badge, "Drink More Milk"	1950-59	35	70	125	local sponsors
Patch, Superman Tim	1942-50	250	500	750	Tim Club
Pennant	1942-50	79	150	200	Tim Club
Pin, Junior Defense League	1938-42	45	90	200	local sponsors
Pin, Superman American	1938-42	30	40	80	local sponsors
Pin, Read Superman Action Comics Magazine	1940s	22	33	45	DC Comics
Premium club set: certificate, button and decoder	1939-49	100	200	400	DC Comics

PEP COMIC PINS

ITEM	DATE	GOOD	FINE	MINT	SPONSOR
Abretha Breeze	1945-47	10	12	18	Pep
Andy Gump	1945-47	10	12	18	Pep
Auntie Blossom	1945-47	10	12	18	Pep
Barney Google	1945-47	10	12	18	Pep
Blondie	1945-47	10	12	18	Pep
Breezi	1945-47	10	12	18	Pep
Brenda Starr	1945-47	10	12	18	Pep
B. O. Plenty	1945-47	10	12	18	Pep
Casper	1945-47	10	12	18	Pep
Chester Gump	1945-47	10	12	18	Pep
Chief Brandon	1945-47	10	12	18	Pep
Cindy	1945-47	10	12	18	Pep
Corky	1945-47	10	12	18	Pep
Dagwood	1945-47	10	12	18	Pep
Daisy	1945-47	10	12	18	Pep
Denny	1945-47	10	12	18	Pep
Dick Tracy	1945-47	12	16	24	Pep
Don Winslow	1945-47	12	16	24	Pep

ITEM	DATE	GOOD	FINE	MINT	SPONSOR
Emma	1945-47	10	12	18	Pep
Fat Stuff	1945-47	10	12	18	Pep
Felix the Cat	1945-47	10	12	18	Pep
Fire Chief	1945-47	10	12	18	Pep
Flash Gordon	1945-47	12	14	26	Pep
Flattop	1945-47	10	12	18	Pep
Fritz	1945-47	10	12	18	Pep
Goofy	1945-47	10	12	18	Pep
Gravel Gertie	1945-47	10	12	18	Pep
Greezie	1945-47	10	12	18	Pep
Hans	1945-47	10	12	18	Pep
Harold Teen	1945-47	10	12	18	Pep
Henry	1945-47	10	12	18	Pep
Herby	1945-47	10	12	18	Pep
Inspector	1945-47	10	12	18	Pep
Jiggs	1945-47	10	12	18	Pep
Judy	1945-47	10	12	18	Pep
Junior Tracy	1945-47	10	12	18	Pep
Kayo	1945-47	10	12	18	Pep
Lillums	1945-47	10	12	18	Pep
Lilums	1945-47	10	12	18	Pep
Little Joe	1945-47	10	12	18	Pep
Little King	1945-47	10	12	18	Pep
Little Moose	1945-47	10	12	18	Pep
Lord Plushbottom	1945-47	10	12	18	Pep
Ma Winkle	1945-47	10	12	18	Pep
Mac	1945-47	10	12	18	Pep
Maggie	1945-47	10	12	18	Pep
Mama De Stross	1945-47	10	12	18	Pep
Mama Katzenjammer	1945-47	10	12	18	Pep
Mamie	1945-47	10	12	18	Pep
Min Gump	1945-47	10	12	18	Pep
Moon Mullins	1945-47	10	12	18	Pep
Mr. Bailey	1945-47	10	12	18	Pep
Mr. Bibbs	1945-47	10	12	18	Pep
Nina	1945-47	10	12	18	Pep
Olive Oyl	1945-47	10	12	18	Pep
Orphan Annie	1945-47	12	16	24	Pep
Pan Patten	1945-47	10	12	18	Pep

ITEM	DATE	GOOD	FINE	MINT	SPONSOR
Pat Patton	1945-47	10	12	18	Pep
Perry Winkle	1945-47	10	12	18	Pep
Phantom	1945-47	10	12	20	Pep
Pop Jenks	1945-47	10	12	18	Pep
Popeye	1945-47	10	12	20	Pep
Punjab	1945-47	10	12	18	Pep
Rip Winkle	1945-47	10	12	18	Pep
Sandy	1945-47	10	12	18	Pep
Shadow (Harold Teen character, not The Shadow)	1945-47	10	12	18	Pep
Skeezix	1945-47	10	12	18	Pep
Smilin' Jack	1945-47	10	12	20	Pep
Smitty	1945-47	10	12	18	Pep
Smoky Stover	1945-47	10	12	18	Pep
Snuffy Smith	1945-47	10	12	18	Pep
Spud	1945-47	10	12	18	Pep
Sundown	1945-47	10	12	18	Pep
Superman (many)	1945-47	12	16	24	Pep
Tess Trueheart	1945-47	10	12	18	Pep
The Captain	1945-47	10	12	18	Pep
Tilda	1945-47	10	12	18	Pep
Tillie the Toiler	1945-47	10	12	18	Pep
Tiny Tim	1945-47	10	12	18	Pep
Toots	1945-47	10	12	18	Pep

A Superman Pep Comic pin

ITEM	DATE	GOOD	FINE	MINT	SPONSOR
Uncle Avery	1945-47	10	12	18	Pep
Uncle Bim	1945-47	10	12	18	Pep
Uncle Walt	1945-47	10	12	18	Pep
Uncle Willie	1945-47	10	12	18	Pep
Vitamin Flintheart	1945-47	10	12	18	Pep
Warbucks	1945-47	10	12	18	Pep
Wilmer	1945-47	10	12	18	Pep
Wimpy	1945-47	10	12	18	Pep
Winnie Winkle	1945-47	10	12	18	Pep
Winnie's twins	1945-47	10	12	18	Pep

PEP MILITARY INSIGNIAS

ITEM	DATE	GOOD	FINE	MINT	SPONSOR
2nd Bomb Squadron	1944-45	3	4	5	Pep
17th Bomb Squadron	1944-45	3	4	5	Pep
24th Bomb Squadron	1944-45	3	4	5	Pep
25th Bomb Squadron	1944-45	3	4	5	Pep
27th Bomb Squadron	1944-45	3	4	5	Pep
29th Bomb Squadron	1944-45	3	4	5	Pep
41th Bomb Squadron	1944-45	3	4	5	Pep
47th Bomb Squadron	1944-45	3	4	5	Pep
48th Bomb Squadron	1944-45	3	4	5	Pep
53rd Bomb Squadron	1944-45	3	4	5	Pep
56th Bomb Squadron	1944-45	3	4	5	Pep
70th Bomb Squadron	1944-45	3	4	5	Pep
70th Bomb Squadron	1944-45	3	4	5	Pep
96th Bomb Squadron	1944-45	3	4	5	Pep
99th Bomb Squadron	1944-45	3	4	5	Pep
306th Bomb Squadron	1944-45	3	4	5	Pep
370th Bomb Squadron	1944-45	3	4	5	Pep
385th Bomb Squadron	1944-45	3	4	5	Pep
391st Bomb Squadron	1944-45	3	4	5	Pep
402nd Bomb Squadron	1944-45	3	4	5	Pep
424th Bomb Squadron	1944-45	3	4	5	Pep
431st Bomb Squadron	1944-45	3	4	5	Pep
44th Fighter Squadron	1944-45	3	4	5	Pep
Marine Bomb Squadron 433	1944-45	3	4	5	Pep
Marine Fighter Squadron VMF-224	1944-45	3	4	5	Pep
Marine Torpedo Bomber Squadron 232	1944-45	3	4	5	Pep
Navy Bomber Fighter Squadron 12	1944-45	3	4	5	Pep

ITEM	DATE	GOOD	FINE	MINT	SPONSOR
Navy Bomber Squadron 11	1944-45	3	4	5	Pep
Navy Cruiser Scot Squadron 2	1944-45	3	4	5	Pep
Navy Patrol Squadron 23	1944-45	3	4	5	Pep
Navy Stagron 14	1944-45	3	4	5	Pep
Navy Torpedo Bomber Squadron 232	1944-45	3	4	5	Pep
Navy Torpedo Squadron 3	1944-45	3	4	5	Pep
Navy Torpedo Squadron 32	1944-45	3	4	5	Pep
103rd Observation Squadron	1944-45	3	4	5	Pep
94th Pursuit Squadron	1944-45	3	4	5	Pep
VB-13	1944-45	3	4	5	Pep
VO-3	1944-45	3	4	5	Pep

APPAREL

ITEM	DATE	GOOD	FINE	MINT	SPONSOR
Buckle and belt	1945	175	350	500	Kellogg's
Masks, ea.	1950-59	10	20	30	
Sweatshirt, Superman Goodstuff, Superman Tim	1942-50	40	50	60	Tim Club
T-shirt	1950-59	8	12	24	

BOOKS AND OTHER PAPER ITEMS

ITEM	DATE	GOOD	FINE	MINT	SPONSOR
Book, Christmas play, Superman Tim	1942-50	10	20	30	Tim Club
Card, member, Defense Club of America	1944	30	65	95	
Cards, membership, Superman Tim, ea.	1942-50	25	50	75	
Cards, puzzle, Superman Tim	1942-50	25	50	75	
Certificate, membership	1938-42	45	90	120	Action Comics
Dangle Dandy	1959	5	12	20	Kellogg's
Manuals, monthly, Superman Tim	1942	30	60	125	Tim Club
Manuals, monthly, Superman Tim	1943	30	60	125	Tim Club
Manuals, monthly, Superman Tim	1946	40	80	200	Tim Club
Manuals, monthly, Superman Tim	1947	30	60	125	Tim Club
Manuals, monthly, Superman Tim	1948	30	60	125	Tim Club
Manuals, monthly, Superman Tim	1949	30	60	125	Tim Club
Manuals, monthly, Superman Tim	1950	30	60	125	Tim Club
Postcards, birthday, Superman Tim, ea.	1942-50	15	30	35	Tim Club
Press card for stamps	1942-50	10	20	40	Tim Club
Red backs, Superman Tim	1942-50	8	12	16	Tim Club
Stamps, Superman Tim, ea.	1942-50	20	40	60	Tim Club

ITEM	DATE	GOOD	FINE	MINT	SPONSOR

RINGS

ITEM	DATE	GOOD	FINE	MINT	SPONSOR
Ring	1950-59	25	50	100	Nestles
Ring, airplane	1948	60	125	250	Pep: not a radio premium
Ring, airplane, F-87, Corn Flakes	1948	55	110	175	Pep
Ring, Crusader's	1947	125	188	250	Kellogg's
Ring, initial, secret compartment, paper picture inside	1938-42	5000	10000	20000	
Ring, Pep airplane	1948	35	70	150	Pep
Ring, Superman Comics Magazine	1938	1500	50000	100000	DC Comics
Ring, Superman Tim Club	1942-50	1500	6000	14000	Tim
Rings, Pep: Jack Kramer, Dennis O'Keefe, Burt Lancaster, Sitting Bull, Pocahontas, Pan American Clipper, Douglas F-3D Sky Knight, Republic XF91, Thundercepter, ea.	1947	10	20	30	Pep

TOYS

ITEM	DATE	GOOD	FINE	MINT	SPONSOR
Airplane, balsa wood, 33 models, ea.	1943-44	12	25	40	Pep
Airplane, cardboard, 40 models, ea.	1943-44	10	20	30	Pep
Parachute rocket	1940	400	2000	3000	H-O Oats
Rocket and launcher, Krypton, red	1949	50	100	200	
Rockets (extra), blue and green, set	1950-59	20	40	80	
Superman, flying	1950-59	75	150	300	
Walkie-talkie	1945	60	125	250	Kellogg's

RECORDINGS

ITEM	DATE	GOOD	FINE	MINT	SPONSOR
Radio episodes, 3 vols., ea., intros by Jim Harmon	1975	5	10	20	Kellogg's

T

ITEM	DATE	GOOD	FINE	MINT	SPONSOR

TARZAN

STATUES

ITEM	DATE	GOOD	FINE	MINT	SPONSOR
Complete set	1932-35	475	700	950	Fould's Products
Tarzan	1932-35	50	100	200	Fould's Products
Cannibal	1932-35	30	60	90	Fould's Products
Cheetah (panther)	1932-35	30	60	90	Fould's Products
D'arnot, French Lieutenant	1932-35	30	60	90	Fould's Products
Jane Porter	1932-35	30	60	90	Fould's Products
Kala (ape mother)	1932-35	30	60	90	Fould's Products
Numa (lion)	1932-35	30	60	90	Fould's Products
Pirate	1932-35	30	60	90	Fould's Products
Three monkeys	1932-35	30	60	90	Fould's Products
Witch doctor	1932-35	30	60	90	Fould's Products
Folder offer	1932-35	30	60	90	Fould's Products
Instruction sheets for figures, ea.	1932-35	30	60	90	Fould's Products

TOYS

ITEM	DATE	GOOD	FINE	MINT	SPONSOR
Paint set, water colors	1932-35	50	100	200	Signal Oil
Map of jungle and treasure hunt and others	1932-35	150	300	600	Weston Biscuit, Kolynos,

BADGES

ITEM	DATE	GOOD	FINE	MINT	SPONSOR
Tarzan Radio Club, name of various sponsors on badge including Burley Coffee, KSL Royal Bakers, Nielen, Signal Oil, etc.	1932-35	175	350	700	
Tarzan Safety Club	1932-35	100	200	400	

TENNESSEE JED

ITEM	DATE	GOOD	FINE	MINT	SPONSOR
Blotter	1945-47	8	15	30	Tip Top Bread

ITEM	DATE	GOOD	FINE	MINT	SPONSOR
Booklet, magic tricks	1945-47	15	20	30	Tip Top Bread
Comic book (8 x 10", 16 p)	1945	30	60	125	Top Top Bread
Gun, atom	1945-47	20	30	40	Tip Top Bread
Gun, paper	1945-47	20	30	40	Tip Top Bread
Lariat	1940s	37	53	75	Tip Top Bread
Mask, paper	1945-47	15	30	45	Tip Top Bread
Pocket puzzle	1945-47	15	30	45	Tip Top Bread
Ring, look around (modified Tom Mix)	1946	125	250	500	Tip Top Bread
Ring, magnet (modified Tom Mix)	1946	125	250	500	Tip Top Bread

TERRY AND THE PIRATES

ITEM	DATE	GOOD	FINE	MINT	SPONSOR
Buttons, set of 5	1953	10	20	25	Canada Dry (TV)
Drawings, comic strip cast, set of 6	1944	100	200	450	Quaker
Comics, pocket size, 36 pages	1953	25	50	100	Canada Dry (TV)
"Dragon Lady in Distress"					
"Forced Landing"					
"Hotshot Charlie Flies Again"					
Contest ad, Terry jingle	1945	9	12	25	Quaker
Game book, "Ruby of Ghenghis Khan"	1942	250	650	1750	Libby, McNeil, Libby
Photo, mascot plane	1943-48	10	22	45	Quaker
Ring, glow in the dark, crocodiles on sides	1947	75	150	350	Quaker
Ring, gold detector	1949	35	70	150	Quaker
Terryscope	1941	150	350	750	Libby, McNeil, Libby
Victory airplane spotter	1942	75	150	300	Libby, McNeil, Libby

TOM CORBETT, SPACE CADET

ITEM	DATE	GOOD	FINE	MINT	SPONSOR
Badge	Early 1950s	35	75	150	Kellogg's
Belt buckle decoder	Early 1950s	75	150	300	Kellogg's

MEMBERSHIP KIT

ITEM	DATE	GOOD	FINE	MINT	SPONSOR
Membership kit, complete	1952	150	300	600	Kellogg's
Decoder, cardboard	1952	30	45	60	Kellogg's
Pinback, membership	1952	10	12	16	Kellogg's
Patch	1952	15	20	25	Kellogg's
Space Cadet News, Vol. 1, No. 1	1952	20	30	40	Kellogg's
Photo, cadet cast	1952	10	15	20	Kellogg's
Certificate, space academy	1952	15	20	25	Kellogg's

ITEM	DATE	GOOD	FINE	MINT	SPONSOR

PAPER ITEMS

ITEM	DATE	GOOD	FINE	MINT	SPONSOR
Package back with space cadet equipment, 4, ea.	1950s	15	20	30	Kellogg's
Album, bread end labels	1950s	15	20	35	Kellogg's
Package, complete	1950s	60	120	240	

RINGS

ITEM	DATE	GOOD	FINE	MINT	SPONSOR
Ring, face	1950s	30	40	50	Kellogg's
Ring, rocket with expansion band	1950s	20	30	60	Kellogg's
Rings, 12: Space Cruiser, Rocket Scout, Space Academy, Space					
Suit, Space Helmet, Corbett-Space Cadet, Cadet dress uniform, girl's space uniform, parallo-ray gun, strate-telescope, sound ray gun, in box, ea.	1950-55	20	30	35	Kellogg's

TOM MIX

BADGES, BUTTONS, MEDALS, AND PATCHES

ITEM	DATE	GOOD	FINE	MINT	SPONSOR
Badge, gold ore	1939	37	56	75	Ralston
Badge, ranch boss	1938	100	250	525	Ralston
Badge, sheriff, Dobie County, siren	1946	23	55	110	Ralston
Badge, six-gun, decoder	1941	65	130	260	Ralston
Badge, Straight shooters, silver or gold	1937	30	45	60	Ralston
Badge, wrangler, 3/4 view of Mix' head	1938	25	50	175	Ralston

Tom Mix six-gun decoder badge

Tom Mix Straight Shooter badge (produced in both silver and gold)

Tom Mix wrangler badge, 3/4 view of Mix's head

Tom Mix Captain spur medal

ITEM	DATE	GOOD	FINE	MINT	SPONSOR
Badge, wrangler, front view Mix' head	1938	25	50	175	Ralston
Buttons, decoder, 5 pieces, set	1946	60	125	250	Ralston

Tom Mix horseshoe nail ring and Tom Mix cloth arm patch, TM-bar Straight Shooters (predominantly blue)

Tom Mix cloth arm patch, TM-Bar Straight Shooters (predominantly black)

ITEM	DATE	GOOD	FINE	MINT	SPONSOR
Buttons, decoder, Curley Bradley, pinback only	1946	18	40	60	Ralston
Medal, Captain, spur	1941	65	125	250	Ralston, Bounceback
Medal, horseshoe and checkerboard ribbon, glow-in-dark plastic	1945	35	65	125	Ralston
Medal, sharpshooter, glow in the dark	1949	75	112	150	Ralston
Medal, straight shooters campaign, gold	1937	37	56	75	Ralston
Medal, straight shooters campaign, silver	1937	37	56	75	Ralston
Patch, arm, TM-Bar Straight Shooters, cloth, predominantly blue	1933	25	50	75	Ralston
Patch, arm, TM-Bar Straight Shooters, cloth, predominantly red	1945	30	60	90	Ralston
Patch, arm, TM-Bar Straight Shooters, cloth, predominantly black	1983	20	30	40	Ralston

APPAREL

Bandanna, TM-Bar	1933	75	150	200	Ralston
Baseball cap	1935	25	38	50	Ralston
Belt and buckle, cowboy, plastic, secret compartment	1950-51	65	125	250	Ralston
Buckle and belt, championship, TM-Bar, cloth	1936	75	155	300	Ralston
Buckle only from championship buckle and belt	1936	35	45	60	Ralston
Cap, skull, TM-Bar	1936	22	45	60	Ralston
Chaps, cowboy, TM-Bar	1935	75	150	300	Ralston

Tom Mix bandanna, TM brand

Tom Mix cowboy plastic belt and buckle with a secret compartment

Tom Mix cloth championship buckle and belt, TM-Bar

Tom Mix leather cuffs

ITEM	DATE	GOOD	FINE	MINT	SPONSOR
Chaps, woolly (cost 35 box tops)	1933	100	200	400	Ralston
Cuffs, leather, TM-Bar (cost 8 box tops)	1933	75	150	300	Ralston
Hat, cowboy (cost 20 box tops)	1933	200	500	1000	Ralston
Shirt, cowboy	1933	125	188	250	Ralston
Skirt, cowgirl, TM-Bar	1935	150	300	600	Ralston
Sweat shirt, TM-Bar	1935	45	90	180	Ralston
T-shirt, Tom Mix and Tony from picture of Curley Bradley and his horse	1950-51	75	150	300	Ralston

1934 advertisement for Tom Mix Cowboy Outfit

Tom Mix Comics Book 1

Tom Mix Comics Book 2

Tom Mix Comics Book 3

Tom Mix Comics Book 4

Tom Mix Comics Book 5

Tom Mix Comics Book 6

Tom Mix Comics Book 7

Tom Mix Comics Book 8

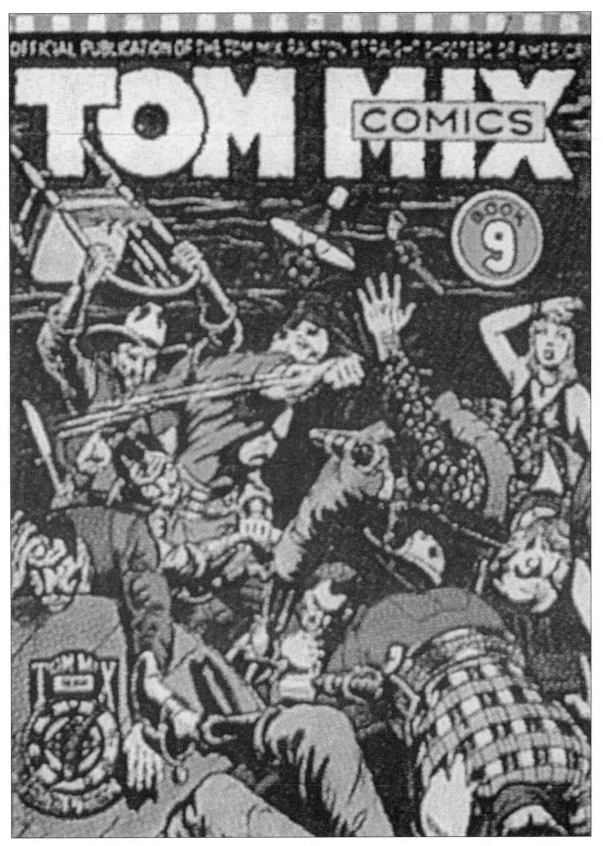

Tom Mix Comics Book 9

Tom Mix Comics Book 10

Tom Mix Comics Book 11

Tom Mix Comics Book 12

ITEM	DATE	GOOD	FINE	MINT	SPONSOR
Vest, cowboy, TM-Bar	1935	60	125	250	Ralston
Vest, sheepskin (cost 15 box tops)	1933	60	120	240	Ralston

BOOKS, COMICS, MANUALS, AND PRINTED MATERIALS

ITEM	DATE	GOOD	FINE	MINT	SPONSOR
Big Little Book, 3 x 3-1/2", "Trail of the Terrible Six" By Tom Mix, 176 pages	1935	20	30	40	Ralston
Book, hard cover, "Radio's Tom Mix and the Mystery of the Flaming Warrior." Contest prize. Also sold in stores.	1947	35	70	100	Ralston
Catalog, premium	1933	15	25	50	Ralston
Catalog, premium	1936	12	30	50	Ralston
Catalog, premium	1937	10	22.5	45	Ralston
Catalog, premium	1938	12	25	50	Ralston
Catalog, premium	1939	15	30	60	Ralston
Catalog, premium	1940	15	30	60	Ralston
Coloring book	1949	17	26	35	doctor's offices

COMIC BOOKS

ITEM	DATE	GOOD	FINE	MINT	SPONSOR
Tom Mix Comics, Book 1	1940-42	200	750	2500	Ralston

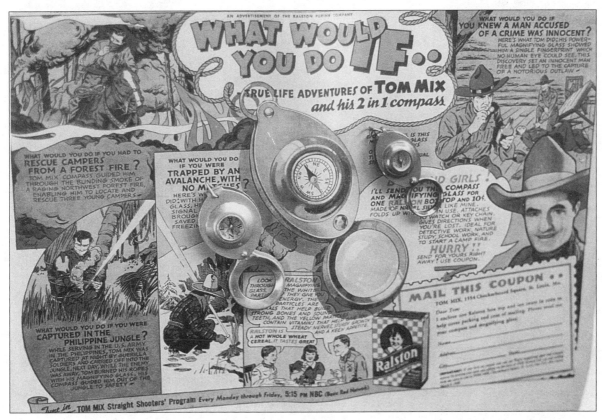

Full-page Tom Mix comics advertisement from a Sunday paper for the Tom Mix "2 in 1 Compass."

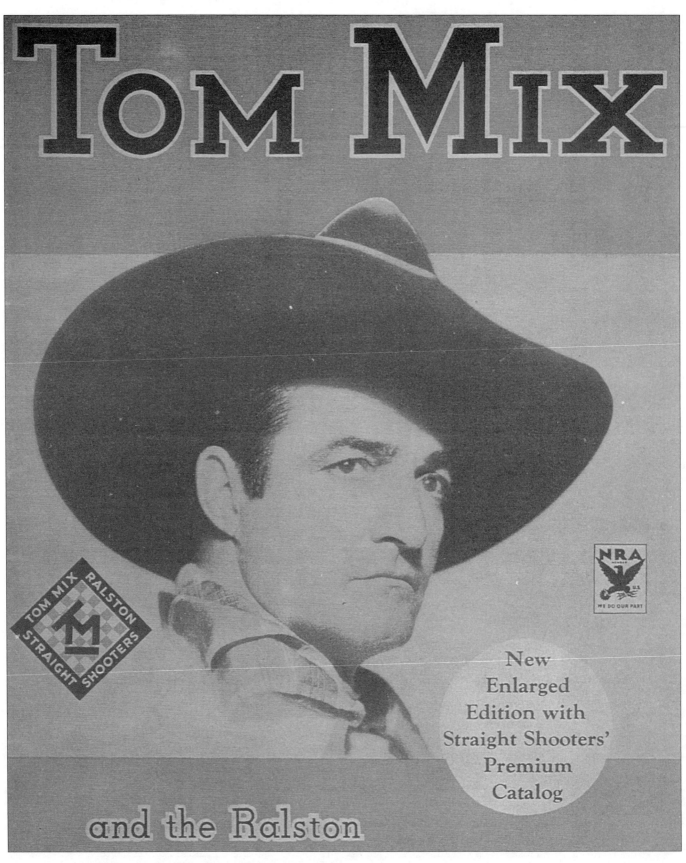

The second edition of the 1933 Tom Mix First Manual

The first ever Tom Mix manual, 1933

ITEM	DATE	GOOD	FINE	MINT	SPONSOR
Tom Mix Comics, Book 2	1940-42	70	250	600	Ralston
Tom Mix Comics, Book 3	1940-42	50	150	450	Ralston
Tom Mix Comics, Book 4	1940-42	50	150	450	Ralston
Tom Mix Comics, Book 5	1940-42	50	150	450	Ralston
Tom Mix Comics, Book 6	1940-42	50	150	450	Ralston
Tom Mix Comics, Book 7	1940-42	50	150	450	Ralston
Tom Mix Comics, Book 8	1940-42	50	150	450	Ralston
Tom Mix Comics, Book 9	1940-42	50	150	450	Ralston
Tom Mix Commandos Comics, Book 10	1940-42	40	120	400	Ralston
Tom Mix Commandos Comics, Book 11	1940-42	40	120	400	Ralston
Tom Mix Commandos Comics, Book 12	1940-42	40	120	400	Ralston
"Tom Mix and the Taking of Grizzly Grebb," 3 x 5" comic book (in cereal box), edited by Jim Harmon.	1983	5	10	15	Ralston
Newspaper Sunday comics advertisements for virtually every premium. Half pages, third pages. Tabloids (scarce). Full pages (rare).	1933-50	15	30	40	Ralston
Enclosures, correspondence, listeners' letters, etc. ave. value	1933-50	18	27	36	Ralston
Instruction sheet, decoder buttons	1946	12	18	24	Ralston
Kit, membership, first, complete. Contains manual, TM-Bar cloth patch, halftone photo of Tom beside Tony, letter, advisory to mother, original mailing envelope, and horseshoe nail ring.	1933	100	175	250	Ralston
Kit, membership, consisting of letter, patch, card, photo, and miniposter	1983	75	100	125	Ralston
Manual, Secret (originals have blank inside front and back covers)	1945	60	55	110	Ralston
Manual, Secret. Reprint.	1970	5	7.50	10	Ralston
Manual, Secret. Tom on rearing horse. Came with siren ring.	1944	35	70	140	Ralston
Manual, "Straight Shooters," Tom in Tony's saddle	1941	40	80	160	Ralston
Manual, "Life of Tom Mix," new enlarged edition, Tom in profile	1933	30	50	100	Ralston
Manual, "Life of Tom Mix," first edition, Tom sitting on fence	1933	32	65	130	Ralston

ITEM	DATE	GOOD	FINE	MINT	SPONSOR

This letter, sent to Jim Harmon, was typed on Tom Mix Straight Shooters stationery

ITEM	DATE	GOOD	FINE	MINT	SPONSOR
Newsletter, "Straight Shooters Newsletter"	1940	22	45	90	Ralston
Photo, Tom Mix, silver frame, autographed to ea. "Straight Shooter" by name from Tom Mix. Not an authentic autograph.	1938	22	45	90	Ralston

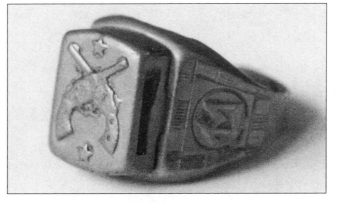

Tom Mix look-around ring

The Tom Mix look-around ring came enclosed in this mailer

ITEM	DATE	GOOD	FINE	MINT	SPONSOR

Tom Mix magnet ring

ITEM	DATE	GOOD	FINE	MINT	SPONSOR
Photos, halftone, 8 x 10", text stories on back. ea.	1933	35	75	150	Ralston
Photos, second set	1933	30	60	90	Ralston
Photo, Tom Mix and Tony	1983	5	10	15	Ralston
Postcard, cast photo, variations	1939	20	30	40	Ralston
Premium sheet	1941	9	18.50	35	Ralston
Stationery, Straight Shooters	1935	20	35	75	Ralston

RINGS, BRACELETS, AND WATCHES

ITEM	DATE	GOOD	FINE	MINT	SPONSOR
Bracelet, dangle, with charms: Tom on Tony, TM-Bar brand, six shooter, steer head	1936	250	550	1100	Ralston

Tom Mix ring, mystery, magnified look-in picture of Tom and Tony

Tom Mix siren ring

Tom Mix slide whistle ring

Tom Mix Straight Shooters ring. Only displays TM-Bar brand against Ralston checkerboard. First TM ring with identifying insignia.

Tom Mix watch fob with gold ore

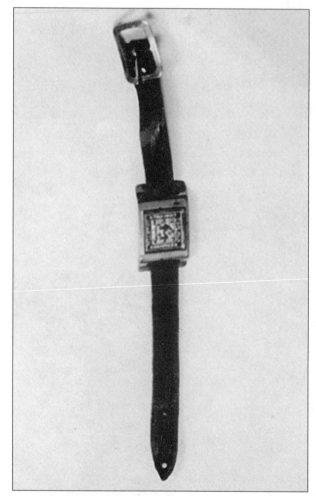

Tom Mix lucky wrist band

ITEM	DATE	GOOD	FINE	MINT	SPONSOR

Tom Mix ring, Tom Mix signature

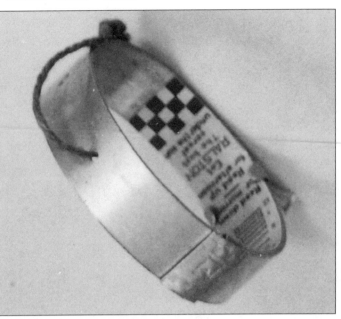

Tom Mix sun watch with circular band. It looks like a bracelet.

ITEM	DATE	GOOD	FINE	MINT	SPONSOR
Bracelet, initial, identification	1947	30	65	120	Ralston
Chain, with magnet gun, signal arrowhead, glows in dark	1948	50	75	100	Ralston
Charm, gold ore, and assay certificate	1940	35	75	150	Ralston
Charm, lucky, horseshoe	1934	22	35	70	Ralston
Ring, circus, spinner	1938	750	1500	2800	Tom Mix Circus

Tom Mix compass gun and whistle arrowhead

Tom Mix glow-in-the-dark plastic compass and magnifying glass

An advertisement for the Tom Mix wooden gun with the turning cylinder

ITEM	DATE	GOOD	FINE	MINT	SPONSOR
Ring, deputy	1934	1200	2500	6200	Tom Mix Gum
Ring, glow in the dark arrowhead, compass, magnifier	1946	48	72	95	Ralston
Ring, horseshoe nail (rounded point identifies original)	1933	20	35	70	Ralston
Ring, look-around	1946	50	75	150	Ralston
Ring, magic tiger-eye. Last Mix ring.	1950	60	125	250	Ralston
Ring, magnet	1947	38	75	150	Ralston
Ring, mystery, magnified look-in picture of Tom and Tony	1938	75	150	300	Ralston
Ring, signet, single initial	1937	32	65	130	Ralston
Ring, siren	1944	32	65	130	Ralston
Ring, slide whistle	1949	32	65	130	Ralston
Ring, Straight Shooters. Only displays TM-Bar brand against Ralston checkerboard. First TM ring with identifying insignia.	1949	32	65	130	Ralston

One view of the Tom Mix brass compass and magnifying glass, TM-Bar brand

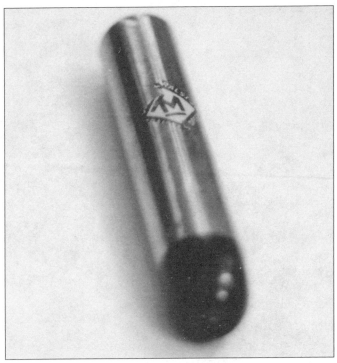

Another view of the Tom Mix brass compass and magnifying glass, TM-Bar brand

Tom Mix TM-Bar brass compass and magnifying glass

Tom Mix bullet flashlight

Tom Mix 1933 wooden gun (open)

Tom Mix 1933 wooden gun (closed)

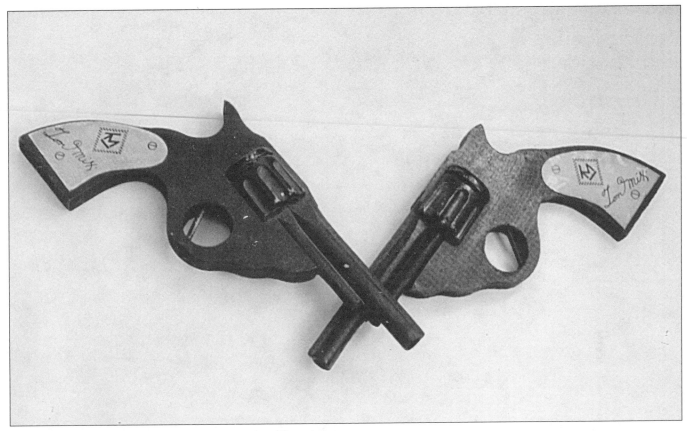

Tom Mix wooden gun; no moving parts, smaller size

Tom Mix first make-up kit

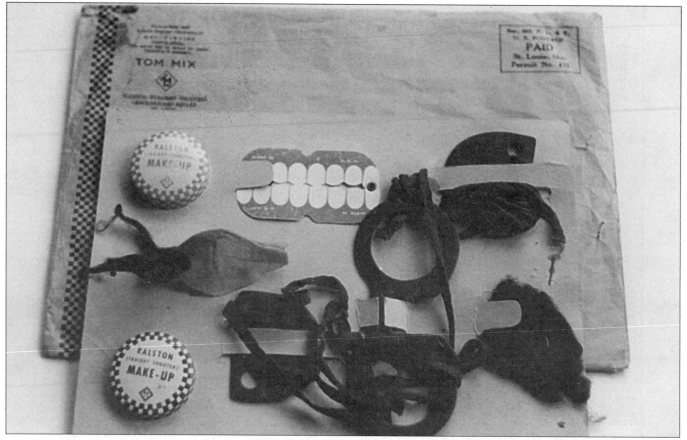

Tom Mix second make-up kit

Tom Mix marbles in a bag; Tom Mix Ralston label

ITEM	DATE	GOOD	FINE	MINT	SPONSOR
Ring, target	1937	150	300	600	Marlin Rifles
Ring, Tom Mix signature	1939	48	95	190	Ralston
Sun watch, circular band. Looks like bracelet.	1935	48	95	190	Ralston
Watch fob, gold ore, and certificate	1940	38	75	150	Ralston
Watch, Swiss-made, windup, 50th anniversary. $19.33 with box top.	1983	50	100	200	Ralston
Wrist band, lucky	1935	25	50	75	Ralston

TOYS

ITEM	DATE	GOOD	FINE	MINT	SPONSOR
Airplane, model kit, balsa wood, TM-Bar brand	1936	150	325	550	Ralston
Airplane and parachute	1938	150	275	450	Ralston
Baseball bat	1935	21	31	42	Ralston
Blow gun, Indian, and target	1940	100	250	600	Ralston
Branding iron and ink pad, TM-Bar	1934	45	95	190	Ralston
Compass gun and whistle arrowhead	1947	45	95	190	Ralston
Compass and magnifying glass,					

Tom Mix checkerboard, TM-Bar brand pocketknife

ITEM	DATE	GOOD	FINE	MINT	SPONSOR
glow in dark, plastic	1946	32	65	130	Ralston
Compass and magnifying glass, TM-Bar, brass	1940	32	65	130	Ralston
Compass/magnifier, silver, no identification	1934	32	65	130	Ralston
Films for toy TV set film viewer	1949	20	35	60	Ralston
Flashlight, bullet	1938	20	35	60	Ralston
Flashlight, three-color lens	1939	30	55	110	Ralston

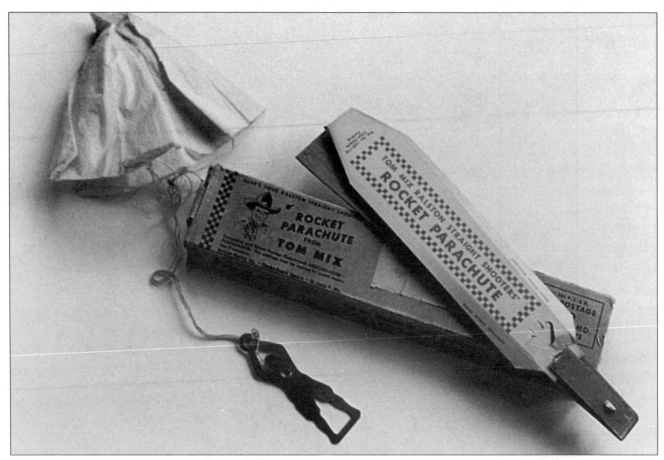

Tom Mix rocket parachute

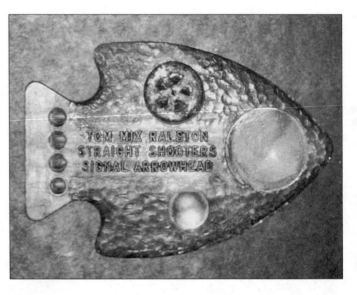

Tom Mix signal arrowhead. It is made of clear plastic and contains a 4-tube whistle, 2-tone siren, magnifying lens and a smallifying lens.

Tom Mix rope, spinning, hemp with wood handle

ITEM	DATE	GOOD	FINE	MINT	SPONSOR
Fountain pen	1938	30	40	50	Ralston
Gun, wooden, no moving parts, smaller size	1939	70	140	200	Ralston
Gun, wooden, opens, cylinder spins	1935	85	160	300	Ralston
Gun, wooden, revolving cylinder, cardboard "ivory" grips, TM-Bar markings	1933	90	180	320	Ralston
Holster and cartridge belt, TM-Bar	1933	125	250	500	Ralston
Make-up kit, movie, including false beard, mustache, five makeup tins saying "Ralston Straight Shooters"	1937	100	200	300	Ralston
Make-up kit, movie, with eye-glasses, mustache, 2 make-up tins	1940	90	175	285	Ralston
Make-up tins only from make-up kit, ea.	1937	10	20	30	Ralston
Marbles, bag, Tom Mix Ralston label	1936	17	26	35	Ralston
Mask, face of Tom Mix	1933	150	300	800	Ralston
Parachute rocket	1947	45	95	175	Ralston
Pen and pencil set	1936	20	40	60	Ralston
Periscope. Cardboard tube with mirrors	1939	35	75	150	Ralston
Pocketknife, checkerboard and TM-Bar brand	1939	45	95	175	Ralston
Rocket parachute. Cardboard/balsa wood. Contains parachute and metal man, all launched by rubber band	1936	52	105	210	Ralston

Tom Mix good luck spinner

Tom Mix glow-in-the-dark spurs came enclosed in this package (back view)

Tom Mix glow-in-the-dark spurs came enclosed in this package (front view)

Tom Mix spurs, TM-Bar, leather straps

ITEM	DATE	GOOD	FINE	MINT	SPONSOR
Rope, spinning, hemp with wood handle	1936	47	72	95	Ralston
Signal arrowhead. Clear plastic containing 4-tube whistle, 2-tone siren, magnifying lens, smallifying lens	1949	35	75	150	Ralston
Spinner, good luck	1933	20	35	60	Ralston
Spurs, glow-in-the dark	1949	50	105	200	Ralston
Spurs, TM-Bar, leather straps	1933	75	150	300	Ralston

Tom Mix TV set film viewer

Tom Mix telescope

ITEM	DATE	GOOD	FINE	MINT	SPONSOR
Telegraph set, postal, blue, with mechanical clicker	1938	30	65	95	Ralston
Telegraph set, red, battery operated, works with second set	1940	75	150	250	Ralston
Telephone set (two metal cups and string)	1938	48	95	175	Ralston
Telescope	1938	30	60	90	Ralston
Television set, toy (3 models known) (double price gold)	1949-50	40	85	150	Ralston
Western movie reel (cardboard and paper pictures)	1935	80	175	250	Ralston
Writing kit, secret ink, decoder dial	1938	75	150	300	Ralston
Zyp gun. No markings. If in original mailer.	1933	175	300	650	Ralston

MISCELLANEOUS

ITEM	DATE	GOOD	FINE	MINT	SPONSOR
Cereal bowl, ceramic, 50th anniversary	1983	20	40	60	Ralston
Mailing box and instructions for live baby turtle	1937	20	30	40	Ralston
Live baby turtle, TM-Bar branded on shell	1937		not found		Ralston

RADIO SHOW RECORDINGS

ITEM	DATE	GOOD	FINE	MINT	SPONSOR
"Vanishing Village," Vol. 1, 30 min.,	1983	10	20	40	Ralston

Curley Bradley (radio's Tom Mix) with Vanishing Village Vol. 1, 30 min.

ITEM	DATE	GOOD	FINE	MINT	SPONSOR
"Vanishing Village," Vol. 2, 30 min., including 1983 production by Jim Harmon. $4.98 ea., or $8.95 both vols.	1983	10	20	40	Ralston

UNCLE DON

ITEM	DATE	GOOD	FINE	MINT	SPONSOR
Booklet, On the Trail of the Secret Formula	1933	15	30	35	Bond Bakers
Letter from Uncle Don	1933	8	12	16	Bond Bakers
Map	1933	25	50	75	Bond Bakers

ITEM	DATE	GOOD	FINE	MINT	SPONSOR

VIC AND SADE

ITEM	DATE	GOOD	FINE	MINT	SPONSOR
Map	1942	50	100	300	Proctor & Gamble

WILD BILL HICKOK

ITEM	DATE	GOOD	FINE	MINT	SPONSOR
Badges, tin star, in pack	1952	3	4	5	Kellogg's
Bunkhouse set w/ pin-ups of Bill, Jingles, guns, ropes, etc. Had theoretical value of $2.50, but given away free	1951-54	25	38	50	appliance stores
Game, breakfast, score card	1951-54	5	8	15	Kellogg's
Guide, secret treasure	1951-54	8	12	16	Kellogg's
Gun, Colt six shooter	1951-54	8	12	16	Kellogg's
Gun kits, old time, plastic, ea.	1951-54	8	12	16	Kellogg's
Map, treasure and guide	1952	48	72	95	Kellogg's
Rifle, model	1952	10	15	20	Kellogg's
Trading cards, Bond Bread, ea.	1952	3	4	5	Kellogg's

WIZARD OF OZ

ITEM	DATE	GOOD	FINE	MINT	SPONSOR
Condensed stories, paperbound	1933-34	30	75	175	Jell-O

Epilogue

The Legend at Sunset

By Jim Harmon

The time was a sunny October morning of a year in the early 1930s.

The place was the nineteenth floor of one of the great towers of the city, housing the editorial offices of the metropolis' great newspaper.

The tall man came out of the express elevator alone. He wore a long, dark overcoat of an expensive cut, a snap-brimmed gray Stetson of a moderately wide Southwestern style, and dark, smoked glasses, now often called sun glasses. He went to the outer door of the executive offices and walked in.

The secretarial trainee was working as a receptionist. She saw the fine looking man come in and was impressed with his magnetic persona. His presence seemed to fill the room. He was a man of indeterminant years, although most people took him for late middle age.

"Good morning. I'm here to see the publisher," he said in one of the most magnificent speaking voices she had ever heard. "Please give him my card."

"Yes, sir."

The publisher had told her that he did not wish to be disturbed, but she made up her own mind. She was sure that order did not include this man.

As she got up from behind her desk, the pretty teenager glanced to the sun slanting through the windows to the caller's dark glasses. "Should I close the drapes while you wait?" she asked.

"I'm fine," he said. He touched his dark glasses. "These protect my health."

As she walked to the door of the inner office, she read the visitor's card.

MR. SILVER
Precision Delivery Systems

"Fast as a Bullet We Come to Your Aid"

There was an embossed silver bullet on the calling card as well.

The publisher was deep in conversation on the telephone, but she approached quietly and put the calling card on the desk blotter in front of him. "A man to see you, sir," she whispered, reducing it to almost a mouthing of the words.

He glanced at the card, then stared. "Admit him at once!" The publisher turned back to the phone. "Forgive me, Governor. I must go."

The man entered them room, and the publisher sprang from his chair, with an energy that belied his graying hair. The two men embraced heartily, strong arms about each other in the Mexican style common along the Texas border.

The newspaper man stood back and examined the visitor. "Sir, it's wonderful to see you. It's been years! Too bad my boy is off at college. Given the restrictions, I was never able to quite explain to him who that fine looking man was who showed up at some of his birthdays."

"I'm sorry that it was impossible for me to be at his mother's funeral," the man said.

"I understand." Little needed to be said among these two. "How is our Faithful Friend?" the publisher said in Indian dialect common along the border of forty years before.

The visitor chuckled. "He's the same as ever. He'll be the same at one hundred. I...sometimes feel selfish keeping him with me in my work. If he had returned to his people and assumed his natural leadership position, he might be a senator or governor by now."

The publisher smiled. "I'd vote for him—or for you—for President."

"He's back at our hotel. You'll see him later. Shall we sit?"

The tall man took the visitor chair and the publisher sat on the edge of his won desk, his eyes intent on the older man. The visitor removed his hat, revealing hair that was still mostly black, but shot through with —appropriately—silver.

"Have you seen any of our old friends lately?"

"I visited Wyatt Earp out on the coast a few years ago. Saw him just months before the end. One of our old foes, Al Jennings, is still working as a production manager in the film business. I think he's making more money at that then he ever did robbing banks."

"Of course he never was a very good bank robber. You know the paper has been running a series of pieces on figures of the Old West...Earp...Buffalo Bill...lone riders, and vigilantes. Tall tales of the old timers, similar to those about Paul Bunyon."

The visitor smiled. "People like to tell stories. I understand a local radio station is running a series of programs about one of those mystery figures. They will soon run through those legends. Certain people in Washington have the facts, if they need to be known."

"Does that hot shot, Elliot Ness, have much work for you?" the publisher asked.

The other man laughed. "Strange you should ask about that. President Hoover didn't seem to have anything for me to do. I don't think he approves of me. But young treasury agent Ness occasionally has little jobs for me. I think he likes it that I don't seek public credit—more for him. As a matter of fact, it is a job for him that brings me to the city."

He grew more serious. "The case doesn't look all that dangerous, but one never knows. I want to renew our agreement. If they follow the instructions I carry on me, and you are contacted, you will see that my body is returned to lay beside your father and our comrades." He paused. "The Big Fellow sleeps nearby."

Tears welled in the other man's eyes. "I haven't asked about him in years. I didn't want to hear it. There were sightings of you on a white horse even into the twenties, but I was afraid it couldn't have been the same."

"Junior and Number Three were fine horses, but there was only one mount. No hooves ever beat the plains like his. He lived well into the Twentieth Century."

"Who can forget him? One of the most magnificent creatures who ever lived."

"He is with me always," the visitor said. He removed a keychain from his pocket, which included a miniature horse-shoe about two inches across. "Made from one of his last shoes. I like to think he is still helping me with his fine senses. I say, 'Big Fellow, which trail shall we take?' And I fancy he helps guide me. A whimsy."

"As you know, his line, and that of his son, once my mount, are carried on at our horse farm in Michigan," the newspaperman said. "There is one new stallion there that I think might be of use to you."

"I'd love to ride him," the man said with enthusiasm. "But not for 'business'. This is the automotive age. Crime has moved to the cities. I use a Cord—silver in color—a conceit. Our friend generally drives. I think he has become more at ease with the Twentieth Century than I have."

"I doubt that!" the publisher said. "There's nothing you can't master."

The man shrugged. "It gives him something useful to do. We'll be going out tonight, on Mr. Ness' business. If all goes well, we'll stop by the house at around midnight." The visitor judged the time of day, from the angle of the sun slating through the window, but checked his wristwatch. "I'm afraid I have to leave. I have preparations to make."

The two men stood up. The publisher said, "It is a pity you never married and gave the world a son to carry on."

The visitor stood, remembering. "Certain women have stirred me. Everything need not be put down on the page. But it was the example of the many dear old Padres I know in the West who showed me that my way was the path of duty."

The visitor placed his hand over the other man's on the desk. "Of course, you are my son, more than only my nephew. Your son carries on our line."

"Sir, could I ask you your present age?"

The tall man smiled. "I'm as old as my teeth. If I give age a number, that will make it real."

"One more thing, sir...Could you remove the dark glasses?"

The visitor removed the glasses.

It was the face he had first seen more than fifty years before, etched with even more character and determination, if that were possible.

"The world should have seen more of the face.'

The visitor put the glasses back on. "No, the mask was better. Now I must go to get ready for my next meeting."

"I hope it will be as pleasant as this one has been for me."

"I think not. A meeting with a traitor is very seldom pleasant." He gave a chest high Indian salute, and turned to leave the room.

The publisher thought, there goes the greatest man I have ever known in two different centuries.

****

The shiny new Cord stood in front of a skyscraper framework of steel under construction, reaching into the night sky. At the wheel sat a dark man in a dark suit, no longer young, but ramrod straight. He was waiting for someone inside the new construction. Somewhere a dog howled. Or was it a wolf? It was said wolves still prowled the hills above the city.

Inside the structure, two men talked in the half light of a small bulb next to an elevator. One was a tall aristocratic man, in a gray European-cut suit. He had a small mustache and a scar on his left cheek. The other was shorter. His round face and his clothes seemed too tight for his round body.

The red-face man spoke. "Count, you will find in this roll of papers the complete plans for the new pursuit plane the Army is going to have built. I want nothing for myself, but the work of the bund must go on."

"Ve already agreed to the twenty thousand pounds—that is, dollars." The mustached man slapped a wallet of thin, fine leather against the palm of his free hand. "Chust hand offer the plans."

Red Face eagerly pushed the roll of papers forward. The receiver started to give up the wallet, but hesitated, and tucked it under his arm. He spread open the roll, slanting it towards the only source of light. "Vat you say seems to be here. Gut, gut...Good. Very good. I'm sure my friend in Washington will be very glad to have these back."

Red Face seemed to go white. "Your voice! Washington? He snatched from the crease in his back a Luger.

A .45 Army Colt automatic appeared in the hand of the man who had been called "Count." The gun spoke once. Red Face shrieked.

"Your fingers sting from the shock of my bullet," the man who had earlier visited the publisher said. "But I fired at and hit your gun. I must say you wouldn't have lived very long with a draw like that back where I come from." He put his automatic in its shoulder holster.

Thirty feet away, on the uncompleted floor, a silver bullet caught a gleam of light, flattened like a coin on the railroad tracks.

"You were a fool to holster your gun," Red Face screamed. "I am strong as a bull!"

Fingers like sausages closed about the supposed "Count's" throat, but fingers like steel bands grabbed wrists above the sausage fingers, and broke the traitorous American's grip like a child's. Arms were twisted behind the round man's back and he was fastened to the nearest upright girder with a pair of handcuffs. The man doing the fastening remembered when he would have used rawhide strips.

The supposed "Count' turned his back, and using an old bandanna, wiped away the make-up scar and mustache. He replaced his smoked glasses which were engineered so that he could see perfectly well at night. In the distance, he heard the wail of a police car. "That will be Mr. Ness' agent coming for you, accompanied by the local police." He tucked one of his "Mr. Silver" calling cards into the round man's shirt pocket.

The sweating traitor glared a the man. In the uncertain light, he could see only that the upper part of his face was blacked out. The greasy one squealed "Who are you, you masked meddler?"

There was a laugh from the other side. "I've been called many names...Certainly not that one for the first time."

The police siren was very near as he ran to the silver Cord. The driver said, "Hear sound of your gun only."

"Right. No need for you to come." He tossed the stolen plans and wallet of supposed pay-off into the back, placed a hand on the door frame, and vaulted into the passenger seat. "Let's travel."

The power of the great car surged through his thighs. The wind rushed by his cheeks. He could believe he was once again riding a white stallion, fine as light. The dark spectacles-masked man now in his seventy-eighth year, lifted his voice to call to the spirit of the horse that seemed to race beside them with a cry ending in the horse's name, to echo among the high rise of building that marched along a trail he first blazed in another century, another world.

INDEX

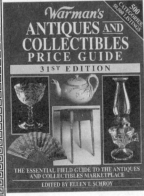